BOOKS BY GREGORY MCNAMEE

Blue Mountains Far Away:
Journeys into the American Wilderness

The Serpent's Tale: Snakes in Folklore and Literature (editor)

Open Range and Parking Lots (with Virgil Hancock)

Grand Canyon Place Names

A World of Turtles (editor)

A Desert Bestiary: Folklore, Literature,
and Ecological Thought from the World's Dry Places

Resist Much, Obey Little: Remembering Ed Abbey (editor)

In the Presence of Wolves (with Art Wolfe)

The Sierra Club Desert Reader (editor)

Gila: The Life and Death of an American River

Named in Stone and Sky (editor)

Christ on the Mount of Olives

Inconstant History: Poems and Translations

The Return of Richard Nixon

Living in Words: Interviews from The Bloomsbury Review,
1981–1988 (editor)

Philoktetes (translator)

The

MOUNTAIN
WORLD

The
MOUNTAIN
WORLD

A
Literary Journey

EDITED BY

Gregory McNamee

SIERRA CLUB BOOKS
SAN FRANCISCO

Copyright © 2000 by Gregory McNamee

Published by Sierra Club Books, in conjunction with Random House, Inc.

Library of Congress Cataloging-in-Publication Data

The mountain world: a literary journey / edited by Gregory McNamee.
    p.   cm.
Includes bibliographical references.
ISBN 0-87156-898-5
1. Mountaineering—Literary collections.   2. Mountain life—Literary collections.
3. Mountains—Literary collections.   I. McNamee, Gregory.
PN6071.M738 M68 2000   808.8'032143—dc21   99-046907

BOOK DESIGN BY DEBORAH KERNER

Contents

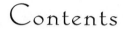

Introduction

The din of the dusty world and the locked-in-ness of human
habitations are what human nature habitually abhors; while, on
the contrary, haze, mist, and the haunting spirits of the mountains
are what human nature seeks, and yet can rarely find.

KUO HSI

Was the earth created with or without mountains? A strange question, perhaps, but one that nonetheless occupied the residents of the Jesuit college of
Coimbre, France, for the better part of the year 1592, when the gold-rich
mountains of the newfound Americas and of Asia were much on the European mind.

Using twists and turns of logic and complex arguments of faith, the sem-
inarians argued pro and con, invoking such contradictory sources as their
near contemporary Saint John of the Cross, who urged seekers after the
truth to retreat to "solitary places, which tend to lift up the soul to God, like

mountains, which furnish no resources for worldly recreations," and the Old Testament prophets, who conversely regarded mountains as frightful places capable of settlement only by Yahweh and assorted demons. But in the end, having determined that the mountains brought living humans as close as they could ever come to the heavens, the Jesuits of Coimbre ruled that mountains were evidence of the earth's perfection as the creation of an infallible God. So the matter rested. Only a century later would it be revived, briefly, when the Protestant theologian Thomas Burnet countered that the earth was inherently "confused by Nature" and that the mountains were "Ruines and Rubbish on a dirty little planet."

Ruins and rubbish, the flatlander's worldview, the notions of someone who has little use for alternate realities. We have since his time made room in our mental and spiritual worlds for mountains, and Burnet has few modern supporters, I suspect, with the notable exception of the confirmed city dweller and sophisticate Roland Barthes, a sometimes Catholic, sometimes Marxist, always interesting literary critic who sniffed at the "Helvetico-Protestant morality" of mountain lovers while arguing that qualities like verticality, "so contrary to the bliss of travel," are the heaven of the Michelin Blue Guide but the hell of ordinary mortals. Poor misguided soul, Barthes was run down while trying to cross a busy Paris street, miles away from the nearest mountain of any account, safe from the imagined terrors of the Alps.

A strange matter, as I say: swirling, heated, passionate arguments over the value and even validity of some of the planet's most characteristic landmasses. We are fortunate to live in a time when the holiness of mountains is almost a given, as the world's religions have always taken it to be.

And for good reason: who, standing on that point of land where Meriwether Lewis exclaimed, "Ocian in view" and taking in the vast magnificent sweep of the central Cascades, could not believe that there, up on 12,300-foot Mount Adams or 14,410-foot Mount Rainier, lies a threshold of heaven? There on those peaks, some native peoples of the Pacific Northwest say, stands the abode of the spirits, of fierce winds, of the very creator. There, Warm Springs storyteller Lucy Miller told the anthropologist Theodora Kroeber, the gods wrestled as Coyote the Trickster mightily conspired to keep Mount Adams and Mount Hood from killing each other in a long-ago time. There the earth shook so badly that the First People all disappeared, leaving only the Klah Klahnee, the Three Sisters, behind to guide the next people to their new homeland.

On another volcanic mountain half a world away—one that probably does not exist in time or space but only in metaphor—Saint Paul rose to behold his God, pointing the way to yet another new homeland. And on still another mountain, a 2,510-foot cinder cone called Cruachán Aigle, Saint Patrick strode forth to conquer the citadel of the ancient Irish harvest god. He did so, and the mountain, now called Croagh Patrick, is Ireland's holiest peak. Patrick played on powerful memories when he conquered that height, sacred before as now, driving away the great bird and the monster serpent who guarded its summit. Mountains, along with wells and caves, were the loci for the Christianization of Ireland, and today thousands of people retrace Patrick's steps on the first Sunday of August.

They are wild places, those mountains, and terrifying. There is something about mountains that sends humans into states of consciousness—fearful, reverential, even awestruck—that are far from our normal modes of being. Some of the reasons are obvious, even deceptively so. As the Jesuits of Coimbre observed, for believers mountains are the closest points on the planet to the abodes of the gods, connecting the spirit world with our own. Mountains hold obvious dominion over the land, stern royalty gazing down on their lowly subjects. And, of course, mountains are high places, and many people fear heights, although a current psychiatric index will show you that many more people fear, in descending order, animals, the sight of blood, and being penned up in enclosed spaces.

From terror grows a kind of grace. It is no surprise, I think, that Saint Francis's notions of "tendance and comforting" should have arisen in the mountains through which he walked, ideas he elaborated while coursing the craggy spine of the Apennines on the way from Assisi to La Verna, for without such kindness, a contemporary remarked, "in those desolate places man could not live." Grace indeed: the nature of mountains embodies the gift by which God enables us to live holy lives, Saint Francis said. They change our being. Thus, as John Muir observed at the beginning of this chewed-up age, "thousands of tired, nerve-shaken, over-civilized people are beginning to find out that going to the mountains is going home."

In mountains were nourished the great religions of the world, nearly all born in the deserts but raised in the high country. The environmental psychologist Bernard S. Aaronson has noted that "the traditional association of mountain tops with the abode of Deity may be less because they are higher than the areas around them than because they make possible those experiences of expanded depth in which the self can invest itself in the world around it and expand across the valleys," a feeling that resembles nothing so much as extrasensory perception. That is just the feeling experienced by human beings deprived of oxygen, a sure step toward coma, and by those who have survived close encounters with death—most mountain climbers, in other words. Alpinist after alpinist reports returning from the mountains filled with an inexplicable sense of inner peace born of that sensory sharpening, filled with something approaching the religious thump on the head that Buddhists call satori, like Maurice Herzog's epiphany atop the 26,502-foot summit of Annapurna: "I had a vision of the life of men. Those who are leaving it for ever are never alone. Resting against the mountain, which was watching over me, I discovered horizons I had never seen. There at my feet, on those vast plains, millions of beings were following a destiny they had not chosen. There is a supernatural power in those close to death." And in those, we might say, who venture close to it, as you will read in the pages of Neville Shulman's fine memoir *Zen in the Art of Climbing Mountains,* an account of terror and redemption on the north face of 15,771-foot Mont Blanc, and in the ninth-century Japanese account of a Buddhist monk named Shodo who climbed the volcanic peak Nantai-zan to confront his mortality:

> *"If I do not reach the top of this mountain, I will never be able to attain Awakening!" After having said these words he moved across the glistening snow and walked on young shoots glimmering like jewels. When he had ascended halfway, all strength left him. He rested for two*

*days and then climbed to the peak. His joy there was complete, like that
of a dream: his dizziness portended the Awakening.*

In the mountains the eyes become clearer, it seems, the ears more finely
tuned; the customary flavors of food take on new nuances; the calls of birds
compose a richer music. The first European known to have climbed a
mountain for the sheer pleasure of it, the Italian poet Petrarch (1304–1374),
devoted many pages of his journals to describing the odd sensations that
overcame him in the highlands, especially on seeing a glacier-lit rainbow
atop the small alp Ventoux: "I stood as one stupefied. I looked down and
saw that the clouds lay beneath my feet. I felt as if another."

As if another, indeed. The English Catholic mystic Dom John Chapman
calls the sense of mountains "unearthly and expanding," echoing the English traveler Freya Stark's notion that the mountains are moving vortexes of
energy on a spinning globe—another strange idea, on the face of it, but one
that has considerable attraction when you consider that everything on the
planet is indeed constantly in motion. I have experienced that "unearthly
and expanding" sense on a number of mountaintops: the Zugspitze, in the
Bavarian Alps; Mount Evans, one of Colorado's "fourteeners"; on Mount
Rainier and, just a few weeks before it blew, on Mount Saint Helens; and,
most profoundly, atop Copperas Peak, an otherwise unimposing mountain
in southwestern New Mexico that overlooks the rushing headwaters of the
Gila River, three streams that pour down from the surrounding highlands
and unite two thousand sheer feet below.

The vista there is dizzying. "Don't go into the Gila if you're scared of
heights," a waitress in Silver City said to me on my first visit there, after
watching me puzzle over a topographic map, trying to make sense out of the
jumble of mountains that fold and unfold, accordionlike, across the landscape. (The Japanese Zen master Dōgen Kigen evoked a similarly topsy-
turvy geology when he wrote in his *Mountain Sutra*, "As for mountains,
there are mountains hidden in jewels; there are mountains hidden in
marshes, mountains hidden in the sky; there are mountains hidden in
mountains. There is a study of mountains hidden in hiddenness.") The

waitress had a point. These streams and their feeders arise in springs and ice caves atop towering ranges—the Mogollon, Black, and Pinos Altos mountains—that ring the Gila Basin on the immediate west side of the Continental Divide. The vertiginous roads that lead over them and down to the water would, I imagine, be an acrophobe's worst nightmare. Atop Copperas Peak, perched tentatively on a narrow shelf of granite with its hundred-mile view on all sides, you have the impression that the horizon is limitless, and that you, mere human, are tiny to the point of insignificance.

There is much value in that humbling experience. In their mountain-studded Alaska homeland, the anthropologist Richard Nelson has observed, Koyukon children learn their place in the order of things from geomorphology itself, having been instructed that they are not to argue over the respective merits of mountains or to compare their sizes. "Your mouth is too small," an offending child will be scolded, meaning that we humans cannot possibly comprehend the vastness of nature. Similarly, the O'od no'ok, or Mountain Pima, of northern Mexico liken themselves to ants who crawl along the ragged canyons and massifs of the western Sierra Madre, singing traditional songs that reinforce the notion of our tininess against the heights. Buddha was likely getting at the same idea when he observed, "In the high places of the earth the being is better to look at himself in the face and learn the truth and true proportion of things."

Terror, vertigo, insignificance: it is odd, perhaps, that these fundamentally dehumanizing elements should lead to the sublime state that characterizes our best spiritual impulses. The human mind is made up of odd stuff, however, and susceptible to seeing in the land whatever it chooses to. In the mountains, those frightening places, it locates the deities. There is no mountain landscape in the world that is not heavily invested with gods, sometimes from many traditions. Chomolungma, or Everest, is sacred to Hindus, Buddhists, Taoists, and Confucianists alike. Similarly, Mount Cuchama, near San Diego, is a mountain island sacred to the now-dispersed Luiseño and Diegueño Indians of the California coast, but also to the far-inland Cocopa, Quechan, and Chemehuevi peoples, for whom the distant mountain, rising above the sere desert floor, was a place of pilgrimage.

Saint Theodoros, a Byzantine mystic, held that "a mountain is the image of the soul rising in meditation." The metaphor is apt. Surely Jesus knew the power of landscape when he took up his position on an unnamed mountainside—perhaps it was Tabor, the site of his transfiguration—to give the Sermon on the Mount. There Jesus commanded a sweeping view of his followers and the valley below them while enjoying a steep, craggy backdrop that symbolically projected him into heaven, ascending to attain the ethereal, the clarity, the shudder that the theologian Rudolf Otto finds in the presence of what he calls the "numinous," lying at the base of all religious impulse. It is no accident, I think, that Jesus chose a mountain site on which to deliver his most powerful address: from on high, there next to God, he spoke of good and evil, of loving one's enemies, of doing's one part in bringing peace to the world. From on high, he taught his followers how to pray.

Just so, throughout time, in religious traditions the world over, holy people have taken themselves into hermitage in the mountains, there to let their souls rise. Just so, throughout time, we have found peace and spiritual succor in the highlands of the world, where, the Hindu Puranas promise, "As the dew is dried up by the morning sun, so are the sins of mankind dried up by the sight of the mountains." Just so, the world over, the architecture of the sacred aims to emulate mountains, as with the ziggurats of Babylon, which bore names like House of the Mountain and Mountain of God; the pyramids of Egypt, the temples of Jerusalem, the stupas of Tibet, the Gothic cathedrals of Europe; even, in this money-worshiping age, the skyscrapers of our urban centers. It is tempting to think that God demolished the Tower of Babel not out of anger for its builders' having attempted to unite humans with their maker but for their hubris in trying to re-create what nature takes millions of years of geological evolution to accomplish: a mountain piercing the heavens.

We cannot undo two million years of our own primate evolution to dissolve the fears and emotions that lie at the center of our beings. Roller coasters, tall buildings, and good portions of the films *Cliffhanger* and *The Eiger Sanction* can still produce those beads of sweat that proclaim our fragility, even though we pretend to be masters of our world. And in that pretense, overlooking the tininess of which those Koyukon mothers so wisely speak, we are increasingly placing the world's mountains at risk.

Sometimes we do so out of greed. Where two thousand years ago Greek priests climbed the slopes of Olympus and Parnassus to search for signs of lightning, indications that sacrifices were propitious and prayers to the gods most likely to be heard, now their descendants build ski lodges. Indian casinos now lie spattered among the once-sacred mountains of Arizona, California, and New Mexico.

And sometimes, with less damage to be sure, we do so out of mere vanity, out of the misplaced drive to conquer nature. N. E. Odell, who accompanied the tragic Mallory expedition to Everest in 1924, wondered whether it was right to climb the mountain: "If it was indeed the sacred ground of Chomolungma, Goddess Mother of the Mountain Snows, had we violated it—was I now violating it?" Today, in the race to deprive the planet of all its mysteries, such questions of propriety are laid aside. Not long ago the famed alpinist Reinhold Messner, having secured permission from Chinese authorities glad to offend Tibetan sensibilities, announced his plan to climb Kailas, the holiest of holy mountains to untold millions of people, despite warnings that to do so would be to profane it.

Whether we climb them or view them from afar, they continue to pull at us, calling us home, those mountains. Watching their peaks pierce the sky, here in the Sonoran Desert, I count myself fortunate to have their sanctuary, their daily reminder of the generosity of the land, and to be able to yield again to tininess, even to terror, and to the ever-expanding universe that lies in the ranges beyond.

This anthology is a celebration of the world's mountains, drawing on a wide body of literature. In making it, I observe the American poet Ezra Pound's dictum that literature "is news that stays news" (and, in passing, to repeat John Muir's injunction, "Climb the mountains and get their good tidings"). I do not pretend to completeness, and this book represents only a fraction of the vast library devoted to mountains. I need also to remark that the record of the world's exploration has been kept mostly by European and American men, who are thus disproportionately represented in this collection. But times are changing, and the work of women and of indigenous writers is now shaping the literature of the mountains, of the land, even as the land is being radically transformed.

For their advice, I thank Don Bahr, Steve Bodio, Brian Doyle, Larry Evers, Julian Hayden, Jane Hirshfield, Barry Lopez, Nanao Sakaki, Gary Snyder, Steve Topping, and Terry Tempest Williams.

For permission to use copyrighted material, I thank Sam Hamill of Copper Canyon Press (for Bill Porter's Han Shan translations from *Collected Poems of Cold Mountain,* © 1984 by Red Pine/Bill Porter), Virginia Kidd and Ursula K. Le Guin (for "At Meta Lake: Autumn 1980," from *In the Red Zone* [John Lord Press], © 1983 by Ursula K. Le Guin), Dennis Maloney of White Pine Press (for Cid Corman and Kaikame Susumu's translations of Bashō, from *Back Roads to Far Towns,* © 1986 by Cid Corman and Kaikame Susumu), Bob Shacochis (for "Bob Versus the Volcano," © 1991 by Bob Shacochis), and Roger Shattuck (for his translation of René Daumal's *Mount Analogue*).

Unless noted otherwise, translations are my own.

AMERICAS

O frightful silent endless space
—Everything goes to the head
   Of the hanging bubble, with men
   The juice is in the head—
   So mountain peaks are points
   Of rocky liquid yearning

JACK KEROUAC

Mount Katahdin

HENRY DAVID THOREAU

After quitting his residence at Walden Pond, Massachusetts, HENRY DAVID THOREAU (1817–1862), in the words of the scholar H. S. Canby, "was no longer content with walks to Wachusett or the Catskills but must pry out the realities of the wilderness itself." In 1846, he and a group of companions set out on foot to explore the interior of Maine. His account of ascending Mount Katahdin was first published in Union Magazine *by Horace Greeley, and later reprinted in Thoreau's* Maine Woods *(1864). The poetic quotations are from John Milton's* Paradise Lost.

At length we reached an elevation sufficiently bare to afford a view of the summit, still distant and blue, almost as if retreating from us. A torrent, which proved to be the same we had crossed, was seen tumbling down in front, literally from out of the clouds. But this glimpse at our whereabouts was soon lost, and we were buried in the woods again. The wood was chiefly yellow birch, spruce, fir, mountain-ash, or round-wood, as the Maine people call it, and moose-wood. It was the worst kind of travelling. . . . The cornel,

3

or bunch-berries, were very abundant, as well as Solomon's seal and moose-berries. Blueberries were distributed along our whole route; and in one place bushes were drooping with the weight of the fruit, still as fresh as ever. It was the 7th of September. Such patches afforded a grateful repast, and served to bait the tired party forward. When any lagged behind, the cry of "blueberries" was most effectual to bring them up. Even at this elevation we passed through a moose-yard, formed by a large flat rock, four or five rods square, where they tread down the snow in winter. At length, fearing that if we held the direct course to the summit we should not find any water near our camping-ground, we gradually swerved to the west, till, at four o'clock, we struck again the torrent which I have mentioned, and here, in view of the summit, the weary party decided to camp that night.

While my companions were seeking a suitable spot for this purpose, I improved the little daylight that was left, in climbing the mountain alone. We were in a deep and narrow ravine, sloping up to the clouds, at an angle of nearly forty-five degrees, and hemmed in by walls of rock, which were at first covered with low trees, then with impenetrable thickets of scraggy birches and spruce-trees and with moss, but at last bare of all vegetation but lichens, and almost continually draped in clouds. Following up the course of the torrent which occupied this—and I mean to lay some emphasis on this word *up*—pulling myself up by the side of perpendicular falls of twenty or thirty feet, by the roots of firs and birches, and then, perhaps, walking a level rod or two in the thin stream, for it took up the whole road, ascending by huge steps, as it were, a giant's stairway, down which a river flowed, I had soon cleared the trees, and paused on the successive shelves, to look back over the country. The torrent was from fifteen to thirty feet wide, without a tributary, and seemingly not diminishing in breadth as I advanced; but still it came rushing and roaring down, with a copious tide, over and amidst masses of bare rock, from the very clouds, as though a waterspout had just burst over the mountain. Leaving this at last, I began to work my way, scarcely less arduous than Satan's anciently through Chaos, up the nearest, though not the highest peak. At first scrambling on all fours over the tops of ancient black spruce-trees (*Abies nigra*), old as the flood, from two to ten or twelve feet in height, their tops flat and spreading, and their foliage blue, and nipt with cold, as if for centuries they had ceased grooving upward against the bleak sky, the solid cold. I walked some good rods erect upon the tops of these trees, which were overgrown with moss and mountain-cranberries. It seemed that in the course of time they had filled up the intervals between the huge rocks, and the cold wind had uniformly levelled all over. Here the principle of vegetation was hard put to it. There was apparently a belt of this kind running quite round the mountain, though, perhaps, nowhere so remarkable as here. Once, slumping through, I looked down ten feet, into a dark and cavernous region, and saw the stem of a spruce, on whose top I stood, as on a mass of coarse basket-work, fully nine inches in diameter at the ground. These holes were bears' dens, and the bears were even then at home. This was the sort of garden I made my way *over,* for an eighth of a mile, at the risk, it is true, of treading on some of the plants, not seeing any path *through* it—certainly the most treacherous and porous country I ever travelled.

> *Nigh foundered on he fares,*
> *Treading the crude consistence, half on foot,*
> *Half flying.*

But nothing could exceed the toughness of the twigs—not one snapped under my weight, for they had slowly grown. Having slumped, scrambled, rolled, bounced, and walked, by turns, over this scraggy country, I arrived upon a sidehill, or rather sidemountain, where rocks, gray, silent rocks, were the flocks and herds that pastured, chewing a rocky cud at sunset. They looked at me with hard gray eyes, without a bleat or a low. This brought me to the skirt of a cloud, and bounded my walk that night. But I had already seen that Maine country when I turned about, waving, flowing, rippling, down below.

When I returned to my companions, they had selected a camping-ground on the torrent's edge, and were resting on the ground; one was on the sick list, rolled in a blanket, on a damp shelf of rock. It was savage and dreary scenery enough; so wildly rough, that they looked long to find a level and open space for the tent. We could not well camp higher, for want of fuel; and the trees here seemed so evergreen and sappy, that we almost doubted if they would acknowledge the influence of fire; but fire prevailed at last, and blazed here, too, like a good citizen of the world. Even at this height we met with frequent traces of moose, as well as of bears. As here was no cedar, we made our bed of coarser feathered spruce; but at any rate the feathers were plucked from the live tree. It was, perhaps, even a more grand and desolate place for a night's lodging than the summit would have been, being in the neighborhood of those wild trees and of the torrent. Some more aerial and finer-spirited winds rushed and roared through the ravine all night, from time to time arousing our fire, and dispersing the embers about. It was as if we lay in the very nest of a young whirlwind. At midnight, one of my bedfellows, being startled in his dreams by the sudden blazing up to its top of a fir-tree, whose green boughs were dried by the heat, sprang up, with a cry, from his bed, thinking the world on fire, and drew the whole camp after him.

In the morning, after whetting our appetite on some raw pork, a wafer of hard bread, and a dipper of condensed cloud or water-spout, we all together began to make our way up the falls, which I have described; this time choosing the right hand, or highest peak which was not the one I had approached before. But soon my companions were lost to my sight behind the mountain ridge in my rear, which still seemed ever retreating before me, and I climbed alone over huge rocks, loosely poised, a mile or more, still edging toward the clouds; for though the day was clear elsewhere, the summit was concealed by mist. The mountain seemed a vast aggregation of loose rocks, as if some time it had rained rocks, and they lay as they fell on the mountain sides, nowhere fairly at rest, but leaning on each other, all rocking-stones, with cavities between, but scarcely any soil or smoother shelf. They were the raw materials of a planet dropped from an unseen quarry, which the vast chemistry of nature would anon work up, or work down, into the smiling and verdant plains and valleys of earth. This was an undone extremity of the globe; as in lignite, we see coal in the process of formation.

At length I entered within the skirts of the cloud which seemed forever drifting over the summit, and yet would never be gone, but was generated out of that pure air as fast as it flowed away; and when, a quarter of a mile farther, I reached the summit of the ridge, which those who have seen in clearer weather say is about five miles long, and contains a thousand acres of table-land, I was deep within the hostile ranks of clouds, and all objects were obscured by them. Now the wind would blow me a yard of clear sunlight, wherein I stood; then a gray, dawning light was all it could accomplish, the cloud-line ever rising and falling with the wind's intensity. Sometimes it seemed as if the summit would be cleared in a few moments and smile in sunshine; but what was gained on one side was lost on another. It was like sitting in a chimney and waiting for the smoke to blow away. It was, in fact, a cloud-factory—these were the cloudworks, and the wind turned them off done from the cool, bare rocks. Occasionally, when the windy columns broke in to me, I caught sight of a dark, damp crag to the right or left; the mist driving ceaselessly between it and me. It reminded me of the creations of the old epic and dramatic poets, of Atlas, Vulcan, the Cyclops, and Prometheus. Such was Caucasus and the rock where Prometheus was bound. Aeschylus had no doubt visited such scenery as this. It was vast, Titanic and such as man never inhabits. Some part of the beholder, even some vital part, seems to escape through the loose grating of his ribs as he ascends. He is more lone than you can imagine. There is less of substantial thought and fair understanding in him, than in the plains where men inhabit. His reason is dispersed and shadowy, more thin and subtle, like the air. Vast, Titanic, inhuman Nature has got him at disadvantage, caught him alone, and pilfers him of some of his divine faculty. She does not smile on him as in the plains. She seems to say sternly, why came ye here before your time? This ground is not prepared for you. Is it not enough that I smile in the valleys? I have never made this soil for thy feet, this air for thy breathing, these rocks for thy neighbors. I cannot pity nor fondle thee here, but forever relentlessly drive thee hence to where I am kind. Why seek me where I have not called thee, and then complain because you find me but a stepmother? Shouldst thou freeze or starve, or shudder thy life away, here is no shrine, nor altar, nor any access to my ear.

Chaos and ancient Night, I come no spy
With purpose to explore or to disturb
The secrets of your realm, but . . .
as my way
Lies through your spacious empire up to lights

The tops of mountains are among the unfinished parts of the globe, whither it is a slight insult to the gods to climb and pry into their secrets and try their effect on our humanity. Only daring and insolent men, perchance, go there. Simple races, as savages, do not climb mountains—their tops are sacred and mysterious tracts never visited by them. [The Abenaki deity] Pomola is always angry with those who climb to the summit of Ktaadn.

According to [Charles T.] Jackson, who, in his capacity of geological surveyor of the State, has accurately measured it, the altitude of Ktaadn is 5,300 feet, or a little more than one mile above the level of the sea, and, he adds, "It is then evidently the highest point in the State of Maine, and is the most abrupt granite mountain in New England." The peculiarities of that spacious table-land on which I was standing, as well as the remarkable semicircular precipice or basin on the eastern side, were all concealed by the mist. I had brought my whole pack to the top, not knowing but I should have to make my descent to the river, and possibly to the settled portion of the State alone, and by some other route, and wishing to have a complete outfit with me. But at length, fearing that my companions would be anxious to reach the river before night, and knowing that the clouds might rest on the mountain for days, I was compelled to descend. Occasionally, as I came down, the wind would blow me a vista open, through which I could see the country eastward, boundless forests, and lakes, and streams, gleaming in the sun, some of them emptying into the East. There were also new mountains in sight in that direction. Now and then some small bird of the sparrow family would flit away before me, unable to command its course, like a fragment of the gray rock blown off by the wind.

I found my companions where I had left them, on the side of the peak, gathering the mountain cranberries, which filled every crevice between the rocks, together with blueberries, which had a spicier flavor the higher up

8

they grew, but were not the less agreeable to our palates. When the country is settled, and roads are made these cranberries will perhaps become an article of commerce. From this elevation, just on the skirts of the clouds, we could overlook the country, west and south, for a hundred miles. There it was, the State of Maine, which we had seen on the map, but not much like that—immeasurable forest for the sun to shine on, that eastern stuff we hear of in Massachusetts. No clearing, no house. It did not look as if a solitary traveler had cut so much as a walking-stick there. Countless lakes—Moosehead in the southwest, forty miles long by ten wide, like a gleaming silver platter at the end of the table; Chesuncook, eighteen long by three wide, without an island; Millinocket, on the south, with its hundred islands; and a hundred other without a name; and mountains also, whose names, for the most part, are known only to the Indians. The forest looked like a firm grass sward, and the effect of these lakes in its midst has been well compared, by one who has since visited this same spot, to that of a "mirror broken into a thousand fragments, and wildly scattered over the grass, reflecting the full blaze of the sun."

Mountain People

(6)

MARTIN FROBISHER

In 1577 MARTIN FROBISHER (1535?-1594) left England in search of the fabled Northwest Passage, a waterway believed to provide easy transit from Europe to Asia. He did not find it, but he sailed through much uncharted territory, including the coast of northern Newfoundland. There Frobisher recorded these notes on the mountainous landscape and its people.

The day following, being the 19th of July, our captain returned to the ship, with report of supposed riches, which showed itself in the bowels of those barren mountains, wherewith we were all satisfied.

Within four days after we had been at the entrance of the straits, the northwest and west winds dispersed the ice into the sea, and made us a large entrance. We entered them, and our general and master with great diligence, sought out and found out a fair harbour for the ship and barks to ride in, and brought the ship, barks, and all their company to safe anchor, except one man, which died by God's visitation.

After the ship rode at anchor, our general, with such company as could well be spared from the ships, in marching order entered the land, having special care that we should all with one voice thank God for our safe arrival: secondly beseech Him, that it would please His divine majesty, long to continue our Queen, for whom he, and all the rest of our company in this order took possession of the country: and thirdly, that by our Christian study and endeavour, those barbarous people trained up in paganism, and infidelity, might be reduced to the knowledge of true religion, and to the hope of salvation in Christ our Redeemer.

We marched through the country, with ensign displayed, so far as was thought needful, and now and then heaped up stones on high mountains, and other places in token of possession, as likewise to signify unto such as hereafter may chance to arrive there, that possession is taken in the behalf of some other prince, by those that first found out the country.

The stones of this supposed continent with America be altogether sparkled, and glisten in the sun like gold: so likewise doth the sand in the bright water, yet they verify the old proverb: all is not gold that glistens.

On this west shore we found a dead fish floating, which had in his nose a horn straight and torqued, of length two yards lacking two inches, being broken in the top, where we might perceive it hollow, into which some of our sailors putting spiders they presently died. I saw not the trial thereof. By the virtue thereof we supposed it to be the sea unicorn [i.e., narwhal].

After our general had found out such store of supposed gold ore as he thought himself satisfied withal, he returned to the *Michael.* Coasting along the west shore not far from whence the ship rode, they perceived a fair harbour, and willing to sound the same, at the entrance thereof, they espied two tents of seal skins, unto which the captain, and other company resorted. At the sight of our men the people fled into the mountains: nevertheless they went to their tents, where leaving certain trifles of ours, as glasses, bells, knives, and such like things they departed, not taking any thing of theirs except one dog. They did in like manner leave behind them a letter, pen, ink, and paper, whereby our men whom the captain lost the year before, and in that people's custody, might (if any of them were alive) be advertised of our presence.

11

At our coming back again to the place where their tents were before, they had removed their tents further into the said bay or sound, where they might if they were driven from the land, flee with their boats into the sea. We parting ourselves into two companies, and compassing a mountain came suddenly upon them by land, who espying us, without any tarrying fled to their boats, leaving the most part of their oars behind them for haste, and rowed down the bay, where our two pinnaces met them and drove them to shore: but if they had had all their oars, so swift are they in rowing, it had been lost time to have chased them.

When they were landed they fiercely assaulted our men with their bows and arrows, who wounded three of them with our arrows: and perceiving themselves thus hurt, they desperately leapt off the rocks into the sea, and drowned themselves. Two women not being so apt to escape as the men were, the one for her age, and the other being encumbered with a young child, we took. The old wretch, whom divers of our sailors supposed to be either a devil, or a witch, had her buskins plucked off, to see if she were cloven footed, and for her ugly hue and deformity we let her go: the young woman and the child we brought away. We named the place where they were slain, Bloody Point.

Having this knowledge of their fierceness and cruelty, we disposed ourselves, contrary to our inclination, something to be cruel, returned to their tents and made a spoil of the same: where we found an old shirt, a doublet, a girdle, and also shoes of our men, whom we lost the year before.

Their riches are not gold, silver or precious drapery, but their said tents and boats, made of the skins of red deer and seal skins: also dogs like unto wolves.

They are men of a large corporature, and good proportion: their colour is not much unlike the sunburnt country man who laboureth daily in the sun for his living.

They wear their hair something long, and cut before either with stone or knife, very disorderly. Their women wear their hair long, and knit up with two loops, showing forth on either side of their faces, and the rest folded upon a knot. Also some of the women raze their faces proportionally, as chin, cheeks, and forehead, and the wrists of their hands, whereupon they lay a colour which continueth dark azurine.

They eat their meat all raw, both flesh, fish, and fowl, or something par-boiled with blood and a little water which they drink. For lack of water they will eat ice that is hard frozen, as pleasantly as we will do sugar candy, or other sugar.

If they for necessity's sake stand in need of the premises, such grass the country yielded they pluck up and eat, not daintily, or saladwise to allure their stomachs to appetite: but for necessity's sake without either salt, oils or washing, like brute beasts devouring the same. They neither use table, stool, nor table cloth for comeliness: but when they are imbrued with blood knuckle deep, and their knives in like sort, they use their tongues as apt in-strument to lick them clean: in doing whereof they are assured to lose none of their victuals.

They frank or keep certain dogs not much unlike wolves, which they yoke together, as we do oxen and horses, to a sled or trail: and so carry their necessaries over the ice and snow from place to place: as the captive, whom we have, made perfect signs. And when those dogs are not apt for the same use: or when with hunger they are constrained for lack of other victuals, they eat them.

They apparel themselves in the skins of such beasts as they kill, sewed together with the sinews of them.

Upon their legs they wear hose of leather, with the fur side inward two or three pair at once, and especially the women. In those hose they put their knives, needles, and other things needful to bear about.

They dress their skins very soft and supple with the hair on. In cold weather or winter they wear the fur side inward: and in summer outward. Other apparel they have none.

Those beasts, fishes, and fowls, which they kill, are their meat, drink, ap-parel, houses, bedding, hose, shoes, thread, and sails for their boats, with many other necessaries whereof they stand in need, and almost all their riches.

Their houses are tents made of seal skins, pitched up with 4 fir quarters foursquare meeting at the top, and the skins sewed together with sinews, and laid thereupon: they are so pitched up, that the entrance into them is al-ways south or against the sun.

Their darts are made of two sorts: the one with many forks of bones in the fore end and likewise in the midst: their proportions are not much unlike our toasting irons but longer: these they cast out of an instrument of wood, very readily. The other sort is greater than the first aforesaid, with a long bone made sharp on both sides not much unlike a rapier, which I take to be their most hurtful weapon.

They have two sorts of boats made of leather, set out on the inner side with quarters of wood, artificially tied together with thongs of the same: the other boat is but for one man to sit and row in with one oar.

What knowledge they have of God, or what idol they adore, we have no perfect intelligence. I think them rather anthropophagi, or devourers of man's flesh than otherwise: for that there is no flesh or fish which they find dead (smell it never so filthily) but they will eat it, as they find it without any other dressing.

The countries on both sides of the straits lie very high with rough stony mountains, and great quantity of snow thereon. There is very little plain ground and no grass, except a little which is much like unto moss that groweth on soft ground, such as we get turfs in. There is no wood at all. To be brief there is nothing fit or profitable for the use of man, which that country with root yieldeth or bringeth forth: howbeit there is great quantity of deer, whose skins are like unto asses, their heads or horns do far exceed, as well in length as also in breadth, any in these our parts or countries: their feet likewise are as great as our oxen's, which we measured to be seven or eight inches in breadth. There are also hares, wolves, fishing bears, and sea fowl of sundry sorts.

Front Range

WALT WHITMAN, ISABELLA LUCY BIRD

At the end of the American Civil War, which he had viewed as "a striving organism with which even Nature was in sympathy," the poet WALT WHITMAN *(1819–1892) was partially paralyzed by a stroke brought on, some suggest, by the horrors he had seen while working as a hospital attendant. As a restorative, Whitman traveled west as far as the Rocky Mountains to seek untrammeled open country, writing pastoral lyrics and fragmentary travel journals along the way. He collected some of those journals, along with his wartime reminiscences, in his last book,* Specimen Days *(1882).*

AN EGOTISTICAL "FIND"

"I have found the law of my own poems," was the unspoken but more and more decided feeling that came to me as I passed, hour after hour, amid all this grim yet joyous elemental abandon—this plenitude of material, entire absence of art, untrammeled play of primitive Nature—the chasm, the gorge, the crystal mountain stream, repeated scores, hundreds of miles—the broad handling and absolute uncrampedness—the fantastic forms, bathed in transparent browns, faint reds and grays, towering sometimes a thousand, sometimes two or three thousand feet high—at their tops now and then huge masses poised, and mixing with the clouds, with only their outlines, hazed in misty lilac, visible. ("In Nature's grandest shows," says an old Dutch writer, an ecclesiastic, "amid the ocean's depth, if so might be, or countless worlds rolling above at night, a man thinks of them, weighs all, not for themselves or the abstract, but with reference to his own personality, and how they may affect him or color his destinies.")

NEW SENSES—NEW JOYS

We follow the stream of amber and bronze brawling along its bed, with its frequent cascades and snow-white foam. Through the canyon we fly—mountains not only each side, but seemingly, till we get near, right in front of us—every rood a new view flashing, and each flash defying description—on the almost perpendicular sides, clinging pines, cedars, spruces, crimson sumac bushes, spots of wild grass—but dominating all, those towering rocks, rocks, rocks, bathed in delicate varicolors, with the clear sky of autumn overhead. New senses, new joys, seem developed. Talk as you like, a typical Rocky Mountain canyon, or a limitless, sealike stretch of the great Kansas or Colorado plains, under favoring circumstances, tallies, perhaps expresses, certainly awakes, those grandest and subtlest element emotions in the human soul, that all the marble temples and sculptures from Phidias to Thorwaldsen—all paintings, poems, reminiscences, or even music, probably never can.

STEAM POWER, TELEGRAPHS, ETC.

I get out on a ten minutes' stoppage at Deer Creek, to enjoy the unequaled combination of hill, stone, and wood. As we speed again, the yellow granite in the sunshine, with natural spires, minarets, castellated perches far aloft—

then long stretches of straight-upright palisades, rhinoceros color—then gamboge and tinted chromos. Ever the best of my pleasures the cool-fresh Colorado atmosphere, yet sufficiently warm. Signs of man's restless advent and pioneerage, hard as Nature's face is—deserted dugouts by dozens in the side-hills—the scantling hut, the telegraph pole, the smoke of some impromptu chimney or outdoor fire—at intervals little settlements of log houses, or parties of surveyors or telegraph builders, with their comfortable tents. Once, a canvas office where you could send a message by electricity anywhere around the world! Yes, pronounced signs of the man of latest dates, dauntlessly grappling with these grisliest shows of the old cosmos. At several places steam sawmills, with their piles of logs and boards, and the pipes puffing. Occasionally Platte Canyon expanding into a grassy flat of a few acres. At one such place, toward the end, where we stop, and I get out to stretch my legs, as I look skyward, or rather mountaintopward, a huge hawk or eagle (a rare sight here) is idly soaring, balancing along the ether, now sinking low and coming quite near, and then up again in stately, languid circles—then higher, higher, slanting to the north, and gradually out of sight.

America's Backbone

I jot these lines literally at Kenosha Summit, where we return, afternoon, and take a long rest, 10,000 feet above sea level. At this immense height the South Park stretches fifty miles before me. Mountainous chains and peaks in every variety of perspective, every hue of vista, fringe the view, in nearer, or middle, or far-dim distance, or fade on the horizon. We have now reached, penetrated the Rockies (Hayden calls it the Front Range) for a hundred miles or so; and though these chains spread away in every direction, especially north and south, thousands and thousands farther, I have seen specimens of the utmost of them, and know henceforth at least what they are and what they look like. Not themselves alone, for they typify stretches and areas of half the globe—are, in fact, the vertebrae or backbone of our hemisphere. As the anatomists say a man is only a spine, topped, footed, breasted, and radiated, so the whole Western world is, in a sense, but an expansion of these mountains. In South America they are the Andes, in Central America and

Mexico the Cordilleras, and in our states they go under different names—in California the Coast and Cascade ranges—thence more eastwardly the Sierra Nevadas—but mainly and more centrally here the Rocky Mountains proper, with many an elevation such as Lincoln's, Gray's, Harvard's, Yale's, Long's, and Pike's Peaks, all over 14,000 feet high. (East, the highest peaks of the Alleghanies, the Adirondacks, the Catskills, and the White Mountains, range from 2,000 to 5,000 feet—only Mount Washington, in the latter, 6,300 feet.)

THE PARKS

In the midst of all here, lie such beautiful contrasts as the sunken basins of the North, Middle, and South Parks (the latter I am now on one side of, and overlooking), each the size of a large, level, almost quadrangular, grassy, western county, walled in by walls of hills, and each park the source of a river. The ones I specify are the largest in Colorado, but the whole of that state, and of Wyoming, Utah, Nevada, and western California, through their sierras and ravines, are copiously marked by similar spreads and openings, many of the small ones of paradisiac loveliness and perfection, with their offsets of mountains, streams, atmosphere, and hues beyond compare.

ART FEATURES

Talk, I say again, of going to Europe, of visiting the ruins of feudal castles, or Colosseum remains, or kings' palaces—when you can come *here*. The alternations one gets, too; after the Illinois and Kansas prairies of a thousand miles—smooth and easy areas of the corn and wheat of ten million democratic farms in the future—here start up in every conceivable presentation of shape, these nonutilitarian piles, coping the skies, emanating a beauty, terror, power, more than Dante or Angelo ever knew. Yes, I think the chyle of not only poetry and painting, but oratory, and even the metaphysics and music fit for the New World, before being finally assimilated, need first and feeding visits here.

Mountain Streams

The spiritual contrast and ethereality of the whole region consists largely to me in its never-absent peculiar streams—the snows of inaccessible upper areas melting and running down through the gorges continually. Nothing like the water of pastoral plains, or creeks with wooded banks and turf or anything of the kind elsewhere. The shapes that element takes in the shows of the globe cannot be fully understood by an artist until he has studied these unique rivulets.

Aerial Effects

But perhaps as I gaze around me the rarest sight of all is in atmospheric hues. The prairies—as I crossed them in my journey hither—and these mountains and parks, seem to me to afford new lights and shades. Everywhere the aerial gradations and sky effects inimitable; nowhere else such perspectives, such transparent lilacs and grays. I can conceive of some superior landscape painter, some fine colorist, after sketching awhile out here, discarding all his previous work, delightful to stock exhibition amateurs, as muddy, raw, and artificial. Near one's eye ranges an infinite variety; high up, the bare white-brown, above timber line; in certain spots afar, patches of snow any time of year (no trees, no flowers, no birds, at those chilling altitudes). As I write I see the Snowy Range through the blue mist, beautiful and far off. I plainly see the patches of snow.

The English traveler Isabella Lucy Bird *(1831–1904), the author of* A Lady's Life in the Rocky Mountains, *was more adventurous than Whitman, scaling Longs Peak to take in a view of the ranges.*

Long's Peak, 14,700 feet high [The mountain is 14,256 feet high. —Ed.], blocks up one end of Estes Park, and dwarfs all the surrounding mountains. From it on this side rise, snow-born, the bright St. Vrain, and the Big and Little Thompson. By sunlight or moonlight its splintered gray crest is the one object which, in spite of wapiti and bighorn, skunk and grizzly, unfailingly arrests the eyes. From it come all storms of snow and wind, and the forked lightnings play round its head like a glory. It is one of the noblest of mountains, but in one's imagination it grows to be much more than a mountain. It becomes invested with a personality. In its caverns and abysses one comes to fancy that it generates and chains the strong winds, to let them loose in its fury. The thunder becomes its voice, and the lightnings do it homage. Other summits blush under the morning kiss of the sun, and turn pale the next moment; but it detains the first sunlight and holds it round its head for an hour at least, till it pleases to change from rosy red to deep blue; and the sunset, as if spell-bound, lingers latest on its crest. The soft winds which hardly rustle the pine needles down here are raging rudely up there round its motionless summit. The mark of fire is upon it; and though it has passed into a grim repose, it tells of fire and upheaval as truly, though not as eloquently, as the living volcanoes of Hawaii. Here under its shadow one learns how naturally nature worship, and the propitiation of the forces of nature, arose in minds which had no better light.

Long's Peak, "the American Matterhorn," as some call it, was ascended five years ago for the first time. I thought I should like to attempt it, but up to Monday, when Evans left for Denver, cold water was thrown upon the project. It was late in the season, the winds were likely to be strong, etc.; but just before leaving, Evans said that the weather was looking more settled, and if I did not get farther than the timber line it would be worth going. Soon after he left, "Mountain Jim" came in, and said he would go up as guide, and the two youths who rode here with me from Longmount and I caught at the proposal. . . .

The ride was one series of glories and surprises of "park" and glade, of lake and stream, of mountains on mountains, culminating in the rent pinnacles of Long's Peak, which looked yet grander and ghastlier as we crossed an attendant mountain 11,000 feet high. The slanting sun added fresh beauty

every hour. There were dark pines against a lemon sky, gray peaks redden-
ing and etherealizing, gorges of deep and infinite blue, floods of golden glory
pouring through canyons of enormous depth, an atmosphere of absolute
purity, an occasional foreground of cottonwood, and aspen flaunting in red
and gold to intensify the blue gloom of the pines, the trickle and murmur of
streams fringed with icicles, the strange sough of gusts moving among the
pine tops—sights and sounds not of the lower earth, but of the solitary,
beast-haunted, frozen upper altitudes. From the dry, buff grass of Estes Park
we turned off up a trail on the side of a pine-hung gorge, up a steep pine-
clothed hill, down to a small valley, rich in fine, sun-cured hay about eighteen inches high, and enclosed by high mountains whose deepest hollow
contains a lily-covered lake, fitly named "The Lake of the Lilies." Ah, how
magical its beauty was, as it slept in silence, while there the dark pines were
mirrored motionless in its pale gold, and here the great white lily cups and
dark green leaves rested on amethyst-colored water!

From this we ascended into the purple gloom of great pine forests
which clothe the skirts of the mountains up to a height of about 11,000
feet, and from their chill and solitary depths we had glimpses of golden atmosphere and rose-lit summits, not of "the land very far off," but of the
land nearer now in all its grandeur, gaining in sublimity by nearness—
glimpses, too, through a broken vista of purple gorges, of the illimitable
Plains lying idealized in the late sunlight, their baked, brown expanse trans-
figured into the likeness of a sunset sea rolling infinitely in waves of misty
gold.

We rode upwards through the gloom on a steep trail blazed through the
forest, all my intellect concentrated on avoiding being dragged off my horse
by impending branches, or having the blankets badly torn, as those of my
companions were, by sharp dead limbs, between which there was hardly
room to pass—the horses breathless, and requiring to stop every few yards,
though their riders, except myself, were afoot. The gloom of the dense, ancient, silent forest is to me awe inspiring. On such an evening it is soundless,
except for the branches creaking in the soft wind, the frequent snap of decayed timber, and a murmur in the pine tops as of a not distant waterfall, all
tending to produce eeriness and sadness. . . .

Day dawned long before the sun rose, pure and lemon colored. The rest
were looking after the horses, when one of the students came running to tell
me that I must come farther down the slope, for Jim said he had never seen
such a sunrise. From the chill, gray Peak above, from the everlasting snows,
from the silvered pines, down through mountain ranges with their depths of
Tyrian purple, we looked to where the Plains lay cold, in blue-gray, like a
morning sea against a far horizon. Suddenly, as a dazzling streak at first, but
enlarging rapidly into a dazzling sphere, the sun wheeled above the gray
line, a light and glory as when it was first created. Jim involuntarily and reverently uncovered his head, and exclaimed, "I believe there is a God!" I felt
as if, Parsee-like, I must worship. The gray of the Plains changed to purple,
the sky was all one rose-red flush, on which vermilion cloud-streaks rested;
the ghastly peaks gleamed like rubies, the earth and heavens were new created. Surely "the Most High dwelleth not in temples made with hands!" For
a full hour those Plains simulated the ocean, down to whose limitless expanse of purple, cliff, rocks, and promontories swept down.

By seven we had finished breakfast, and passed into the ghastlier solitudes above, I riding as far as what, rightly or wrongly, are called the "Lava
Beds," an expanse of large and small boulders, with snow in their crevices.
It was very cold; some water which we crossed was frozen hard enough to
bear the horse. Jim had advised me against taking any wraps, and my thin
Hawaiian riding dress, only fit for the tropics, was penetrated by the keen
air. The rarefied atmosphere soon began to oppress our breathing, and I
found that Evans' boots were so large that I had no foothold. Fortunately, before the real difficulty of the ascent began, we found, under a rock, a pair of
small overshoes, probably left by the Hayden exploring expedition, which
just lasted for the day. As we were leaping from rock to rock, Jim said, "I was
thinking in the night about your traveling alone, and wondering where you
carried your Derringer, for I could see no signs of it." On my telling him that
I traveled unarmed, he could hardly believe it, and adjured me to get a re-
volver at once.

On arriving at the "Notch" (a literal gate of rock), we found ourselves absolutely on the knifelike ridge or backbone of Long's Peak, only a few feet
wide, covered with colossal boulders and fragments, and on the other side

shelving in one precipitous, snow-patched sweep of 3,000 feet to a picturesque hollow, containing a lake of pure green water. Other lakes, hidden among dense pine woods, were farther off, while close above us rose the Peak, which, for about 500 feet, is a smooth, gaunt, inaccessible-looking pile of granite. Passing through the "Notch," we looked along the nearly inaccessible side of the Peak, composed of boulders and debris of all shapes and sizes, through which appeared broad, smooth ribs of reddish-colored granite, looking as if they upheld the towering rock mass above. I usually dislike bird's-eye and panoramic views, but, though from a mountain, this was not one. Serrated ridges, not much lower than that on which we stood, rose, one beyond another, far as that pure atmosphere could carry the vision, broken into awful chasms deep with ice and snow, rising into pinnacles piercing the heavenly blue with their cold, barren, gray, on, on for ever, till the most distant range upbore unsullied snow alone. There were fair lakes mirroring the dark pine woods, canyons dark and blue-black with unbroken expanses of pines, snowlashed pinnacles, wintry heights frowning upon lovely parks, watered and wooded, lying in the lap of summer; North Park floating off into the blue distance, Middle Park closed till another season, the sunny slopes of Estes Park, and winding down among the mountains the snowy ridge of the Divide, whose bright waters seek both the Atlantic and Pacific Oceans. There, far below, links of diamonds showed where the Grand River takes its rise to seek the mysterious Colorado, with its still unsolved enigma, and lose itself in the waters of the Pacific, and nearer the snow-born Thompson bursts forth from the ice to begin its journey to the Gulf of Mexico. Nature, rioting in her grandest mood, exclaimed with voices of grandeur, solitude, sublimity, beauty, and infinity, "Lord, what is man, that Thou art mindful of him? or the son of man, that Thou visitest him?" Never-to-be-forgotten glories they were, burnt in upon my memory by six succeeding hours of terror.

You know I have no head and no ankles, and never ought to dream of mountaineering; and had I known that the ascent was a real mountaineering feat I should not have felt the slightest ambition to perform it. As it is, I am only humiliated by my success, for Jim dragged me up, like a bale of goods, by sheer force of muscle. At the "Notch" the real business of the ascent began. Two thousand feet of solid rock towered above us, four thousand feet of broken rock shelved precipitously below; smooth granite ribs, with barely foothold, stood out here and there; melted snow refrozen several times, presented a more serious obstacle; many of the rocks were loose, and tumbled down when touched. To me it was a time of extreme terror. I was roped to Jim, but it was of no use; my feet were paralyzed and slipped on the bare rock, and he said it was useless to try to go that way, and we retraced our steps. I wanted to return to the "Notch," knowing that my incompetence would detain the party, and one of the young men said almost plainly that a woman was a dangerous encumbrance, but the trapper replied shortly that if it were not to take a lady up he would not go up at all. He went on to explore, and reported that further progress on the correct line of ascent was blocked by ice; and then for two hours we descended, lowering ourselves by our hands from rock to rock along a boulder-strewn sweep of 4,000 feet, patched with ice and snow, and perilous from rolling stones. My fatigue, giddiness, and pain from bruised ankles, and arms half pulled out of their sockets, were so great that I should never have gone halfway had not Jim, nolens volens, dragged me along with a patience and skill, and withal a determination that I should ascend the Peak which never failed. After descending about 2,000 feet to avoid the ice, we got into a deep ravine with inaccessible sides, partly filled with ice and snow and partly with large and small fragments of rock, which were constantly giving away, rendering the footing very insecure. That part to me was two hours of painful and unwilling submission to the inevitable; of trembling, slipping, straining, of smooth ice appearing when it was least expected, and of weak entreaties to be left behind while the others went on. Jim always said that there was no danger, that there was only a short bad bit ahead, and that I should go up even if he carried me!

Slipping, faltering, gasping from exhausting toil in the rarefied air, with throbbing hearts and panting lungs, we reached the top of the gorge and squeezed ourselves between two gigantic fragments of rock by a passage called the "Dog's Lift," when I climbed on the shoulders of one man and then was hauled up. This introduced us by an abrupt turn round the southwest angle of the Peak to a narrow shelf of considerable length, rugged, uneven, and so overhung by the cliff in some places that it is necessary to crouch to pass it all. Above, the Peak looks nearly vertical for 400 feet; and below, the most tremendous precipice I have ever seen descends in one un-broken fall. This is usually considered the most dangerous part of the as-cent, but it does not seem so to me, for such foothold as there is is secure, and one fancies that it is possible to hold on with the hands. But there, and on the final, and, to my thinking, the worst part of the climb, one slip, and a breathing, thinking, human being would lie 3,000 feet below, a shapeless, bloody heap!

From thence the view is more magnificent even than that from the "Notch." At the foot of the precipice below us lay a lovely lake, wood embo-somed, from or near which the bright St. Vrain and other streams take their rise. I thought how their clear cold waters, growing turbid in the affluent flats, would heat under the tropic sun, and eventually form part of that great ocean river which renders our far-off islands habitable by impinging on their shores. Snowy ranges, one behind the other, extended to the distant horizon, folding in their wintry embrace the beauties of Middle Park. Pike's Peak, more than one hundred miles off, lifted that vast but shapeless summit which is the landmark of southern Colorado. There were snow patches, snow slashes, snow abysses, snow forlorn and soiled looking, snow pure and dazzling, snow glistening above the purple robe of pine worn by all the mountains; while away to the east, in limitless breadth, stretched the green-gray of the endless Plains. Giants everywhere reared their splintered crests. From thence, with a single sweep, the eye takes in a distance of 300 miles—that distance to the west, north, and south being made up of mountains ten, eleven, twelve, and thirteen thousand feet in height, dominated by Long's Peak, Gray's Peak, and Pike's Peak, all nearly the height of Mont Blanc! On the Plains we traced the rivers by their fringe of cottonwoods to the distant Platte, and between us and them lay glories of mountain, canyon, and lake, sleeping in depths of blue and purple most ravishing to the eye.

Sacred Geography

NAVAJO TEXT

*The native peoples of the Americas use mountains to mark tribal and sa-
cred territories, which, as the Tewa scholar Alfonso Ortiz has noted, often
overlap. The Santa Catalina Mountains north of Tucson, Arizona, have
a role in the religions of not only the nearby Tohono O'odham and White
Mountain Apaches but also the distant Luiseño and Diegueño peoples of
the southern California coast; the mountains of the Colorado Plateau are
sacred to Zuni, Pueblo, Navajo, and Hopi alike. The supernatural beings
who live in these mountains, the "mountain people," are protectors, trans-
mitters of special knowledge, and teachers of song and custom.*

*Here a Navajo shaman named SANDOVAL describes the sacred geogra-
phy of his people's defining mountains: Blanca Peak (East) and Mount
Taylor (South) in New Mexico, the San Francisco Peaks (West) of Arizona, and the La Plata Mountains (North) of Colorado.*

First Man and First Woman formed six sacred mountains from the soil that
First Man had gathered from the mountains in the Third World and kept in

his medicine bag. As before, they placed Sis na 'jin in the East, Tso dzil in the South, Dook 'oslid in the West, and Debe'ntsa in the North. They placed a sacred mountain, which they called Choli'i'i, on the earth, and they made the mountain, Dzilna' odili, around which the people were to travel.

There were four Holy Boys. These beings First Man called to him. He told the White Bead Boy to enter the mountain of the East, Sis na 'jin. The Turquoise Boy he told to go into the mountain of the South, Tso dzil. The Abalone Shell Boy entered the mountain of the West, Dook 'oslid. And into the mountain of the North, Debe'ntsa, went the Jet Boy.

Now the mountains to the East and South were dissatisfied. The East wanted the Turquoise Boy and the South wanted the White Bead Boy for their bodies. There was quite a lot of trouble; the mountains would tremble as though they were not satisfied. The other mountains were happy in their bodies and there was no trouble between them. First Man and First Woman called other Holy Beings to them. They put the Beautiful Mixed Stones Boy and Girl into the sacred mountain called Choli'i'i. They put the Pollen Boy and Grasshopper Girl into Dzilna 'odili. They asked the Rock Crystal Girl to go into Sis na 'jin. They put the White Corn Girl into Tso dzil; the Yellow Corn Girl into Dook 'oslid; and the Darkness Girl into Debe'ntsa.

After the Holy Beings had entered the Sacred Mountains First Man and First Woman dressed them according to their positions on the earth. They fastened Sis na 'jin to the earth with a bolt of white lightning. They covered the mountain with a blanket of daylight, and they decorated it with white shells, white lightning, black clouds, and male rain. They placed the white shell basket on the summit; and in this basket two eggs of the hasbi'delgai, the pigeon. They said that the pigeons were to be the mountain's feather; and that is why there are many wild pigeons in this mountain today. And, lastly they sent the bear to guard the doorway of the White Bead Boy in the East.

Tso dzil, they fastened to the earth with a stone knife. They covered this mountain of the South with a blue cloud blanket; and they decorated it with turquoise, white corn, dark mists, and the female rain. They placed a turquoise basket on the highest peak, and in it they put two eggs of the blue-bird, doli. Bluebirds are Tso dzil's feathers. They sent the big snake to guard the doorway of the Turquoise Boy in the South.

Dook 'oslid was fastened to the earth with a sunbeam. They covered the mountain of the West with a yellow cloud. They adorned it with haliotis shell, yellow corn, black clouds, and the male rain, and they called many animals to dwell upon it. They placed the abalone shell basket on the summit; and in it they placed the two eggs of the tsidiltsoi, the yellow warbler. These birds were to become its feather. The Black Wind was told to go to the West and guard the doorway of the Abalone Shell Boy.

They fastened the mountain of the North, Debe'ntsa, to the earth with a rainbow. Over it they spread a blanket of darkness. They decorated it with bash'zhini' obsidian, black vapors, and different plants and animals. The basket they placed on its highest peak was of obsidian; and in it they put two eggs of the Chagi, the blackbird. The blackbirds are the mountain's feather. The lightning was sent to guard the Jet Boy's doorway in the North.

First Man and First Woman fastened the Sacred Mountain Choli'i'i to the earth with a streak of rain. They decorated it with the pollens, mixed chips of stone precious to them, the dark mists, and the female rain. And they fastened Dzilna' odili to the earth with the 'hadahonige, the mirage stone, and those people associate the Mirage Boy and the Carnelian Girl with the mountain. All the mountains have their prayers and chants which are called Dressing the Mountains. All the cornerposts have their prayers and chants, as have the stars and markings in the sky and on the earth. It is their custom to keep the sky and the earth and the day and the night beautiful. The belief is that if this is done, living among the people of the earth will be good.

Songs for the Mountain World

AKIMEL O'ODHAM, CHIRICAHUA APACHE,
CHEYENNE, SOUTHERN PAIUTE,
WIND RIVER SHOSHONE, TEWA,
TOHONO O'ODHAM, AND PAIUTE TEXTS

Greasy Mountain,
Greasy Mountain stands.
There inside
Green flowers
Cover me.
There inside
Manic is.

Broad Mountain stands.
There below, waters primed to spurt.
And I below there go,
On stick's end cling:
Stick glitters,
then enter.

Does your singing speak?
I'm going but dead
And wander here.
Long Mountain
there manic calls.
Behind I circle,
Suddenly dizziness
Makes lines back and forth.

Do you hear me?
Do you hear me?
All earth sounding,
Circles stomped on top,
On top, eagle down puffing,
Cloud entering.

(AKIMEL O'ODHAM)

Earth Magician shapes this world.
    Behold what he can do!
Round and smooth he molds it.
    Behold what he can do!
Earth Magician makes the mountains.
    Heed what he has to say!
He is that which makes the mesas.
    Heed what he has to say!
Earth Magician shapes this world.
    Earth Magician makes its mountains.

(AKIMEL O'ODHAM)

Big Blue Mountain Spirit,
The home made of blue clouds,
The cross made of the blue mirage,
There, you have begun to live,
There, is the life of goodness,
I am grateful for that made of goodness there.

Big Yellow Mountain Spirit in the south,
Your spiritually hale body is made of yellow clouds;
Leader of the Mountain Spirits, holy Mountain Spirit,
You live by means of the good of this life.

Big White Mountain Spirit in the west,
Your spiritually hale body is made of the white mirage;
Holy Mountain Spirit, leader of the Mountain Spirits,
I am happy over your words,
You are happy over my words.

Big Black Mountain Spirit in the north,
Your spiritually hale body is made of black clouds;
In that way, Big Black Mountain Spirit,
Holy Mountain Spirit, leader of the Mountain Spirits,
I am happy over your words,
You are happy over my words,
Now it is good.

(CHIRICAHUA APACHE)

The mountain,
The mountain,
It is circling around,
It is circling around.

A'hiya'e'yee'heye!
A'hiya'e'yee'heye!

(CHEYENNE)

The rocks are ringing,
The rocks are ringing,
The rocks are ringing.
They are ringing in the mountains,
They are ringing in the mountains,
They are ringing in the mountains.

(SOUTHERN PAIUTE)

Sunlit showers on the mountains, sunlit showers on the mountains ena.
Sunlit showers on the mountains, sunlit showers on the mountains ena.
Pine needles in pools of mountainside gullies after sunlit showers on the
mountains ena.

(WIND RIVER SHOSHONE)

My home over there, my home over there,
My home over there, now I remember it.
And when I see that mountain far away,
I weep. What can I do?
What can I do? What can I do?
My home over there, now I remember it.

(TEWA)

A sandy land I saw
And in this land
I make my home.
A sandy land mountain
I learned
I am going to make my home there.

(TOHONO O'ODHAM)

At first the world was all water, and remained so a long time. The water began to go down and at last Kura'ngwa [Mount Grant] emerged from the water, near the southwest end of Walker Lake. There was fire on its top, and when the wind blew hard the water dashed over the fire and would have extinguished it, but that the sage-hen nestled down over it and fanned away the water with her wing. The heat scorched the feathers on the breast of the sage-hen, and they remain black to this day. Afterward the Paiute got their first fire from the mountain through the help of the rabbit, who is a great wonder-worker, the same as a god. As the water subsided other mountains appeared, until at last the earth was left as it is now.

Then the great ancestor of the Paiute, whom they call *Numi'naa'*, "Our Father," came from the south in the direction of Mount Grant, upon which his footprints can still be seen, and journeyed across to the mountains east of Carson sink and made his home there. A woman, *Ibidsíí*, "Our Mother," followed him from the same direction, and they met and she became his wife. They dressed themselves in skins, and lived on the meat of deer and mountain sheep, for there was plenty of game in those days. They had children, two boys and two girls. Their father made bows and arrows for the boys, and the mother fashioned sticks for the girls with which to dig roots. When the children grew up, each boy married his sister, but the two families quarreled until their father told them to separate. So one family went to Walker Lake and became *Aga'ihtikara*, "fish eaters" (Walker Lake Paiute), while the other family went farther north into Idaho and became *Kot-*

so'tikara, "buffalo eaters" (Bannock), but both are one people and have the same language. After their children had left them, the parents went on to the mountains farther east, and there *Numi'naa'* went up to the sky and his wife followed him.

(PAIUTE)

Sierra Nevada

❧

JOHN MUIR, MARY AUSTIN

*The naturalist and outdoorsman JOHN MUIR (1838–1914), who founded
the Sierra Club, spent much of his life exploring the desert and mountain
West, especially his beloved Sierra Nevada. In* The Mountains of California, *he describes a thunderstorm in the high country.*

The weather of spring and summer in the middle region of the Sierra is usually well flecked with rains and light dustings of snow, most of which are far
too obviously joyful and life-giving to be regarded as storms; and in the picturesque beauty and clearness of outlines of their clouds they offer striking
contrasts to those boundless, all-embracing cloud-mantles of the storms of
winter. The smallest and most perfectly individualized specimens present a
richly modeled cumulus cloud rising above the dark woods, about 11 A.M.,
swelling with a visible motion straight up into the calm, sunny sky to a
height of 12,000 to 14,000 feet above the sea, its white, pearly bosses relieved by gray and pale purple shadows in the hollows, and showing outlines as keenly defined as those of the glacier-polished domes. In less than

35

an hour it attains full development and stands poised in the blazing sunshine like some colossal mountain, as beautiful in form and finish as if it were to become a permanent addition to the landscape. Presently a thunderbolt crashes through the crisp air, ringing like steel on steel, sharp and clear, its startling detonation breaking into a spray of echoes against the cliffs and cañon walls. Then down comes a cataract of rain. The big drops sift through the pine-needles, plash and patter on the granite pavements, and pour down the sides of ridges and domes in a network of gray, bubbling rills. In a few minutes the cloud withers to a mesh of dim filaments and disappears, leaving the sky perfectly clear and bright, every dust-particle wiped and washed out of it. Everything is refreshed and invigorated, a steam of fragrance rises, and the storm is finished—one cloud, one lightning-stroke, and one dash of rain. This is the Sierra midsummer thunder-storm reduced to its lowest terms. But some of them attain much larger proportions, and assume a grandeur and energy of expression hardly surpassed by those bred in the depths of winter, producing those sudden floods called "cloudbursts," which are local, and to a considerable extent periodical, for they appear nearly every day about the same time for weeks, usually about eleven o'clock, and lasting from five minutes to an hour or two. One soon becomes so accustomed to see them that the noon sky seems empty and abandoned without them, as if Nature were forgetting something. When the glorious pearl and alabaster clouds of these noonday storms are being built I never give attention to anything else. No mountain or mountain-range, however divinely clothed with light, has a more enduring charm than those fleeting mountains of the sky—floating fountains bearing water for every well, the angels of the streams and lakes; brooding in the deep azure, or sweeping softly along the ground over ridge and dome, over meadow, over forest, over garden and grove; lingering with cooling shadows, refreshing every flower, and soothing rugged rock-brows with a gentleness of touch and gesture wholly divine.

The most beautiful and imposing of the summer storms rise just above the upper edge of the Silver Fir zone, and all are so beautiful that it is not easy to choose any one for particular description. The one that I remember best fell on the mountains near Yosemite Valley, July 19, 1869, while I was encamped in the Silver Fir woods. A range of bossy cumuli took possession of the sky, huge domes and peaks rising one beyond another with deep cañons between them, bending this way and that in long curves and reaches, interrupted here and there with white upboiling masses that looked like the spray of waterfalls. Zigzag lances of lightning followed each other in quick succession, and the thunder was so gloriously loud and massive it seemed as if surely an entire mountain was being shattered at every stroke. Only the trees were touched, however, so far as I could see,—a few firs 200 feet high, perhaps, and five to six feet in diameter, were split into long rails and slivers from top to bottom and scattered to all points of the compass. Then came the rain in a hearty flood, covering the ground and making it shine with a continuous sheet of water that, like a transparent film or skin, fitted closely down over all the rugged anatomy of the landscape.

It is not long, geologically speaking, since the first raindrop fell on the present landscapes of the Sierra; and in the few tens of thousands of years of stormy cultivation they have been blest with, how beautiful they have become! The first rains fell on raw, crumbling moraines and rocks without a plant. Now scarcely a drop can fail to find a beautiful mark: on the tops of the peaks, on the smooth glacier pavements, on the curves of the domes, on moraines full of crystals, on the thousand forms of yosemitic sculpture with their tender beauty of balmy, flowery vegetation, laving, plashing, glinting, pattering; some falling softly on meadows, creeping out of sight, seeking and finding every thirsty rootlet, some through the spires of the woods, sifting in dust through the needles, and whispering good cheer to each of them; some falling with blunt tapping sounds, drumming on the broad leaves of veratrum, cypripedium, saxifrage; some falling straight into fragrant corollas, kissing the lips of lilies, glinting on the sides of crystals, on shining grains of gold; some falling into the fountains of snow to swell their well-saved stores; some into the lakes and rivers, patting the smooth glassy levels, making dimples and bells and spray, washing the mountain windows, washing the wandering winds; some plashing into the heart of snowy falls and cascades as if eager to join in the dance and the song and beat the foam yet finer. Good work and happy work for the merry mountain raindrops, each one of them a brave fall in itself, rushing from the cliffs and hollows of the clouds into the cliffs and hollows of the mountains; away from the thunder of the sky into the thunder of the roaring rivers. And how far they have to go, and how many cups to fill—cassiope-cups, holding half a drop, and lake basins between the hills, each replenished with equal care—every drop God's messenger sent on its way with glorious pomp and display of power—silvery new-born stars with lake and river, mountain and valley—all that the landscape holds—reflected in their crystal depths.

Mary Austin (1868–1934) also spent much of her life exploring the American West. In this passage from her 1903 book The Land of Little Rain, *she describes the southern Sierra.*

All streets of the mountains lead to the citadel; steep or slow they go up to the core of the hills. Any trail that goes otherwise must dip and cross, sidle and take chances. Rifts of the hills open into each other, and the high meadows are often wide enough to be called valleys by courtesy; but one keeps this distinction in mind,—valleys are the sunken places of the earth, cañons are scored out by the glacier ploughs of God. They have a better name in the Rockies for these hill-fenced open glades of pleasantness; they call them parks. Here and there in the hill country one comes upon blind gullies fronted by high stony barriers. These head also for the heart of the mountains; their distinction is that they never get anywhere.

All mountain streets have streams to thread them, or deep grooves where a stream might run. You would do well to avoid that range uncomforted by singing floods. You will find it forsaken of most things but beauty and madness and death and God. Many such lie east and north away from the mid Sierras, and quicken the imagination with the sense of purposes not revealed, but the ordinary traveler brings nothing away from them but an intolerable thirst.

The river cañons of the Sierras of the Snows are better worth while than most Broadways, though the choice of them is like the choice of streets, not very well determined by their names. There is always an amount of local history to be read in the names of mountain highways where one touches the successive waves of occupation or discovery, as in the old villages where the neighborhoods are not built but grow. Here you have the Spanish California in Cerro Gordo and piñon; Symmes and Shepherd, pioneers both; Tunawai, probably Shoshone; Oak Creek, Kearsarge,—easy to fix the date of that christening,—Tinpah, Paiute that; Mist Cañon and Paddy Jack's. The streets of the west Sierras sloping toward the San Joaquin are long and winding, but from the east, my country, a day's ride carries one to the lake regions. The next day reaches the passes of the high divide, but whether one gets passage depends a little on how many have gone that road before, and much on one's own powers. The passes are steep and windy ridges, though not the highest. By two and three thousand feet the snow-caps overtop them. It is even possible to wind through the Sierras without having passed above timber-line, but one misses a great exhilaration.

The shape of a new mountain is roughly pyramidal, running out into long shark-finned ridges that interfere and merge into other thunder-splintered sierras. You get the sawtooth effect from a distance, but the nearby granite bulk glitters with the terrible keen polish of old glacial ages. I say terrible; so it seems. When those glossy domes swim into the alpenglow, wet after rain, you conceive how long and imperturbable are the purposes of God.

Never believe what you are told, that midsummer is the best time to go up the streets of the mountain—well—perhaps for the merely idle or sportsmanly or scientific; but for seeing and understanding, the best time is when you have the longest leave to stay. And here is a hint if you would attempt the stateliest approaches; travel light, and as much as possible live off the land. Mulligatawny soup and tinned lobster will not bring you the favor of the woodlanders.

Every cañon commends itself for some particular pleasantness; this for pines, another for trout, one for pure bleak beauty of granite buttresses, one for its far-flung irised falls; and as I say, though some are easier going, leads each to the cloud-shouldering citadel. First, near the cañon mouth you get the low-heading full-branched, one-leaf pines. That is the sort of tree to know at sight, for the globose, resin-dripping cones have palatable, nourishing kernels, the main harvest of the Paiutes. That perhaps accounts for their growing accommodatingly below the limit of deep snow, grouped somberly on the valleyward slopes. The real procession of the pines begins in the rifts with the long-leafed *Pinus jeffreyi,* sighing its soul away upon the wind. And it ought not to sigh in such good company. Here begins the manzanita, adjusting its tortuous stiff stems to the sharp waste of boulders, its pale olive leaves twisting edgewise to the sleek, ruddy, chestnut stems; begins also the meadowsweet, burnished laurel, and the million unregarded trumpets of the coral-red penstemon. Wild life is likely to be busiest about the lower pine border. One looks in hollow trees and hiving rocks for wild honey. The drone of bees, the chatter of jays, the hurry and stir of squirrels, is incessant; the air is odorous and hot. The roar of the stream fills up the morning and evening intervals, and at night the deer feed in the buckthorn thickets. It is worth watching the year round in the purlieus of the long-leafed pines. One month or another you get sight or trail of most roving mountain dwellers as they follow the limit of forbidding snows, and more bloom than you can properly appreciate.

Whatever goes up or comes down the streets of the mountains, water has the right of way; it takes the lowest ground and the shortest passage. Where the rifts are narrow, and some of the Sierra cañons are not a stone's throw from wall to wall, the best trail for foot or horse winds considerably above the watercourses; but in a country of cone-bearers there is usually a good strip of swardy sod along the cañon floor. Pine woods, the short-leafed Balfour and Murryana of the high Sierras, are somber, rooted in the litter of a thousand years, hushed, and corrective to the spirit. The trail passes insensibly into them from the black pines and a thin belt of firs. You look back as you rise, and strain for glimpses of the tawny valley, blue glints of the Bitter Lake, and tender cloud films on the farther ranges. For such pictures the pine branches make a noble frame. Presently they close in wholly; they draw mysteriously near, covering your tracks, giving up the trail indifferently, or with a secret grudge. You get a kind of impatience with their locked ranks, until you come out lastly on some high, windy dome and see what they are about. They troop thickly up the open ways, river banks and brook borders; up open swales of dribbling springs swarm over old moraines; circle the peaty swamps and part and meet about clean still lakes; scale the stony gullies, tormented, bowed, persisting to the door of the storm chambers tall priests to pray for rain. The spring winds lift clouds of pollen dust, finer than frankincense, and trail it out over high altars, staining the snow. No doubt they understand this work better than we; in fact they know no other. "Come," say the churches of the valleys, after a season of dry years, "let us pray for rain." They would do better to plant more trees.

It is a pity we have let the gift of lyric improvisation die out. Sitting islanded on some gray peak above the encompassing wood, the soul is lifted up to sing the Iliad of the pines. They have no voice but the wind, and no sound of them rises up to the high places. But the waters, the evidences of their power, that go down the steep and stony ways, the outlets of ice-bordered pools, the young rivers swaying with the force of their running, they sing and shout and trumpet at the falls, and the noise of it far out-reaches the forest spires. You see from these conning towers how they call and find each other in the slender gorges; how they fumble in the meadows, needing the sheer nearing walls to give them countenance and show the way; and how the pine woods are made glad by them.

Nothing else in the streets of the mountains gives such a sense of pageantry as the conifers; other trees, if there are any, are home dwellers, like the tender fluttered, sisterhood of quaking aspen. They grow in clumps by spring borders, and all their stems have a permanent curve toward the down slope, as you may also see in hillside pines, where they have borne the weight of sagging drifts.

Well up from the valley, at the confluence of cañons, are delectable summer meadows. Fireweed flames about them against the gray boulders; streams are open, go smoothly about the glacier slips and make deep bluish pools for trout. Pines raise statelier shafts and give themselves room to grow,—gentians, shinleaf, and little grass of Parnassus in their golden checkered shadows; the meadow is white with violets and all outdoors keeps the clock. For example, when the ripples at the ford of the creek raise a clear half tone,—sign that the snow water has come down from the heated high ridges,—it is time to light the evening fire. When it drops off a note—but you will not know it except the Douglas squirrel tells you with his high, fluty chirrup from the pines' aerial gloom—it is a sign that some star watcher has caught the first far glint of the nearing sun. Whitney cries it from his vantage tower; it flashes from Oppapago to the front of Williamson; LeConte speeds it to the weltering peaks. The high rills wake and run, the birds begin. But down three thousand feet in the cañon, where you stir the fire under the cooking pot, it will not be day for an hour. It goes on, the play of light across the high places, rosy, purpling, tender, glint and glow, thunder and windy flood, like the grave, exulting talk of elders above a merry game.

Who shall say what another will find most to his liking in the streets of the mountains. As for me, once set above the country of the silver firs, I must go on until I find white columbine. Around the amphitheaters of the lake regions and above them to the limit of perennial drifts they gather flock-wise in splintered rock wastes. The crowds of them, the airy spread of sepals, the pale purity of the petal spurs, the quivering swing of bloom, obsesses the sense. . . .

Lingering on in the alpine regions until the first full snow, which is often before the cessation of bloom, one goes down in good company. First snows are soft and clogging and make laborious paths. Then it is the roving inhabitants range down to the edge of the wood, below the limit of early storms. Early winter and early spring one may have sight or track of deer and bear and bighorn, cougar and bobcat, about the thickets of buckthorn on open slopes between the black pines. But when the ice crust is firm above the twenty-foot drifts, they range far and forage where they will. Often in midwinter will come, now and then, a long fall of soft snow piling three or four feet above the ice crust, and work a real hardship for the dwellers of these streets. When such a storm portends the weather-wise blacktail will go down across the valley and up to the pastures of Waban where no more snow falls than suffices to nourish the sparsely growing pines. But the bighorn, the wild sheep, able to bear the bitterest storms with no signs of stress, cannot cope with the loose shifty snow. Never such a storm goes over the mountains that the Indians do not catch them floundering belly deep among the lower rifts. I have a pair of horns, inconceivably heavy, that were borne as late as a year ago by a very monarch of the flock whom death overtook at the mouth of Oak Creek after a week of wet snow. He met it as a king should, with no vain effort or trembling, and it was wholly kind to take him so with four of his following rather than that the night prowlers should find him.

There is always more life abroad in the winter hills than one looks to find, and much more in evidence than in summer weather. Light feet of hare that make no print on the forest litter leave a wondrously plain track in the snow. We used to look and look at the beginning of winter for birds to come down from the pine lands; looked in the orchard and stubble; looked north and south on the mesa for their migratory passing, and wondered that they never came. Busy little grosbeaks picked about the kitchen doors, and woodpeckers tapped the eaves of the farm buildings, but we saw hardly any other of the frequenters of the summer cañons. After a while when we grew bold to tempt the snow borders we found them in the street of the mountains. In the thick pine woods where the overlapping boughs hung with snow-wreaths make wind-proof shelter tents, in a very community of dwelling, winter the bird-folk who get their living from the persisting cones and the larvae harboring bark. Ground inhabiting species seek the dim snow chambers of the chaparral. Consider how it must be in a hill-slope overgrown with stout-twigged, partly evergreen shrubs, more than man high, and as thick as a hedge. Not all the cañon's sifting of snow can fill the intricate spaces of the hill tangles. Here and there an overhanging rock, or a stiff arch of buckthorn, makes an opening to communicating rooms and runways deep under the snow.

The light filtering through the snow walls is blue and ghostly, but serves to show seeds of shrubs and grass, and berries, and the wind-built walls are warm against the wind. It seems that live plants, especially if they are evergreen and growing, give off heat; the snow wall melts earliest from within and hollows to thinness before there is a hint of spring in the air. But you think of these things afterward. Up in the street it has the effect of being done consciously; the buckthorns lean to each other and the drift to them, the little birds run in and out of their appointed ways with the greatest cheerfulness. They give almost no tokens of distress, and even if the winter tries them too much you are not to pity them. You of the house habit can hardly understand the sense of the hills. No doubt the labor of being comfortable gives you an exaggerated opinion of yourself, an exaggerated pain to be set aside. Whether the wild things understand it or not they adapt themselves to its processes with the greater ease. The business that goes on in the street of the mountain is tremendous, world-formative. Here go birds, squirrels, and red deer, children crying small wares and playing in the street, but they do not obstruct its affairs. Summer is their holiday; "Come now," says the lord of the street, "I have need of a great work and no more playing."

But they are left borders and breathing-space out of pure kindness. They are not pushed out except by the exigencies of the nobler plan which they adopt with a dignity the rest of us have not yet learned.

Mount Saint Helens

@

URSULA K. LE GUIN

Mount Saint Helens, one of the volcanic Pacific Cascades, took all but a few seismologists by surprise when it erupted on May 18, 1980. The mountain lost its 2,000-foot cap in the blow, the destruction seemed all but total, and many scientists predicted that the landscape would remain nearly lunar for generations to come. But, as URSULA K. LE GUIN remarks in her poem "At Meta Lake: Autumn 1980," from which this is excerpted, new life came almost immediately from the ashes.

There are no mirrors here.

This is a labyrinth where none of the ways
        leads in or out
but all the arrows point in the same direction.

It is easy to compare to Hell,
but then where are you?

Hell has to do with justice.
This has not.
This has nothing to do with us at all
   except as we are fir, are fern,
   are trout, are jay, are elk.

The bones of deer are in this ash.
This is not punishment.
We have no claim on it. It does not regard us.
Our crimes can only imitate.
It is we who hold the mirror up.
This is not Hell.

But is it wrong to say the names of hope?
The names break through the gray crust,
   tough, sweet, and seedy:
   fireweed,
   pearly everlasting,
   vetch.
  Some grass. Some bracken fern.
  A brownish-orange mushroom the size of a thumbtack
   down in the hollow of the huge dead trees
   by the stinking shores
   of the little, sick, dark lake.
(Imagine!
  morning sunlight filtering through leaves
  to the clear water, and the birds waking!)

Yet there are wings:
  migrants,
  a sudden quickness in the dull air,
  gone.
And the seeds, the spores, break through.
The germ is powerful.

Thumb-high seedlings under blue shadow of May snow,
ignorant when the black blast came:
now they stand one here
one there,
small green prayersticks,
feathers, powers,
in this steep dust encumbered with the dead.

Popocatepetl

FRAY LÓPEZ DE GOMARA

At 17,887 feet, Popocatepetl is the highest mountain in Mexico. It is also an active volcano, threatening to erupt even as I write. FRAY LÓPEZ DE GOMARA, a late contemporary of the first wave of Spanish conquistadores to enter Mexico, describes it in this passage, first anthologized in English in the book of travels Purchas His Pilgrimes *in 1625.*

There is a hill eight leagues from Cholula, called Popocatepec, which is to say, a hill of smoake, for many times it casteth out smoake and fire. Cortes sent thither ten Spaniards, with many Indians, to carry their victuall, and to guide them in the way. The ascending up was very troublesome, and full of craggie rocks. They approached so nigh the top, that they heard such a terrible noise which proceeded from thence, that they durst not goe unto it, for the ground did tremble and shake, and great quantity of ashes which disturbed the way: but yet two of them who seemed to be most hardie, and desirous to see strange things, went up to the top, because they would not returne with a sleevelesse answer, and that they might not be accounted cowards, leaving their fellowes behinde them, proceeding forwards. The Indians said, what meane these men? for as yet never mortall man tooke such a journey in hand.

These two valiant fellowes passed through the Desart of Ashes, and at length came under a great smoake very thicke, and standing there a while, the darkenesse vanished partly away, and then appeared the vulcan and concavity, which was about halfe a league in compasse, out of which the ayre came abounding, with a great noise, very shrill, and whistling, in such sort that the whole hill did tremble. It was to be compared unto an Oven where Glasse is made. The smoake and heate was so great, that they could not abide it, and of force were constrained to returne by the way that they had ascended: but they were not gone farre, when the vulcan began to lash out flames of fire, ashes, and imbers, yea and at the last, stones of burning fire: and if they had not chansed to finde a Rocke, where under they shadowed themselves, undoubtedly they had there beene burned. When with good tokens they were returned where they left their fellowes, the other Indians kissed their garments as an honour due unto gods. They presented unto them such things as they had, and wondred much at their fact.

The simple Indians thought, that that place was an infernal place, where all such as governed not well, or used tyrannic in their offices, were punished when they died, and also beleeved, that after their purgation, they passed into glory. This Vulcan is like unto the Vulcan of Sicilia, it is high and round, and never wanteth snow about it, and is scene afarre off in the night, it lasheth out flames of fire. There is neere about this Hill many Cities, and Huexozinco is one of the nighest. In tenne yeeres space this strange hill of working did expell no vapour or smoke: but in the yeere 1540 it began againe to burne, and with the horrible noyse thereof, the Neighbours that dwelt foure leagues from thence were terrified, for the especiall strange smoakes that then were scene, the like to their Predecessors had not beene scene. The ashes that proceeded from thence came to Huexozinco, Quelaxcopan, Tepiacac, Quauhquecholla, Chololla, and Tlaxcallan, which standeth ten leagues from thence, yea some say, it extended fifteene leagues distant, and burned their hearties in their Gardens, their Fieldes of Corne, Trees, and cloathes that lay a drying.

He left the way that the Mexicans had perswaded him to come, for it was both evill and dangerous, as the Spaniard which went to the Vulcan had scene, he went another plainer way, and neerer. He ascended up a Hill covered with snow, which was sixe miles of height, where if the 30,000 soldiers had waited for them, they might easily have taken them, by reason of the great cold: and from the top of that Hill, they discovered the Land of Mexico, and the great Lake, with his Villages round about, which is an exceeding goodly sight. But when Cortes saw that beautifull thing, his joy was without comparison.

Climbing to the
Middle of the World

⑥

AIMÉ FELIX TSCHIFFELY

*Born in the highlands of Switzerland, AIMÉ FELIX TSCHIFFELY
(1895–1950) moved to Argentina as a young man and tried his hand at
several trades, including ranching and journalism. The skills Tschiffely
learned served him well when he decided to ride two fifteen-year-old
criollo ponies ten thousand miles, from the desert pampas north to Washington, D.C., in 1903. His account of his long, adventure-filled trip,*
Southern Cross to Pole Star, *is a little-read classic of travel literature,
full of keen observations and still useful information. (The great English
traveler Eric Newby wryly observes, "Anyone who is thinking of riding
10,000 miles on horseback through South, Central, and North America
should read this book.") Here Tschiffely describes the difficult passage over
the Cerro de la Muerte from Palmares to San Juan, Costa Rica.*

I knew that the horses would have some very bad days until we reached the
other side of the mountain, so I gave them a good rest and all the fodder we
could find. When we left the settlement the people came to give us all sorts

of little gifts, consisting chiefly of the finest tobacco leaves they had picked out of their stock, but I could not accept all that was offered to us, for the pack was already full. It nearly made my guide weep when I refused some of the offers, but it could not be helped. I often tried to roll a cigar, but never succeeded in performing this seemingly simple trick. However, the guide was very clever at it, so we were sure that we would at least have plenty to smoke for the next week or so, by which time I hoped to reach San José. I purchased a few provisions, and although I hated to do it, I packed three live chickens into a small basket and strapped it on top of the pack.

Many were the terrible stories I heard about the Cerro de la Muerte. Some said the mountain had formerly been bewitched and that the devils had been tamed by firing guns. One man told me that there was a place where the dead were standing up like tree trunks, frozen stiff, and the devils danced among them at night.

Before we reached the foot of the mountain it began to rain and the ground became so slippery that the horses continually slipped and fell. We would only scramble a few yards and then we had to stop for breath or hack steps so that the animals could get a grip with their hoofs. This went on for some hours until we reached higher altitudes, where we entered oak forests. There the temperature was cool but the perspiration was falling off us in drops. The guide's pony had fallen so often and was so tired that it began to refuse to get up, so every time it fell again one of us had to pull in front while the other helped the animal by lifting it by the tail. Late in the evening we came to a shelter that had been built by government men some years before. We cut small palm leaves which formed the only fodder we could find, but in spite of their toughness and bitter taste all had disappeared by morning. The night was bitterly cold but we built a fire and one of the hens was soon in our cooking-pot with some rice and yucca.

Next day we continued the difficult ascent, stumbling over a regular network of roots of the huge, lichen-covered oak trees. I feared that a horse might break a leg at any moment, but luck was with us. After some anxious hours we came out of the timberline and from there had a wonderful view of the jungles below. Through holes in the shifting fogs we could sometimes get a glance of both the Pacific and Atlantic oceans in the distance.

Finally we found another shelter where we prepared to spend the night. It was bitter cold and a little spring nearby was completely surrounded by ice. It was easy to see that my horses were accustomed to this, for they did not step on the icy edge but began to paw and break it to make sure that they would not fall into a deep hole. The guide's animal seemed puzzled and nervous and only drank when I offered him the water in my sombrero. Some coarse grass grew near there, so I turned the animals loose. This point—slightly over 11,500 feet above sea level—is called Muerte (Death), but this fantastic name did not seem to affect our spirits as, puffing away at our cigars, we watched the second hen broiling in the pot. During the night the moon was so bright that I thought it was early morning, and as I could sleep no more I went out to keep the horses company. They seemed glad when they saw me and all followed me when I went where the grass was better and where they had feared to go alone, their instinct for danger having kept them near the shelter where we slept.

I sat down and wrapped a heavy poncho and a blanket about me and blew puffs of smoke into the icy night air. I observed that the animals felt the cold, for every now and again they gave some of those peculiar little snorts horses give when the cold air freezes their nostrils. Sitting out there on the mountain all alone, my thoughts began to wander, as they had often done before when I was on some lonely Andean peak. The soft, cold, silvery light of the moon gave the mists below a ghostly appearance. I felt lonely but happy and did not envy king, potentate or ruler. Here was I between two continents and two mighty oceans, with my faithful friends of thousands of miles both making the best of a bad meal beside me. But I knew they were satisfied, for experience had taught the three of us to be contented, even with the worst.

My thoughts wandered back to my boyhood and to the school bench for which I always had an inborn dislike. Then I recalled some incidents of my boisterous age and chuckled to myself. As I tried to penetrate the infinite distance, pictures of city life appeared before me, the strife for wealth and fame, the hurry and worry of mankind, some rising, others falling, foolish pleasures, the struggle of humanity, and then I came back to reality. Where was I?—La Muerte.

When the first purple streaks on the horizon announced the arrival of a new day I returned to the shelter to prepare coffee. The horses followed me in hopes of something good and, although we had none to spare, each one received a good chunk of unrefined sugar which they munched until their mouths foamed and dribbled. After a welcome can of hot coffee we started out, following the bare ridges for some time, and then we began the descent. We slipped over rocks and stones and had to pick our way step by step. Dark clouds began to collect, and suddenly a terrific downpour set in. With it a strong wind blew that made it impossible to protect ourselves against the icy water that soon seemed to penetrate to the very marrow.

The guide stumbled along, head down and teeth chattering. I always carried a flask of aguardiente in case of sickness, and knowing this the poor man could resist no longer. He asked me for a cupful which I gladly gave him and took one myself. To this day I cannot explain how we got the horses down these slopes without crippling them. Towards evening we found another shelter where we warmed and dried ourselves near a fire we had built. My boots were all in pieces now, and my feet had been cut by the sharp rocks. We were again in an oak forest, and once more the animals had to be content with a feed of leaves of small woolly palms that grew here and there among the hoary giants of the primeval forest. The rain lasted throughout the night, and I realized that we had beaten the rainy season—and defeat— by barely twenty-four hours.

Andes

KECHUA AND SPANISH FOLK SONGS,
SIMÓN BOLÍVAR, IDA PFEIFFER,
CHARLES DARWIN

The KECHUA sing this lovely tune to the gods of the high Andes.

Hailli, little shepherdess!
You go to the hill,
where the condor hovers.

Hailli, little shepherd!
You go to the mountain,
where the hawk flies and flies.

Hailli, shepherds!
You climb to the ridges,
and leave the fleeting fox
trailing in your steps.

The SPANISH CONQUISTADORES *rejoined with a song of their own.*

> I am lonesome for you,
> country that suckled me.
> If unlucky I should die,
> bury me high in these mountains
> so that my interred body
> will not miss the land for which I long.
> Bury me as high as you can,
> so that I can see from there
> the country for which I shed these tears.

That altitude sickness induces hallucinations, we know. Few of those
strange visions are so powerful, so history altering, as the one that came
late in 1823 to the war-weary South American liberator SIMÓN BOLÍVAR
(1783–1830) atop 20,702-foot Mount Chimborazo, in what is now
Ecuador. The "mantle of Iris" refers to Bolívar's rainbow battle flag,
which he had been carrying for a decade.

I came wrapped in the mantle of Iris to the place where the stream-rich
Orinoco pays tribute to the god of waters. I had visited the enchanted Ama-
zonian fountains, and I wanted to climb the watchtower of the universe. I
looked for the tracks of La Condamine and Humboldt; I followed them dar-
ingly, nothing held me back; I came to the glacial region, the ether suffocated
my breath. No human sole had trod on the diamantine crown that the hands
of Eternity had placed atop the lofty temples of the dominator of the Andes.
I said to myself: this mantle of Iris that has served as my battle-standard has
journeyed in my hands across infernal regions; it has crossed rivers and
oceans; it has climbed the gigantic shoulders of the Andes; the land has
yielded itself to the new Columbia, and time has not been able to slow the

march of liberty. Belona was humiliated before the splendor of Iris; could I not climb the cane-covered tresses of this giant of the earth? I could! And seized by the violence of a spirit unknown to me, one that seemed to me divine, I left behind the path of Humboldt, battling the eternal crystals that surround Chimborazo. I came as if driven by the genius that animated me, and I grew weak as I touched with my head the cup of the firmament: I had at my feet the deep shadows of the abyss.

A delirious fever seized my mind. I felt burned by a strange, superior fire. It was the god of Columbia that possessed me.

Soon Time presented itself to me. Under the guise of an old venerable man it bore the plunder of the ages: frowning, bent, bald, wrinkled, a sickle in its hand. . . .

"I am the father of the centuries, I am the arcanum of fame and of secrecy, my mother was Eternity; Infinity signals the borders of my empire; I have no grave, because I am more powerful than Death; I see the past, I see the future, and the present passes through my hands. Why do you take vain pride in yourself, young man or old, man or hero? Do you really believe your universe is anything? What makes you more than an atom of creation? Do you think that the seconds you call centuries can solve my mysteries? Do you imagine that you have seen the holy Truth? Do you madly suppose that your actions have any merit in my eyes? Everything is less than a speck in the presence of Infinity, who is my brother."

Surprised by this holy terror, I answered, "What, O Time! Is there nothing for this miserable mortal who has climbed so high to take pride in? I have surpassed all other men in fortune, because I have lifted myself above all their heads. I dominate the earth with my footprints; I arrive at Eternity with my hands; I feel the infernal prisons bubbling beneath my legs; I am looking at the same time at gleaming stars and infinite suns; I see without fear the space that encloses all matter, and in your face I read the history of the past and the thoughts of destiny."

"Observe," he said to me. "Learn, keep in your mind what you have seen, use your eyes to describe for your fellow men this plan of the physical universe, of the moral universe; hide no secrets that the universe has revealed to you; tell the truth to men."

The phantasm disappeared.

Lost in thought, frozen in place, as it were, I remained weak for a long time, spread out across some immense diamond that served as my bed. At last, the tremendous voice of Columbia shouted. I revive, I incorporate, I open with my hands my heavy eyelids, I become once again a human being, and I write of my delirium.

In 1855, the British traveler IDA PFEIFFER *retraced Bolívar's path.*

The 30th of March was one of the most remarkable days of my life, for on this day I crossed the grand Cordillera of the Andes, and that at one of its most interesting points, the Chimborazo. When I was young this was supposed to be the highest mountain in the world; but the discovery since then of some points in the Himalaya, which far exceed its height of 21,000 feet, has thrown it into the second class.

We set off at a very early hour in the morning, for we had eleven leagues, mostly over dreadful roads, and on a constant steep ascent, before us. For this distance there was no kind of shelter in which to pass the night.

At first it was really terrible. I was compelled as before to dismount at the worst places; and the sharp mountain air had begun to affect my chest severely. I was oppressed by a feeling of terror and anxiety, my breath failed me, my limbs trembled, and I dreaded every moment that I should sink down utterly exhausted; but the word was still "forwards," and forwards I went, dragging myself painfully over rocks, through torrents and morasses, and into and out of holes filled with mire. Had I been at the top of the Chimborazo, I should have ascribed the painful sensations I experienced to the great rarefaction of the air, since it frequently produces symptoms of the kind; indeed the feeling is so common as to have had a name given to it. It is called "veta," and lasts with some people only a few days, but with others, if they remain in the high regions, as many weeks.

After the first two leagues the way became more rocky and stony, and I could at least keep my seat on my mule. We had continual torrents of rain, and now and then a fall of snow, which mostly melted, however, as soon as it touched the ground, though it remained lying in some few places, so that I may say I travelled over the snow; but the clouds and mists never parted for a single moment, and I got no sight of the top of the Chimborazo—a thing that I grieved at much more than at my bodily sufferings.

From Guaranda to the summit of the pass is reckoned six leagues, and the mountain there spreads into a sort of small plain or table-land, around which it falls abruptly on every side except the north, where the cone of the Chimborazo rises almost perpendicularly. On this small elevated plain a heap of stones has been thrown together by travellers; according to some merely as a sign that the highest point of the pass is here attained, but others consider the stones as the memorial of a murder committed here, some years ago, on an Englishman, who undertook to cross the Chimborazo accompanied only by a single *arriero*. Perhaps, he might have done so in safety, had he not had the imprudence, on all occasions when there was anything to pay, to display a purse well filled with gold. This glittering temptation the guide could not withstand, and when he found himself alone with the unfortunate traveller in this solitary region, he struck him a fatal blow on the back of the head with a great stone wrapped in a cloth—a common method of murder in this country. He concealed the body in the snow; but both deed and doer were discovered very soon by his offering one of the gold pieces to change.

Wearied as I was, I alighted from my mule, and got a stone to furnish my contribution to the heap; and I then climbed a little way down the western side of the mountain till I came to water, when I filled a pitcher, drank a little, and then took the rest and poured it into a stream that fell down the eastern side, and then, reversing the operation, carried some thence to the western. This was an imitation on my part, of the Baron Von Tschuddi, who did this on the watershed of the Pasco de Serro, and amused himself as I did with the thought of having now sent to the Atlantic some water that had been destined to flow into the Pacific, and vice versa.

The precise height of the summit of this pass I could not ascertain, as some said it was 14,000, others 16,000 feet. Probably the truth lies somewhere between the two. The perpetual snow-line under the Equator is at the height of 15,000 feet; and to reach this we should have had, at most, two or three hundred feet more to ascend, as it seemed almost close to us. The thermometer stood here at the freezing point.

In The Voyage of the Beagle *(1845),* CHARLES DARWIN *recounts a passage of the Chilean Andes.*

March 18th.—We set out for the Portillo pass. Leaving Santiago we crossed the wide burnt-up plain on which that city stands, and in the afternoon arrived at the Maypu, one of the principal rivers in Chile. The valley, at the point where it enters the first Cordillera, is bounded on each side by lofty barren mountains; and although not broad, it is very fertile. Numerous cottages were surrounded by vines, and by orchards of apple, nectarine, and peach trees—their boughs breaking with the weight of the beautiful ripe fruit. In the evening we passed the custom-house, where our luggage was examined. The frontier of Chile is better guarded by the Cordillera, than by the waters of the sea. There are very few valleys which lead to the central ranges, and the mountains are quite impassable in other parts by beasts of burden. . . .

At night we slept at a cottage. Our manner of traveling was delightfully independent. In the inhabited parts we bought a little firewood, hired pasture for the animals, and bivouacked in the corner of the same field with them. Carrying an iron pot, we cooked and ate our supper under a cloudless sky, and knew no trouble. My companions were Mariano Gonzales, who had formerly accompanied me in Chile, and an "arriero," with his ten mules and a "madrina." The madrina (or godmother) is a most important personage: she is an old steady mare, with a little bell round her neck; and wherever she goes, the mules, like good children, follow her. The affection of these animals for their madrinas saves infinite trouble. If several large troops are turned into one field to graze, in the morning the muleteers have only to lead the madrinas a little apart, and tinkle their bells; and although there may be two or three hundred together, each mule immediately knows the bell of its own madrina, and comes to her. It is nearly impossible to lose an old mule; for if detained for several hours by force, she will, by the power of smell, like a dog, track out her companions, or rather the madrina, for, according to the muleteer, she is the chief object of affection. The feeling, however, is not of an individual nature; for I believe I am right in saying that any animal with a bell will serve as a madrina. In a troop each animal carries on a level road, a cargo weighing 416 pounds (more than 29 stone), but in a mountainous country 100 pounds less; yet with what delicate slim limbs, without any proportional bulk of muscle, these animals support so great a burden! The mule always appears to me a most surprising animal. That a hybrid should possess more reason, memory, obstinacy, social affection, powers of muscular endurance, and length of life, than either of its parents, seems to indicate that art has here outdone nature. Of our ten animals, six were intended for riding, and four for carrying cargoes, each taking turn about. We carried a good deal of food, in case we should be snowed up, as the season was rather late for passing the Portillo.

March 19th.—We rode during this day to the last, and therefore most elevated house in the valley. The number of inhabitants became scanty; but wherever water could be brought on the land, it was very fertile. All the main valleys in the Cordillera are characterized by having, on both sides, a fringe or terrace of shingle and sand, rudely stratified, and generally of considerable thickness. These fringes evidently once extended across the valleys, and were united; and the bottoms of the valleys in northern Chile, where there are no streams, are thus smoothly filled up. On these fringes the roads are generally carried, for their surfaces are even, and they rise with a very gentle slope up the valleys: hence, also, they are easily cultivated by irrigation. They may be traced up to a height of between 7000 and 9000 feet, where they become hidden by the irregular piles of debris. At the lower end or mouths of the valleys, they are continuously united to those land-locked plains (also formed of shingle) at the foot of the main Cordillera, which I have described in a former chapter as characteristic of the scenery of Chile, and which were undoubtedly deposited when the sea penetrated Chile, as it now does the more southern coasts. No one fact in the geology of South America interested me more than these terraces of rudely-stratified shingle. They precisely resemble in composition, the matter which the torrents in each valley would deposit, if they were checked in their course by any cause, such as entering a lake or arm of the sea; but the torrents, instead of depositing matter, are now steadily at work wearing away both the solid rock and these alluvial deposits, along the whole line of every main valley and side valley. It is impossible here to give the reasons, but I am convinced that the shingle terraces were accumulated, during the gradual elevation of the Cordillera, by the torrents delivering, at successive levels, their detritus on the beachheads of long narrow arms of the sea, first high up the valleys, then lower and lower down as the land slowly rose. If this be so, and I cannot doubt it, the grand and broken chain of the Cordillera, instead of having been suddenly thrown up, as was till lately the universal, and still is the common opinion of geologists, has been slowly upheaved in mass, in the same gradual manner as the coasts of the Atlantic and Pacific have risen within the recent period. A multitude of facts in the structure of the Cordillera, on this view receive a simple explanation.

The rivers which flow in these valleys ought rather to be called mountain-torrents. Their inclination is very great, and their water the colour of mud. The roar which the Maypu made, as it rushed over the great rounded fragments, was like that of the sea. Amidst the din of rushing waters, the noise from the stones, as they rattled one over another, was most distinctly audible even from a distance. This rattling noise, night and day, may be heard along the whole course of the torrent. The sound spoke eloquently to the geologist; the thousands and thousands of stones, which, striking against each other, made the one dull uniform sound, were all hurrying in one direction. It was like thinking on time, where the minute that now glides past is irrecoverable. So was it with these stones; the ocean is their eternity, and each note of that wild music told of one more step towards their destiny.

It is not possible for the mind to comprehend, except by a slow process, any effect which is produced by a cause repeated so often, that the multiplier itself conveys an idea, not more definite than the savage implies when he points to the hairs of his head. As often as I have seen beds of mud, sand, and shingle, accumulated to the thickness of many thousand feet, I have felt inclined to exclaim that causes, such as the present rivers and the present beaches, could never have ground down and produced such masses. But, on the other hand, when listening to the rattling noise of these torrents, and calling to mind that whole races of animals have passed away from the face of the earth, and that during this whole period, night and day, these stones have gone rattling onwards in their course, I have thought to myself, can any mountains, any continent, withstand such waste?

In this part of the valley, the mountains on each side were from 3000 to 6000 or 8000 feet high, with rounded outlines and steep bare flanks. The general colour of the rock was dullish purple, and the stratification very distinct. If the scenery was not beautiful, it was remarkable and grand. We met during the day several herds of cattle, which men were driving down from the higher valleys in the Cordillera. This sign of the approaching winter hurried our steps, more than was convenient for geologising. The house where we slept was situated at the foot of a mountain, on the summit of which are the mines of S. Pedro de Nolasko. Sir F. Head marvels how mines have been discovered in such extraordinary situations, as the bleak summit of the mountain of S. Pedro de Nolasko. In the first place, metallic veins in this country are generally harder than the surrounding strata: hence, during the gradual wear of the hills, they project above the surface of the ground. Secondly, almost every labourer, especially in the northern parts of Chile, understands something about the appearance of ores. In the great mining provinces of Coquimbo and Copiapo, firewood is very scarce, and men search for it over every hill and dale; and by this means nearly all the richest mines have there been discovered. Chanuncillo, from which silver to the value of many hundred thousand pounds has been raised in the course of a few years, was discovered by a man who threw a stone at his loaded donkey, and thinking that it was very heavy, he picked it up, and found it full of pure silver: the vein occurred at no great distance, standing up like a wedge of metal. The miners, also, taking a crowbar with them, often wander on Sundays over the mountains. In this south part of Chile, the men who drive cattle into the Cordillera, and who frequent every ravine where there is a little pasture, are the usual discoverers.

March 20th.—As we ascended the valley, the vegetation, with the exception of a few pretty alpine flowers, became exceedingly scanty; and of quadrupeds, birds, or insects, scarcely one could be seen. The lofty mountains, their summits marked with a few patches of snow, stood well separated from each other; the valleys being filled up with an immense thickness of stratified alluvium. The features in the scenery of the Andes which struck me most, as contrasted with the other mountain chains with which I am acquainted, were,—the flat fringes sometimes expanding into narrow plains on each side of the valleys,—the bright colours, chiefly red and purple, of the utterly bare and precipitous hills of porphyry,—the grand and continuous wall-like dikes,—the plainly-divided strata which, where nearly vertical, formed the picturesque and wild central pinnacles, but where less inclined, composed the great massive mountains on the outskirts of the range,—and lastly, the smooth conical piles of fine and brightly-coloured detritus, which sloped up at a high angle from the base of the mountains, sometimes to a height of more than 2000 feet.

I frequently observed, both in Tierra del Fuego and within the Andes, that where the rock was covered during the greater part of the year with snow, it was shivered in a very extraordinary manner into small angular fragments. Scoresby has observed the same fact in Spitzbergen. The case appears to me rather obscure: for that part of the mountain which is protected by a mantle of snow, must be less subject to repeated and great changes of temperature than any other part. I have sometimes thought, that the earth and fragments of stone on the surface, were perhaps less effectually removed by slowly percolating snow water than by rain, and therefore that the appearance of a quicker disintegration of the solid rock under the snow, was deceptive. Whatever the cause may be, the quantity of crumbling stone on the Cordillera is very great. Occasionally in the spring, great masses of this detritus slide down the mountains, and cover the snow-drifts in the valleys, thus forming natural ice-houses. We rode over one, the height of which was far below the limit of perpetual snow.

The *Tepuis*
of Guyana

⟲

SIR ARTHUR CONAN DOYLE

Seventy years before Jurassic Park *filled the world's multiplex screens, the English mysterian and novelist* SIR ARTHUR CONAN DOYLE *(1859–1930) enjoyed an unexpected success with his novel* The Lost World, *an adventure set on an islandlike* tepui *in the Guyanan jungle. He had been reading newspaper accounts of the exploration of Roraima, a 9,094-foot-tall, 25-square-mile plateau on which were found animal and plant species quite unlike those of the surrounding lowlands, and he took the idea of its antiquity to its logical extreme: what if these ancient uplifts, formed some 1,750 million years ago, sheltered prehistoric life-forms?*

Doyle was not the first English writer to puzzle over tepuis. *Sir Walter Raleigh, the sixteenth-century explorer, recorded that in Guyana he had been told of "the mountain of Christall. . . . Berreo told me it hath diamonds and other precious stones on it, and that they shined very farre off; but what it hath I knowe not, neither durst he or any of his men ascende to the toppe of the saide mountaine, those people adjoyning beeing his enemies and the way to it is so impassible." Raleigh's contemporaries seemed*

*content to let those diamonds lie, and it was not until the late nineteenth
century that a* tepui *was scaled. Even today, these geological formations
remain little explored.*

*Here Doyle writes of the strange discoveries that await a party led by
the intrepid George Edward Challenger.*

The peaceful penetration of Maple White Land was the pressing subject before us. We had the evidence of our own eyes that the place was inhabited by
some unknown creatures, and there was that of Maple White's sketchbook
to show that more dreadful and more dangerous monsters might still appear. That there might also prove to be human occupants and that they were
of a malevolent character was suggested by the skeleton impaled upon the
bamboos, which could not have got there had it not been dropped from
above. Our situation, stranded without possibility of escape in such a land,
was clearly full of danger, and our reasons endorsed every measure of caution which Lord John's experience could suggest. Yet it was surely impossible that we should halt on the edge of this world of mystery when our very
souls were tingling with impatience to push forward and to pluck the heart
from it.

We therefore blocked the entrance to our zareba by filling it up with several thorny bushes, and left our camp with the stores entirely surrounded by
this protecting hedge. We then slowly and cautiously set forth into the unknown, following the course of the little stream which flowed from our
spring, as it should always serve us as a guide on our return.

Hardly had we started when we came across signs that there were indeed
wonders awaiting us. After a few hundred yards of thick forest, containing
many trees which were quite unknown to me, but which Summerlee, who
was the botanist of the party, recognized as forms of Coniferae and of cy-
cadaceous plants which have long passed away in the world below, we entered a region where the stream widened out and formed a considerable
bog. High reeds of a peculiar type grew thickly before us, which were pronounced to be equisetums, or mare's tails, with tree ferns scattered amongst
them, all of them swaying in a brisk wind. Suddenly Lord John, who was
walking first, halted with uplifted hand.

"Look at this!" said he. "By George, this must be the trail of the father of all birds!"

An enormous three-toed track was imprinted in the soft mud before us. The creature, whatever it was, had crossed the swamp and had passed on into the forest. We all stopped to examine that monstrous spoor. If it were indeed a bird—and what animal could leave such a mark?—its foot was so much larger than an ostrich's that its height upon the same scale must be enormous. Lord John looked eagerly round him and slipped two cartridges into his elephant gun.

"I'll stake my good name as a shikari," said he, "that the track is a fresh one. The creature has not passed ten minutes. Look how the water is still oozing into that deeper print! By Jove! See, here is the mark of a little one!"

Sure enough, smaller tracks of the same general form were running parallel to the large ones.

"But what do you make of this?" cried Professor Summerlee, triumphantly, pointing to what looked like the huge print of a five-fingered human hand appearing among the three-toed marks.

"Wealden!" cried Challenger, in an ecstasy. "I've seen them in the Wealden clay. It is a creature walking erect upon three-toed feet, and occasionally putting one of its five-fingered forepaws upon the ground. Not a bird, my dear Roxton—not a bird."

"A beast?"

"No; a reptile—a dinosaur. Nothing else could have left such a track. They puzzled a worthy Sussex doctor some ninety years ago; but who in the world could have hoped—hoped—to have seen a sight like that?"

His words died away into a whisper, and we all stood in motionless amazement. Following the tracks, we had left the morass and passed through a screen of brushwood and trees. Beyond was an open glade, and in this were five of the most extraordinary creatures that I have ever seen. Crouching down among the bushes, we observed them at our leisure.

There were, as I say, five of them, two being adults and three young ones. In size they were enormous. Even the babies were as big as elephants, while the two large ones were far beyond all creatures I have ever seen. They had slate-colored skin, which was scaled like a lizard's and shimmered where the sun shone upon it. All five were sitting up, balancing themselves upon their broad, powerful tails and their huge three-toed hind feet, while with their small five-fingered front feet they pulled down the branches upon which they browsed. I do not know that I can bring their appearance home to you better than by saying that they looked like monstrous kangaroos, twenty feet in length, and with skins like black crocodiles.

I do not know how long we stayed motionless gazing at this marvelous spectacle. A strong wind blew toward us and we were well concealed, so there was no chance of discovery. From time to time the little ones played round their parents in unwieldy gambols, the great beasts bounding into the air and falling with dull thuds upon the earth. The strength of the parents seemed to be limitless, for one of them, having some difficulty in reaching a bunch of foliage which grew upon a considerable-sized tree, put his forelegs round the trunk and tore it down as if it had been a sapling. The action seemed, as I thought, to show not only the great development of its muscles, but also the small one of its brain, for the whole weight came crashing down upon the top of it, and it uttered a series of shrill yelps to show that, big as it was, there was a limit to what it could endure. The incident made it think, apparently, that the neighborhood was dangerous, for it slowly lurched off through the wood, followed by its mate and its three enormous infants. We saw the shimmering slaty gleam of their skins between the tree trunks, and their heads undulating high above the brushwood. Then they vanished from our sight.

I looked at my comrades. Lord John was standing at gaze with his finger on the trigger of his elephant gun, his eager hunter's soul shining from his fierce eyes. What would he not give for one such head to place between the two crossed oars above the mantelpiece in his snuggery at the Albany! And yet his reason held him in, for all our exploration of the wonders of this un-known land depended upon our presence being concealed from its inhabi-tants. The two professors were in silent ecstasy. In their excitement they had unconsciously seized each other by the hand, and stood like two little chil-dren in the presence of a marvel, Challenger's cheeks bunched up into a seraphic smile, and Summerlee's sardonic face softening for the moment into wonder and reverence.

"*Nunc dimittis!*" he cried at last. "What will they say in England of this?"

"My dear Summerlee, I will tell you with great confidence exactly what they will say in England," said Challenger. "They will say that you are an infernal liar and a scientific charlatan, exactly as you and others said of me."

"In the face of photographs?"

"Faked, Summerlee! Clumsily faked!"

"In the face of specimens?"

"Ah, there we may have them! Malone and his filthy Fleet Street crew may be all yelping our praises yet. August the twenty-eighth—the day we saw five live iguanodons in a glade of Maple White Land. Put it down in your diary, my young friend, and send it to your rag."

"And be ready to get the toe end of the editorial boot in return," said Lord John. "Things look a bit different from the latitude of London, young fellah my lad. There's many a man who never tells his adventures, for he can't hope to be believed. Who's to blame them? For this will seem a bit of a dream to ourselves in a month or two. What did you say they were?"

"Iguanodons," said Summerlee. "You'll find their footmarks all over the Hastings sands, in Kent, and in Sussex. The south of England was alive with them when there was plenty of good lush green stuff to keep them going. Conditions have changed, and the beasts died. Here it seems that the conditions have not changed, and the beasts have lived."

"If ever we get out of this alive, I must have a head with me," said Lord John. "Lord, how some of that Somaliland-Uganda crowd would turn a beautiful pea green if they saw it! I don't know what you chaps think, but it strikes me that we are on mighty thin ice all this time."

I had the same feeling of mystery and danger around us. In the gloom of the trees there seemed a constant menace and as we looked up into their shadowy foliage vague terrors crept into one's heart. It is true that these monstrous creatures which we had seen were lumbering, inoffensive brutes which were unlikely to hurt anyone, but in this world of wonders what other survivals might there not be—what fierce, active horrors ready to pounce upon us from their lair among the rocks or brushwood? I knew little of prehistoric life, but I had a clear remembrance of one book which I had read in which it spoke of creatures who would live upon our lions and tigers as a cat lives upon mice. What if these also were to be found in the woods of Maple White Land!

It was destined that on this very morning—our first in the new country— we were to find out what strange hazards lay around us. It was a loathsome adventure, and one of which I hate to think. If, as Lord John said, the glade of the iguanodons will remain with us as a dream, then surely the swamp of the pterodactyls will forever be our nightmare. Let me set down exactly what occurred.

We passed very slowly through the woods, partly because Lord Roxton acted as scout before he would let us advance, and partly because at every second step one or other of our professors would fall, with a cry of wonder, before some flower or insect which presented him with a new type. We may have traveled two or three miles in all, keeping to the right of the line of the stream, when we came upon a considerable opening in the trees. A belt of brushwood led up to a tangle of rocks—the whole plateau was strewn with boulders. We were walking slowly toward these rocks, among bushes which reached over our waists, when we became aware of a strange low gabbling and whistling sound, which filled the air with a constant clamor and appeared to come from some spot immediately before us. Lord John held up his hand as a signal for us to stop, and he made his way swiftly, stooping and running, to the line of rocks. We saw him peep over them and give a gesture of amazement. Then he stood staring as if forgetting us, so utterly entranced was he by what he saw. Finally he waved us to come on, holding up his hand as a signal for caution. His whole bearing made me feel that something wonderful but dangerous lay before us.

Creeping to his side, we looked over the rocks. The place into which we gazed was a pit, and may, in the early days, have been one of the smaller volcanic blowholes of the plateau. It was bowl shaped and at the bottom, some hundreds of yards from where we lay, were pools of green-scummed, stagnant water, fringed with bulrushes. It was a weird place in itself, but its occupants made it seem like a scene from the Seven Circles of Dante. The place was a rookery of pterodactyls. There were hundreds of them congregated within view. All the bottom area round the water edge was alive with their young ones, and with hideous mothers brooding upon their leathery, yellowish eggs. From this crawling flapping mass of obscene reptilian life came the shocking clamor which filled the air and the mephitic, horrible, musty odor which turned us sick. But above, perched each upon its own stone, tall, gray, and withered, more like dead and dried specimens than actual living creatures, sat the horrible males, absolutely motionless save for the rolling of their red eyes or an occasional snap of their rat-trap beaks as a dragonfly went past them. Their huge, membranous wings were closed by folding their forearms, so that they sat like gigantic old women, wrapped in hideous web-colored shawls, and with their ferocious heads protruding above them. Large and small, not less than a thousand of these filthy creatures lay in the hollow before us.

Our professors would gladly have stayed there all day, so entranced were they by this opportunity of studying the life of a prehistoric age. They pointed out the fish and dead birds lying about among the rocks as proving the nature of the food of these creatures, and I heard them congratulating each other on having cleared up the point why the bones of this flying dragon are found in such great numbers in certain well-defined areas, as in the Cambridge Green sand, since it was now seen that, like penguins, they lived in gregarious fashion.

Finally, however, Challenger, bent upon proving some point which Summerlee had contested, thrust his head over the rock and nearly brought destruction upon us all. In an instant the nearest male gave a shrill, whistling cry, and flapped its twenty-foot span of leathery wings as it soared up into the air. The females and young ones huddled together beside the water, while the whole circle of sentinels rose one after the other and sailed off into the sky. It was a wonderful sight to see at least a hundred creatures of such enormous size and hideous appearance all swooping like swallows with swift, shearing wing strokes above us; but soon we realized that it was not one on which we could afford to linger. At first the great brutes flew round in a huge ring, as if to make sure what the exact extent of the danger might be. Then, the flight grew lower and the circle narrower, until they were whizzing round and round us, the dry, rustling flap of their huge slate-colored wings filling the air with a volume of sound that made me think of Hendon aerodrome upon a race day.

"Make for the wood and keep together," cried Lord John, clubbing his rifle. "The brutes mean mischief."

AFRICA

Have we not made the Earth as a cradle
and the mountains as pegs?

THE QURAN

Mountains
of Africa

⑥

ASHANTI, WACHAGGA, GIKUYU,
XAN, AND !KUNG FOLKTALES,
PLINY THE ELDER

The advertising copywriters who dreamed up the wondrous tales of Paul Bunyan and Babe the Blue Ox doubtless did not know this Ashanti tale of the origins of rivers and mountains, but it belongs alongside the Bunyan stories in the annals of fabulous creation. The folklorist HAROLD COUR-LANDER recorded this story in Accra, Ghana.

Once there was a boy named Toddu, who lived in the grass country north of Kumasi in Ashanti. He had to care for his father's cattle, and day after day he took them to the watering places and watched them graze. His father's herd had many cows and only one bull, but it was the largest bull in all Africa. Its name was Only One. Whenever a bull calf was born, Only One would kill it, for he thought one bull was enough for the herd.

One time a bull calf was born, and Toddu liked him very much. Only One didn't know about the calf yet, so Toddu carried him away into the bush country and hid him. Every day he crept back to the herd to get milk for the calf from its mother. The old bull, Only One, was getting suspicious about things, so when the calf was a little bigger Toddu took him far into the back country.

The calf grew up. When he was four years old he was almost as big as Only One. Then Toddu took him to a great rock that lay in the middle of the plains and said, "You look like a bull, and you act like a bull. But you aren't full-grown until you're strong enough to move this rock."

The bull put his head down and pushed against the great rock, but nothing happened.

"You're too young, you're still a calf," Toddu said. "Wait another year."

The young bull was so provoked because he couldn't move the rock that he pawed the ground with his foot. He pawed so deep and wide that a lake came up, and that was Lake Bouro.

The next year the boy took his bull to the rock again and said, "Put your horns to it and try again."

The young bull put his head down and tried to toss the great rock, but it didn't budge.

"You're too young yet," Toddu said. "You're not grown up."

The bull was so angry he put one horn in the ground and charged through the bush, plowing a deep furrow. He plowed so deep and far that water came up and began to flow, and that was the Adifofu River.

They waited another year, and again Toddu said, "You're bigger now. Put your horns to the rock and push it."

The bull put his head down and pushed so hard his eyes got red and white foam came out on his hide, but the rock didn't move. He was so angry that he ran into the forest, tearing down all the trees for miles around. This was the great hurricane that Ashanti people still talk about.

Another year came, and the boy said to his bull, "Try again." This time the bull dug his feet in and his muscles bulged and the rock swayed a little.

"Next year you'll do it," Toddu said.

But the bull was unhappy. He bellowed, and down in Komasi it sounded like thunder and the people ran for shelter.

The next year the bull was eight years old, and his horns were as thick as the trunk of a baobab tree.

"Try it again," Toddu said.

The bull tried the rock gently with his horns. Then he went a mile away across the flat grasslands. He pawed the ground, and then he began to run. He charged across the plains with his head down low, and struck the great rock in the middle. It smashed into many pieces and flew into the air in all directions. Wherever the pieces fell they became the mountains of Africa.

The WACHAGGA PEOPLE of Tanzania tell this story.

How the mountains came into being: Ages ago, the earth was everywhere flat and uniform. Then it arose in order to speak with the sky. As it departed again it did not return home in all places at once. The parts which got tired on the way home failed to complete the descent and remained where they were. These became the earth's mountains and hills.

The GIKUYU PEOPLE of Kenya believe that the spirit of the creator god Mwene-Nyaga invests the summit of Mount Kenya. Jomo Kenyatta, an anthropologist and politician, writes that Gikuyu elders sing this song to the mountain in a sacrificial ceremony meant to bring on rain.

Reverend Elder who lives on Kere-Nyaga. You who make mountains tremble and rivers flood, we offer to you this sacrifice that you may bring us rain. People and children are crying; sheep, goats, and cattle are crying. Mwene-Nyaga, we beseech you, with the blood and fat of this lamb which we are going to sacrifice to you. Refined honey and milk we have brought for you. We praise you in the same way as our forefathers used to praise you under this very same tree, and you heard them and brought them rain. We beseech you to accept this, our sacrifice, to bring us rain of prosperity. Peace, we beseech you, peace be with us.

*The X*ᴀɴ *tell this story about the mountain wind.*

The Wind was formerly a man. He became a bird. And he was flying, no longer walking as he once did; and he dwelled in a mountain cave. He flies around from it, he flies around from it, and he returns, and he sleeps.

Smoke's Man once saw this wind on Haarfontein Mountain, and he threw a stone at it, thinking it was a bird. The wind did not blow gently, but blew dust, because Smoke's Man had thrown a rock at it. The wind raised dust, and then flew away, back to the mountain. That is why you do not throw rocks at the wind, for it will kick up the dust.

*The !K*ᴜɴɢ *tell this story about a feature in the mountains of the Kalahari.*

Lizard was going, and he sang,

> *For*
> *I intend to go*
> > *Passing through*
> guru-'na *pass.*

> *And*
> *I therefore intend to go*

Passing through
xe khwai *pass.*

And, when he was passing through, the mountains squeezed together and broke him in two, for he thought he could just go through them although the pass is so narrow. The mountains bit him, and he broke in two, and half is up there on *guru-'na* pass, and the other on *xe khwai* pass. You can see Lizard there today.

In his Historia Naturalis, PLINY THE ELDER (A.D. 23–79) *passes on these reports of the Atlas Mountains from Roman explorers.*

Mount Atlas has more legends attached to it than any other mountain in Africa. It is reported that it rises out of the sand desert high into the sky, rugged and jagged on the side facing the coastline of the Atlantic Ocean, which is named for the mountain, whereas on the side facing the interior of Africa it is shaded by forests and watered by gushing springs. Fruits of all kinds grow there on their own and in such abundance that no one ever wants for food.

In the Atlas region no person is ever seen in the daytime. Everything is as starkly silent there as it is in the desert, and anyone approaching the quiet summit, which reaches nearly to the moon, is dumbstruck with a certain dread. At night Atlas is covered with many fires, or so I have heard, illuminating the orgies of Goat-Pans and Satyrs, and it rings with echoes of their wild flutes, bagpipes, drums, and cymbals. Noted writers have published accounts of these things, along with the exploits of Hercules and Perseus that took place on the mountain. Mount Atlas is a tremendous distance away from Rome and must be approached across unmapped territory.

Some notes have survived made by the Punic general Hanno, who, at the height of Carthage's power, was ordered by its leaders to circumnavigate the continent of Africa. Most Greek and Roman writers follow Hanno in re-counting both his legends and accounts of the many settlements he founded in Africa. No one remembers where these settlements were, and no trace of them remains.

When Scipio Aemilianus was the Roman commanding general in Africa, the historian Polybius took a fleet to explore the continent. Sailing along the coast, Polybius reported that west of Mount Atlas lie forests full of wild animals. In the River Bambolus, he said, there are many crocodiles and hippopotamuses.

The first time Roman forces fought in Mauretania was during Claudius's reign. Caligula had murdered Ptolemy, and his freeman Aedemon sought to avenge him in the desert. Most people believe that our soldiers went as far as Mount Atlas, where the natives fled from them.

Five Roman colonies now lie in the province. According to widespread reports, you might think them to be easily accessible, but that is simply not true. Well-born people, too lazy to find out the truth for themselves, are nonetheless not ashamed to tell lies if by not doing so they admit to ignorance. Credibility never more quickly collapses than when an important authority supports a lie. As for me, I am less surprised that our knights, some of whom are now entering the Senate, do not know the truth about these things than that anything at all is to Luxury, an immensely influential power that causes people to fell whole forests and the creatures within them for ivory and citrus-wood, to sift through all the rocky shores of Algeria for murex and purple-fish.

Suetonius Paulinus, who was consul in my day [ca. A.D. 66], was the first Roman leader to cross over the Atlas Mountains, and he went further into Mauretania. His estimate of their height generally accords with what other authorities say, but he adds that the lower slopes are covered with dense forests of tall trees, the species of which he does not record; they have very tall, lustrous trunks that have no knots. The leaves, like cypress but heavily scented, are covered with a silky down from which clothing can be made, just as it can from the down of the silkworm. The summit of Mount Atlas, he says, is covered with deep snow, even in summer.

The Mountains
of the Moon

Abu El Fadel

"Around the bay [of Zanzibar] the cannibal Aethiopians dwell, and from there toward the west are the Mountains of the Moon from which the lakes of the Nile receive snow water," wrote the Egyptian naturalist Ptolemy. In the Middle Ages, Arab cartographers assigned the name of the uplift they called the Gebl Gumr, or Mountains of the Moon, to the Ruwenzori Massif of Uganda. One of them, Abu El Fadel, wrote this account.

As for the Nile, it starts from the mountains of Gumr beyond the equator, from a source from which flow ten rivers, every five of these flowing into a separate lake, then from each one of these two lakes, two rivers flow out; then all four of these rivers flow into one great lake in the first zone and from this great lake flows out the Nile.

Some say that its rise is caused by snows melted in summer, and according to the quantity of snowfall will be the greater or lesser rise. Others say that the rise is caused by the different directions of the winds; that is to say, that when the north wind blows strongly, it stirs up the Mediterranean and pushes the waters thereof backwards so that it overflows the land, and when the south wind blows the Mediterranean ceases to storm, and the waters that were dammed up flow away again. Others say that the rise is caused by fountains upon its banks that have been seen by travellers who have reached to the highest point.

Others say that the Nile flows from snowy mountains, and they are the mountains called Kaf. That it passes through the Green Sea, and over gold and silver and emerald and ruby mines, flowing on *ad infinitum* until it reaches the lake of the Zingh and they say were it not to enter into the salt sea and be mixed up with the waters thereof it could not be drunk for great sweetness.

Some say that people have ascended the mountain, and one of them began to laugh and clap his hands, and threw himself down on the further side of the mountain. The others were afraid of being seized with the same fit and so came back. It is said that those who saw it, saw bright snows like white silver glistening with light. Whoever looked at them became attracted and stuck to them until they died, and this science is called Human Magnetism.

It is said that a certain king sent an expedition to discover the Nile sources, and they reached copper mountains, and when the sun rose, the rays reflected were so strong that they were burnt. Others say that these people arrived at bright mountains like crystal, and when the rays of the sun were reflected these mountains burned them.

The Ascent
of Kilimanjaro

H. H. JOHNSTON

*In 1884 the British geographer H. H. JOHNSTON received a commission
from the British Association for the Advancement of Science to study the
relationship of altitude to animal and plant speciation. He chose 19,340-
foot Kilimanjaro, "a snow-clad mountain mass that lies in the Equatorial zone, and exhibits an extraordinary range of climates on its broad
slopes," as his laboratory largely because similar equatorial mountains in
South America had already been well studied, and he did not wish to du-
plicate earlier efforts. During the course of his work, he joined the ranks
of the first Europeans to ascend the mountain, although he did not attain
the summit, the height of which was not then known. This passage from
his 1885 memoir* The Kilima-njaro Expedition *tells why he did not reach
the top.*

Starting at nine, I walked upwards, with few stoppages, until 1:30. At first
we crossed grassy, undulating hillocks, the road being fairly easy. Then we
entered a heathy tract, scorched and burnt with recent bush fires, but higher

up, where the blaze had not reached, the vegetation was fairly abundant and green. Small pink irises studded the ground in numbers, an occasional gladiolus of a vivid crimson gleamed brightly out from the tufted grass. About 12,600 feet we struck a pretty little stream, flowing S.S.W., and lower down carving its way through a tremendous ravine, the sides of which were clothed with thick vegetation and gaily lit up with the brilliant red-leaf shoots of the protea (*Protea abyssinica*) shrub. At the place where we crossed the stream the banks were shelving, and above the little ford the water fell in pretty cascades through a rift in the higher ridge of rock. About this spot the surrounding scenery had lost much of its accustomed asperity. On the further side of the stream was a patch of level green sward, somewhat spoilt by the buffaloes who came thither to drink and sport, and who had rucked up and befouled much of this little natural lawn. Strange sessile thistles grew here, nearly five feet in circumference, belonging to the genus *Carduus,* also an extraordinary lobelia (*Lobelia deckeni*), three to four feet in height, with a teazle-like crown of silvery green bracts and bright blue blossoms. Other remarkable plants were the lovely *Cynoglossum amplifolium,* with rich ultramarine flowers, and an extraordinary arborescent plant, since named *Senecio johnstoni,* looking somewhat like a banana in the distance, but in reality consisting of a tall, black, smooth trunk, twenty to thirty feet in height, and surmounted by a huge crown of broad leaves interspersed or headed up with bunches of yellow blossom. This strange composite grew abundantly in the streamlet's bed, and its trunk was so superficially rooted and so rotten that, in spite of its height and girth, I could pull it down with one hand.

Tufts of chervil and other tall *Umbelliferae,* with patches of vivid green moss, overhung the water which itself was lovely in its absolute clearness and in the bright wavelets and streaks of foam which marked its hurried descent. At this altitude of nearly 13,000 feet bees and wasps were still to be seen—their very presence, too, seemed to account for the vivid colours of the flora—and bright little sunbirds darted from bush to bush, gleaning their repast of honey.

As we ascended on the further side of the stream-valley we came to some strange boulders or smoothed masses of rock. They had been eaten away underneath into small caverns, large enough for a man to creep into. I went inside several, but detected nothing whatever resembling either past or present animal occupation. The last fern I saw on Kilima-njaro, as I went upwards, I picked from under a sheltered shelf of one of these caverns. Beyond and about these huge slabs of rock the ground became pappy and boggy with water, in fact some three or four small springs issued from about the rocks, and seemed to have done their work in carving the cavelike hollows within. Putting down my hand to gather a small plant by the roots, I was surprised to find the water warm. At first I fancied it an illusion, and called to one of the men to try, when he also exclaimed at the unexpected warmth. Then getting out my thermometer I found the temperature of the trickling mud—for it was little else in this bog—to be 91° Fahr.

Mounting high above the rivulet the scenery became much harsher. Vegetation only grew in dwarfed patches as we passed the altitude of 13,000 feet, and the ground was covered with boulders, more or less big, apparently lying in utter confusion, and without any definite direction. These slabs of rock were singularly shaped, and marked like huge tortoise-shells, being divided by lines and seams into a tesselated surface. They were not very difficult to climb over, and even seemed to act as irregular stone steps upwards. In their interstices heaths of the size of large shrubs grew with a certain luxuriance, and bright yellow euryops flowers studded the occasional patches of bare earth, while every now and then my eye alighted with pleasure on lovely clusters of pink everlasting flowers growing, where they did grow, so thickly that they presented a blushing sheet of rosy bloom. About 13,700 feet I saw the last resident bird, a kind of stonechat. It went in little cheery flocks, and showed such absence of fear that I had to walk away from it before shooting, to avoid shattering my specimen. After this, with the exception of an occasional high-soaring kite or great-billed raven, I saw no other bird.

On reaching a height a little above 14,000 feet, I stopped again to boil the thermometer and refresh myself with a little lunch. The result of my observations gave this altitude as 14,117 feet. Throughout this ascent, which was easy to climb, I suffered absolutely nothing from want of health or mountain-sickness, although my three Zanzibari followers lagged behind, panting and exhausted, and complained much of their lungs and head. Moreover, every gust of wind breaking the silence of the mountain made them look round with ashy countenances, convinced that the Bogy of Kilima-njaro was upon them, coming *in propria persona* to chastise our presumption. I often dreaded that their panic would overcome them, and that they would turn and flee, carrying with them my collecting things, instruments, and provisions. Moreover, about this time we occasionally heard distant rumblings of thunder echoing among unseen cliffs and valleys; and although these weird sounds might be only referable to that cause, still I confess they did resemble somewhat the rising murmurs of an angry spirit— or, at least, they did to my men's imaginations, for I myself, never having heard an angry spirit murmur, was not in a position to discriminate. However, I resolved not to try their powers of endurance much longer, so, on arriving at the place where I stopped to lunch—a protected hollow surrounded by huge flattened boulders—I determined to fix on this as our sleeping-place for the night, and accordingly directed the men to collect the dry roots of the heaths and other fair-sized shrubs as firewood. They were further instructed to proceed to the small stream which rose hard by and fill our gourds there with water, and afterwards to stretch out a macintosh in guise of a tent, so that we might have some shelter against possible rain and wind. Other directions for rendering our instalment as comfortable as the unfavourable circumstances would permit were also given; and having left the men in seemingly better spirits, I hastened to continue my ascent while the weather would permit.

Climbing up a few hundred feet higher than the last stopping-place, and rounding an unsuspected and deep ravine, I arrived close to the base of a small peak which had been a continual and useful point to aim at during the whole journey from my station. I was now at an elevation of 15,150 feet, and on the central connecting ridge of Kilima-njaro, and could see a little on both sides, though the misty state of the atmosphere prevented my getting any good view of the country. This ridge, which from below looks so simple and straight, is in reality dotted with several small monticules and cut up into many minor ridges, the general direction of which is, on the southern side, from north-east to south-west. To the eastward I could see the greater part of Kimawenzi rising grandly with its jagged peaks and smooth glissades of golden sand. Westward I still looked vainly in the piled-up clouds, for the monarch of the chain still remained obstinately hidden, and I was at a loss how to best approach his awful crown of snow. At length, and it was so sudden and so fleeting that I had no time to fully take in the majesty of the snowy dome of Kibo, the clouds parted and I looked on a blaze of snow so blinding white under the brief flicker of sunlight that I could see little detail. Since sunrise that morning I had caught no glimpse of Kibo, and now it was suddenly presented to me with unusual and startling nearness. But before I could get out my sketch-book and sharpen my chalk-pencil the clouds had once more hidden everything, indeed had enclosed me in a kind of London fog, very depressing in character, for the decrease in light was rather alarming to one who felt himself alone and cut off at a point nearly as high as the summit of Mont Blanc. However, knowing now the direction of my goal, I rose from the clammy stones, and clutching up my sketch-book with benumbed hands, began once more to ascend westwards. Seeing but a few yards in front of me, choked with mist, I made but slow progress; nevertheless, I continually mounted along a gently sloping, hummocky ridge where the spaces in between the masses of rock were filled with fine yellowish sand. There were also fragments of stone strewn about, and some of these I put into my knapsack. The slabs of rock were so slippery with the drizzling mist that I very often nearly lost my footing, and I thought with a shudder what a sprained ankle would mean here. However, though reflection told me it would be better to return to my followers and recommence the climb tomorrow, I still struggled on with stupid persistency, and at length, after a rather steeper ascent than usual up the now smoother and sharper ridge, I suddenly encountered snow lying at my very feet, and nearly plunged headlong into a great rift filled with snow that here seemed to cut across the ridge and interrupt it. The dense mist cleared a little in a partial manner, and I then saw to my left the black rock sloping gently to an awful gulf of snow so vast and deep that its limits were concealed by fog. Above me a line of snow was just discernible, and altogether the prospect was such a gloomy one with its all-surrounding curtain of sombre cloud and its uninhabited wastes of snow and rock, that my heart sank within me at my loneliness. Nevertheless, I thought "only a little farther and perhaps I may ascend above the clouds and stand gazing down into the crater of Kilima-njaro from its snowy rim." So turning momentarily northwards I rounded the rift of snow, and once more dragged myself, now breathless and panting, and with aching limbs, along the slippery ridge of bare rock which went ever mounting upwards. I continued this for nearly an hour, and then dropped exhausted on the ground, overcome with what I suppose was an ordinary attack of mountain-sickness.

It is not necessary to dilate on my sensations at this moment. Possibly there are some among my readers who have scaled the giant peaks of South America, India, and Armenia, and who would laugh at the puny difficulties that Kilima-njaro presents—a mountain that can be climbed without even the aid of a walking-stick, and where the most serious obstacles arise from mist and cold which would scarcely deter a cockney from ascending Snowdon. But the feeling that overcame me when I sat and gasped for breath on the wet and slippery rocks at this great height was one of overwhelming isolation. I felt as if I should never more regain the force to move, and must remain and die amid this horrid solitude of stones and snow. Then I took some brandy-and-water from my flask, and a little courage came back to me. I was miserably cold, the driving mist having wetted me to the skin. Yet the temperature recorded here was above freezing point, being 35° Fahr. I boiled my thermometer, and the agreeable warmth of the spirit-lamp put life into my benumbed hands. The mercury rose to 183.8. This observation when properly computed, and with the correction added for the temperature of the intermediate air, gives a height of 16,315 feet as the highest point I attained on Kilima-njaro. I thus came within a little more than 2000 feet of the summit, which is usually estimated to reach an altitude of 18,800 feet.

Having looked at my watch, I found it was now nearly half-past four, so I resolved to hasten back as quickly as possible to my improvised shelter, for the clouds were thickening, and thin showers of sleety snow were falling. A high wind arose and whipped my face with the icy rain, and made it very difficult to keep my footing on the slippery ridge. At length I reached the boulders and the sand, then descending with greater ease entered once more, at about an altitude of 15,000 feet, the region of vegetation. Keeping in view the small hillock I have already mentioned as such a useful landmark, I ultimately found my way back to the spot where I had left the men. What was my agonized surprise to find on searching the sheltered hollow, that it was deserted and abandoned! I hesitated but little. Sooner than remain there without blankets, food, or fire, I would endeavour to regain my station, even though I had to wander all night on the lonely flanks of the mountain; so starting off in the waning daylight, I hurried over the now easy descent at a pace that soon quickened into an irregular run. I crossed the stream at the well-remembered ford; and cheered with the sight of old landmarks, and warmed with the violent exercise, I marched straight on in the direction of my little village. The mists dispersed, the moon shone out brightly, I could clearly distinguish familiar hill-tops, and on reaching once more the banks of my own river, I then had an unfailing guide to follow until the glimmering watch-fires of my settlement glanced out from our bushy stockade, and the loud voices of men broke the still and frosty air. As I stepped in through the palisade, and appeared before my almost terror-stricken men, I saw I was at first taken for my own ghost, but when I had spoken a few sentences in a very real and energetic tone to the three culprits who had deserted me, the other men crowded round me in an ecstasy of joy, kissing my hands, patting me all over to assure themselves that I was back in the flesh, and assuring me that if I had taken *them,* they would never have left me to perish in the snowy solitudes above—no! not if the Demon of the Mountain had appeared visibly in all his terrors to confront them. It appeared that my three followers had remained for about an hour in the place I had left them, and then seeing I did not return, had been seized with an irresistible panic, had caught up their loads, and had returned helter-skelter to the station. Fortunately they had not lost the collections, so after a short rebuke I was disposed to condone their fault; the more so, as I felt so thankful to return to warmth and shelter and familiar faces, that I little cared to pass the night in unprofitable scolding.

Mysteries of the
Highlands

6

JOHN BARROW

JOHN BARROW (1764–1848) arrived in South Africa just as European colonists were making their first extended ventures into the interior. When not keeping the government's accounts, he spent much of his time there combing the mountains for the unicorn, which he believed to live there. The Bushman cave paintings he describes likely depict the oryx, a creature easy enough to mistake for a unicorn. This passage is taken from Barrow's memoir An Account of Travels in the Interior of Southern Africa, *published in 1801.*

On the fifteenth we made another long excursion into the Tarka mountains, near where they united with the great chain that runs along the upper part of the Kaffer country. Our object was to find among the drawings, made by the Bosjesmans [Bushmen], the representation of an unicorn. One of the party promised to bring us directly to the spot where he knew such a drawing stood. We set off at an early hour, and rode through several defiles along the beds of temporary streamlets. In one place was a very large and curious cavern formed by a waterfall, that from time to time had deposited a vast mass of stalactitical matter; many of the ramifications were not less than forty or fifty feet in length. Some were twisted and knotted like the roots of an old tree, and others were cellular and cavernous. This great mass, reflected from a sheet of deep water beneath, clear as crystal, hemmed in by two steep faces of solid rock, and fronted by two old weeping-willows, made as fine a piece of wild and romantic scenery as fancy could design. A little on one side of the cavern, and under a long projecting ridge of smooth white sand-stone, were several sketches of animals, and satirical attempts to represent the colonists in ridiculous situations and attitudes, characterizing them by some of their most common and striking habits. But the grand object of our research was still wanting. The long-necked camelopardalis was easily distinguished among the rest; as was also the rhinoceros and the elephant.

The same kind of black matter that had been found along with the native nitre, was here abundantly adhering to the rocks, and oozing down the sides of the cave. A Bosjesman that belonged to one of the party informed us that his countrymen mixed it with water, and drank it as tea. This cavern was near the source of the Riet river, a small stream that falls into the Fish river.

We still continued our search in the kloofs [cliffs] of the mountains, in the hope of meeting with the figure of the unicorn, the peasantry being equally sanguine to convince me of the truth of their assertions as I was to gratify curiosity. We came, at length, to a very high and concealed kloof, at the head of which was a deep cave covered in front by thick shrubbery. One of the party mounted up the steep ascent, and having made his way through the close brushwood, he gave us notice that the sides of the cavern were covered with drawings. After clearing away the bushes to let in the light, and examining the numerous drawings, some of which were tolerably well executed, and other caricatures, part of a figure was discovered that was certainly intended as the representation of a beast with a single horn projecting from the forehead. . . . The body and legs had been erased to give place to the figure of an elephant that stood directly before it.

Nothing could be more mortifying than such an accident; but the peasantry, who could form no idea of the consequence I attached to the drawing of such an animal, seemed to enjoy my chagrin. One being told however, that a thousand, or even five thousand, rixdollars would be given to any one who would produce an original, they stood gaping with open mouths, and were ready to enlist for an expedition behind the Bambosberg, where some of them were quite certain the animal was to be found. Imperfect as the figure was, it was sufficient to convince me that the Bosjesmans are in practice of including, among their representations of animals, that of an unicorn; and it also offered a strong argument for the existence of a living original. Among the several thousand figures of animals that, in the course of the journey, we had met with, none had the appearance of being monstrous, none that could be considered as works of the imagination, "creatures of the brain," on the contrary, they were generally as faithful representations of nature as the talents of the artist would allow. An instance of this appeared in the cavern we last visited. The black shell of the testudo geometrica was lying on the ground; and the regular figures with which it is marked and from which it takes its name, had been recently, and very accurately, copied on the side of a smooth rock. It was thought, indeed, from several circumstances, that the savages had slept in the cavern the preceding night.

The unicorn, as it is represented in Europe, is unquestionably a work of fancy; but it does not follow from thence that a quadruped with one horn, growing out of the middle of the forehead, should not exist. The arguments, indeed, that might be offered are much stronger for its existence than the objections are against it. The first idea of such an animal seems to have been taken from Holy Writ; and from the description there given, a representation of the unicorn, very illy conceived, has been assumed as a supporter to regal arms. The animal, to which the writer of the Book of Job, who was no mean historian, puts into the mouth of the Almighty a poetical allusion, has been supposed, with great plausibility, to be the one-horned rhinoceros: "Canst thou bind the unicorn with his band in the furrow? Or will he harrow the valleys after thee? Wilt thou trust him because his strength is great, or wilt thou leave thy labor to him?" Moses also very probably meant the rhinoceros when he mentions the unicorn as having the strength of God. Aristotle had a very different idea of the animal, to which he gives the name of unicorn, for he ascribes it as a species of wild ass with solidungulous feet.

The African rhinoceros, having invariably two horns, cannot be supposed as the prototype of the Bosjesmans' paintings of the unicorn. Besides, the former frequently occurs among their productions, and is represented as the thick short-legged figure that it really is, whilst the latter is said by the peasantry to be uniformly met with as a solidungulous animal resembling the horse, with an elegantly shaped body, marked from the shoulders to the flanks with longitudinal stripes or bands. The greatest number of such drawings are said to be met with in the Bambosberg; and, as the people who make them live on the north side of this great chain of mountains, the original may of be also found there.

This part of Africa is as yet untrodden ground, none of the peasantry having proceeded beyond the mountains. It may be said, perhaps, that if such an animal existed, and was known to the natives inhabiting a part of the country not very distant from the borders of the colony, the fact would certainly before this time have been ascertained. This, however, does not follow. Very few of the colonists have crossed the Orange river, or have been higher along its banks than the part where we were under the necessity of turning off to the southward; and the sort of communication that the peasantry have with the Bosjesmans is not of that nature to supply much information respecting the country they inhabit. The mouth of the Orange river is much nearer to the Cape than the plains behind the Kaffer mountains; yet it was but the other day that the existence of the camelopardalis was ascertained near the former place; though no savage nation, but a civilized tribe of Hottentots only, intervened. Certain animals, as well as plants, confine themselves to certain districts of the same country. The animal above mentioned was never known to have passed the Orange river. It would appear also that in Northern Africa it has its limited range; for, since the time of Julius Caesar, when one was publicly exhibited in Rome, it has been lost to Europe till within the present century. The accounts given of it by ancient writers were looked upon as fabulous. The gnoo is found only in certain parts of Southern Africa; and the blue antelope (the leucophaea), which confined itself to the banks of one small river in the vicinity of Zwellendam, is now entirely lost to the colony. The springbok, seen in the northern parts in troops of thousands, never made its appearance in any part of the district of Zwellendam.

The Bosjesmans have no knowledge of any doubts concerning the existence of such an animal as the unicorn; nor do they seem to think there is any thing extraordinary that a beast should have one horn only. The colonists take it for granted that such an animal exists beyond the limits of the colony.

Table Mountain

⑥

JOSHUA PENNY

JOSHUA PENNY, an American, was press-ganged into the British Navy during the War of 1812 and taken to South Africa, where he had lived for a brief time some years earlier, as a hand on the frigate Sceptre. *He feigned sickness on the ship's arrival in Cape Town and was brought ashore to see a doctor. He escaped, as he describes here, and for the next fourteen months he lived atop Table Mountain, a 3,563-foot rise overlooking the Cape of Good Hope. His* Life and Adventures of Joshua Penny, *published on his return to New York, became an early American best-seller.*

The doctor's mate ordered the men to follow him through town in single rank, and I was in the rear of this procession. We had not proceeded far before we came to a wine-house, where I begged the sailors to set me down, as I was very thirsty. They very readily complied, knowing they should get some wine. I called on the landlord, as we entered his house, for a bottle of Constantia wine and three tumblers. I took my glass, and paid the landlord while the sailors were drinking theirs. I proposed going immediately, judg-

95

ing however that they would never budge while any wine remained. As soon as they became engaged, I pretended an occasion of necessity to retire out of the back door, and helped myself by the chairs until fairly out, and it was safe to become as well as ever I was in my life.

I went hastily through the back yard into another street, which enabled me to get through the town and reach the thicket of bushes at the skirts of Table mountain, which I had often looked to as a place of refuge. I had this in contemplation long before, because I had been acquainted with the mode of living in similar places, and had taken the precaution to provide myself with a belt to fasten around me, containing a knife, a small brass tinder-box, and eleven dollars.

Here, feeling myself secure from pursuit, I meditated leisurely, and at length determined to spend the residue of my days on this mountain, if the British ships should not leave the Cape. I resolved to become a breakfast for a lion, sooner than be taken to another floating dungeon.

I returned into the town in the dark, and laid in my supply of goods— this was two loaves of bread, a calabash of brandy and a flint. This was as much as I could take, although my money was not all spent, which had been saved out of my rations of grog for this purpose. My dress was composed of one shirt, one Guernsey frock, and one pair of duck trowsers, with a hospital cap.

Thus equipped I marched on my tour up the mountain, without waiting to hear what return the doctor's mate would make to our captain of the sick Jonas Ingleberg, for that was my name on board the ship. My destiny seemed providential; for the first news I had of the *Sceptre,* was that she sunk soon after I left her, in a gale of wind, without weighing her anchors, and every soul on board perished in her.

There are no trees on Table mountain, and I climbed the cragged rocks through the bushes, and ascended, or attempted to ascend, all night; yet frequently returned to the place last left. I was much fatigued, and sometimes found a spring of water, where my calabash was very useful. It was unsafe to make a fire that night on a mountain fronting the ships, yet I was in danger from the wild beasts, who were often near me, and seemed reluctant to get out of my way. I knew the wild beasts were numerous here, and of almost every species. The next morning, I perceived that the ships lay far below, and could not discover me.

This mountain is green in every season, and it seems, from the water, that a cat might be discovered upon it: but I found nothing else than gullies, cragged rocks piled on each other, and scrubby bushes in their crevices. Here I began to think of preparing for subsistence, and, on searching, soon found a hive of bees among the rocks. This wild honey is so plenty, that a man from Cape Town will return home, loaded, the same day he leaves it.

The Hottentots had taught me the process of obtaining this honey, and having a wooden pipe, I proceeded to the cavity of the rock, covered with wax, and introducing the stem of my pipe through the entrance of the bees, blew in the smoke, which caused the bees to retreat into the interior. The second night I could make a fire under the cover of a rock, and regale myself with brandy and honey.

When I had ascended four days from the mountain's foot, I lost sight of the fleet and the bay. My course now was over level rocky spots, of 30 or 40 feet in width, on which I saw innumerable herds of goats, hosts of antelopes, wolves, tygers, and leopards. The three latter are the only animals considered dangerous here, except the venomous snakes. The baboons are here numerous and large. At first, they would apparently take no notice of me; but soon after would be seen on a precipice, 100 feet above, throwing stones at me.

At last I reached the summit, and selected a spot, in view of the Western Ocean, for my residence. I occupied a cavern which secured me from storms, near a spring of good water. My whole stock of provisions being nearly exhausted, I thought it time to recruit. Necessity invents the means in these cases. I sallied out with a stone in my hand, and had not advanced a great distance when I espied an antelope on the brow of a precipice. I threw the stone at the back of his head, and tumbled him to the bottom; where, by a circuitous route, I found my game, whose skin I drew over his head, and cutting the meat into strings, hung it on sticks put into the crevices of my habitation. This meat when dried, I broiled and ate with toad-sorrel for my sauce. Besides this I had honey and good water. It seemed rather hard at first, to live without bread, salt, and articles deemed necessary in former days; but at the end of two or three weeks I lived very contentedly. While among the Hottentots I had learned their method of making a very pleasant beverage resembling metheglin. I was fortunate enough to find an old hollow tree, which I cut off with my knife, and seized a green hide on one end for a bottom. Into this tub honey and water was put to stand twenty-four hours; then was added some pounded root to make it foment. This root, in use among the frontier Hottentots, does not resemble any of my acquaintance in America, but makes an excellent drink in this preparation. I had ground-nuts and a root with a stem one inch above the ground, with three leaves as small as those of the garden pink. This root, of the size of a junk bottle, is eatable; yet is not as good as the water-melon, which the Dutch call it. It is probably the *kameroo* from the description given me of its size and shape.

My clothes, by creeping through the rocks and bushes, were so tattered that I had become almost naked. In this extremity I made a needle from the bone of a beast; the eye of which being made with my sharp pointed knife, enabled me to sew with the sinews of my antelopes. With the skins I equipped myself completely from head to foot. The skins were dressed by rubbing sand on the flesh side with a stone; and furnished me with moccasins, shin-fenders, or leggings to the knee; a short petticoat fastened round my waist, and a hunting frock. The hair was worn inside when cold, and turned outside when warm. It is almost unnecessary to add that I wore a superb cap.

Thus accoutred, it is natural to suppose me somewhat elevated, although without a looking-glass. Pride must have a fall—I was soon afflicted with lice. By procuring an entire new suit, and changing my residence, these tenants of the skin abandoned me. It was not troublesome to change my quarters; and by often shifting my abode for a new tenement, I acquired by occupation dwellings enough to make my territory called a city. Thus I lived, unannoyed by wild beasts or press-gangs; until one day I crept out of some cragged rocks, and came inadvertently into a large concourse of wolves, in their season of making love. They soon surrounded me; some within 20 feet. I stood ready with my knife to defend myself; when at last, one turned off, another followed, till they all had sneaked off apparently ashamed of themselves and left me alone. I used to kill darsies or mountain rats, which eat grass, and are choice food.

At each full moon I cut a notch in the root, which hung to a silken cord about my neck; and this was the only account I kept of time.

Once I undertook to descend the western side of the mountain to the sea shore, where I could often see vessels in clear weather; but the mountain being very steep on that side, with so many rocks that I frequently let myself down by taking hold of bushes, until I seemed sliding into the sea without power to stop. In two days I returned, and gave up experiments in that direction. My practice was to eat twice in the day; and when cooking in the evening always heard the howling of wild beasts, and often saw the light of their eyes, when attracted about me by the smell of meat.

My residence was not on the summit, but in a convenient place for hunting; near some height, on which I could cramp my game. I often went over to the eastern front to view the ships; and continued to do so until twelve notches were made upon the calendar fastened to my neck. I had become perfectly reconciled to my condition—had abundance of meat, sorrel, honey and water; and every night could sing my song with as much pleasure as at any period of my life. In fine, I never enjoyed life better than while I lived among the ferocious animals of Table mountain; because I had secured myself against the more savage English. I now discovered some vessels at sea, on the western side of the mountain, but was unable to distinguish them as ships or other vessels, the clouds being so far below me. However, I suspected the fleet had sailed from the Cape—mustered my provisions, and stowed them in a knapsack, made of a skin drawn over the head, after splitting it on the hind-legs. The skin of each hind leg was tied to that of the foreleg on the same side, and my arms passed through the loop, the neck hung at the bottom down my back.

I now left my numerous habitations for the last time. During my residence I had never been able to discover the vestige of a human being, except myself, having ever ventured here. I travelled one day and part of a night, without being able to discover any shipping, on account of intervening clouds. I often was compelled to travel five miles on the mountain, without gaining in descent one hundred rods. The second day in my descent, the air being clear, I saw the bay, and one vessel only. I concluded to pursue my course until I could ascertain her character. Continuing on the next day, I perceived that vessel to be a brig; and having no top-gallant-masts, took her for a merchantman.

Determined to push for her immediately, I descended to the foot of the mountain, and rested there till after day break. It was only half a mile to the shore. A British regiment I supposed to be stationed in the town; yet I thought no person would know me after so long an absence; especially in my mountain dress: but to avoid their notice of my uncouth habit, I turned the hair side inwards. I marched through the town unobserved by any one except two or three servants, who continued to gaze obliquely at me as long as I could see them. The boat was coming to the shore as I approached it, with two men and the captain, as I supposed.

I tried my power of speech to prepare myself. The captain landing advanced guardedly towards me, I stepped up to meet him and asked if he wanted to ship a man? He was surprised to hear me speak, and asked "What in the name of God are you! man or beast?" He at last stepped up to me and giving me his hand, said "This is no place to talk—jump into the boat and go on board." The boat was ordered to return for him in half an hour; into it I sprung, and was soon snug on board.

When the captain returned he sent for me in the cabin and ordered me two suits of clothes. I put them on, and took my beard off for the first time in fourteen months. He then heard a short story of myself, and said he supposed me to be a deserter; but that I had nothing to fear if I would go with him.

This brig was under Danish colors, but the captain and property were English, as he told me—and was bound to St. Helena, and thence to London. On learning that I had deserted the *Sceptre,* he informed me that she had been sunk fourteen months: He pointed to a monument on shore over the bodies of her crew which had been driven on shore and there interred.

ASIA

Cloudbank curling low?
Ah! Mount Yoshino rises high:
Cherry-blossom clouds.

RYOTA

You see the mountains.
You think them firm,
yet they move like clouds.

THE QURAN

High Japan

JAPANESE MYTHS, DŌGEN KIGEN, BASHŌ,

NANAO SAKAKI, ASUKA GASEI, YOSHINORI,

OTA DOKAN, KAYANO SHIGERU

In this episode from the ancient Japanese mythological cycle Nihongi, *the hunter-creator god* AME-WAKA-HIKO *has just been slain by one of his own arrows. Through his death, the etiological legend tells, rose one of the Japanese Alps.*

The sound of the weeping and mourning of Ame-waka-hiko's wife Shita-teru-hime reached Heaven. At this time, Ame no Kuni-dama, hearing the voice of her crying, straightway knew that her husband, Ame-waka-hiko, was dead, and sent down a swift wind to bring the body up to Heaven. Forthwith a mortuary house was made, in which it was temporarily deposited. The river-geese were made the head-hanging bearers and broom-bearers.

For eight days and eight nights they wept and sang dirges.

Before this, when Ame-waka-hiko was in the Central Land of Reed Plains, he was on terms of friendship with Aji-suki-taka-hiko-ne no Kami. Therefore Aji-suki-taka-hiko-ne no Kami ascended to Heaven and offered condolence on his decease. Now this God was exactly like in appearance to Ame-waka-hiko when he was alive, and therefore Ame-waka-hiko's parents, relations, wife, and children all said:—"Our Lord is still alive," and clung to his garments and to his girdle, partly rejoiced and partly distracted. Then Aji-suki-taka-hiko-ne no Kami became flushed with anger and said:—"The way of friends is such that it is right that mutual condolence should be made. Therefore I have not been daunted by the pollution, but have come from afar to make mourning. Why then should I be mistaken for a dead person?" So he drew his sword, Oho-hakari, which he had in his girdle, and cut down the mortuary house, which fell to earth and became a mountain. It is now in the province of Mino, by the upper waters of the River Ayumi. This is the mountain of Moyama [Mourning Mountain]. This is why people take care not to mistake a living for a dead person.

The Nihongi *also reports that an early emperor,* Yuriaku, *was so happy on seeing the mountains of the northern province of Hatsuse that he composed this song.*

> *The mountains of Hatsuse,*
>   *The secluded—*
> *They stand out,*
> *Excellent mountains!*
> *They run out,*
> *Excellent mountains!*
> *The mountains of Hatsuse,*
>   *The secluded—*
> *Are full of various beauties!*
> *Are full of various beauties!*

TRANSLATED BY W. G. ASTON

DŌGEN KIGEN, the thirteenth-century founder of Soto Zen Buddhism,
spent much time in the mountains of Japan and China, from which he
drew his famous Mountains and Rivers Sutra, *excerpted here.*

From time immemorial the mountains have been the dwelling-place of the
great sages; wise men and sages have all made the mountains their own
chambers, their own body and mind. And through these wise men and sages
the mountains have been actualized. However many great sages and wise
men we suppose have assembled in the mountains, ever since they entered
the mountains no one has met a single one of them. There is only the actu-
alization of the life of the mountains; not a single trace of their having entered remains. . . .

Although we say that mountains belong to the country, actually they belong to those who love them. When the mountains love their master, the
wise and the virtuous inevitably enter the mountains. And when sages and
wise men live in the mountains, because the mountains belong to them, trees
and rocks flourish and abound, and the birds and beasts take on a supernatural excellence. This is because the sages and wise men have covered them
with virtue. We should realize that the mountains actually take delight in
wise men and sages.

Throughout the ages we have excellent examples of emperors who have
gone to the mountains to pay homage to wise men and seek instruction from
great sages. At such times the emperors respected the sages as teachers, and
honored them without abiding by worldly forms. For the imperial authority
has no power over the mountain sage, and the emperors knew that the
mountains are beyond the mundane world.

In ancient times we have the examples of K'ung-Fung and Hua Feng.
When the Yellow Emperor made his visit to Kuang Ch'eng-tzu, he went on
his knees, prostrated himself, and begged instruction. Again, Sakyamuni
Buddha left his father's palace and went into the mountains; yet his father
felt no resentment toward the mountains, nor distrust of those in the mountains who instructed the prince. His twelve years of cultivating the way were

spent largely in the mountains, and it was in the mountains that the Dharma King's auspicious event occurred. Even a veritable cakravartin does not wield authority over the mountains.

We should understand that the mountains are not within the human realm, nor within the realm of heaven. They are not to be viewed with the suppositions of human thought. If only we did not compare them with flowing in the human realm, who would have any doubt about such things as the mountains flowing or not flowing? . . .

As for mountains, there are mountains hidden in jewels; there are mountains hidden in marshes, mountains hidden in the sky; there are mountains hidden in mountains. There is a study of mountains hidden in hiddenness.

In the spring of 1689, a forty-six-year-old poet named BASHŌ *left the Japanese capital of Edo, today's Tokyo, and wandered into the highlands of northern Honshū. There he spent nine months in pilgrimage, visiting temples and small villages, seeing acquaintances, and locating his "heart's mountain." The centerpiece of his journey, recorded in his* Oku-no-hosomichi, *or "Path to the Deep North," was an ascent of Gassan, or Moon Mountain, the highest of northern Japan's sacred peaks. The haikai poems he wrote describing his ascent are among the most famous in Japanese literature.*

In the demesne of Yamagata the mountain temple called Ryushakuji. Founded by Jikaku Daishi, unusually well-kept quiet place. "You must go and see it," people urged; from here, off back towards Obanazawa, about seven *li.* Sun not yet down. Reserved space at dormitory at bottom, then climbed to temple on ridge. This mountain one of rocky steeps, ancient pines and cypresses, old earth and stone and smooth moss, and on the rocks temple-doors locked, no sound. Climbed along edges of and crept over boulders, worshipped at temples, penetrating scene, profound quietness, heart/mind open clear.

silence itself is
in the rock absorbing
cicada sounds

Third day of the sixth moon, climbed Haguroyama. Visited Zushi Sakichi and received in audience by the *betto-dai*, Egaku Ajari. Lodged at side-temple at Minamidani and he eagerly and cordially welcomed us.

The fourth, at main temple building, *haikai* party.

thank you *very much*
for all your perfuming snow
Minamidani

On the fifth worshipped at Gongen temple. Its founder, Nojo Daishi, but date unknown. In the *Engishiki* given as date of Ushusatoyama. Whoever did the copying wrote "satoyama" for "kuro" by mistake probably. One of the Ushukuroyama *kanji* dropped out and so it became Hagurogama. The idea of Dewa seems clarified in the *Fudoki*, where payments in down and feathers are mentioned as a form of local tribute. Gassan and Yudono with it compose a trinity. This temple affiliated with Toei in Buko, the moon of the Tendai shi-kan clear, by way of *endonyuzu*, light increased, ridge to temple ridge extending, the devout encouraging each other in austere duties, the grace revealed (*genko*) in heart's mountains and heart's land calls forth reverence and awe in folk. Prosperity unconfined and the mountains may be said to bestow blessings.

Eighth, climbed Gassan. Yushime hanging from our necks, heads covered by hokan, led by a goriki, up into mountain air, clouds, mist, walking ice and snow, going some eight *li* up until it seemed near the gateway to the clouds, sun and moon passing over, each breath a last one, numb, reached peak, sun down, moon out. Spread bamboo grass, used shino as pillows, lay down, waited for daybreak. Sun up, clouds gone, headed down towards Yudono.

At valley's edge place known as the Swordsmiths' Hut. Smiths in these parts fetch holy water here to purify themselves and to temper blades in which they eventually carve: Gassan: a mark of wide repute. Said that swords were tempered at Ryusen too. Reminiscent of ancient Kansho and Bakuya. That their dedication to their craft not superficial, well-known. Perched on rock resting a while, saw half-opened buds of three-foot cherry trees. Buried under piled-up reluctant snow, slow blossoms don't forget spring, remarkable stubbornness. As if the "plum under blazing heaven" were suddenly seen here. Recalled Gyoson Sojo's poem, which made buds seem to bud the more. By and large against code to disclose what goes on here. And with that the brush stops, won't write. Went back to dormitory and at the Ajari's insistence wrote poems of our visit to the Three Mountains on *tanzaku.*

coolness itself ah
the dimlit three day crescent's
Haguro-san

the summits of clouds
but how many giving way
to the moon's mountain

prohibited speech
at Yudono moistening
the edge of a sleeve

Yudono-yama
pennies for the stepping-stones
and many a tear

TRANSLATED BY CID CORMAN AND KAMAIKE SUSUMU

Nanao Sakaki, Japan's foremost poet-ecologist, is a modern heir of Bashō's.

> *Why climb a mountain?*
> *Look! A mountain there.*
>
> *I don't climb mountain.*
> *Mountain climbs me.*
>
> *Mountain is myself.*
> *I climb on myself.*
>
> *There is no mountain*
>   *nor myself.*
>   *Something*
>   *moves up and down*
>   *in the air.*

As today, MEDIEVAL JAPANESE POETS celebrated Fujiyama, Japan's most sacred mountain. These haikai *honor the peak.*

> *How could we forget the sight of Mount Fuji*
> *blooming amid the clouds of the rising sun*
> *in the bright autumn morning?*

ASUKA GASEI

As the morning sun darts his golden light,
the snow on Mount Fuji
is more beautiful than ever.

YOSHINORI

My dwelling place faces open sea
along the pine grove
and from beneath the eaves of my house
Mount Fuji is glimpsed.

OTA DOKAN

The Ainu are the aboriginal people of Japan, believed to descend from a
branch of an eastern Caucasian group, who were largely displaced by the
arrival of the present Japanese, themselves descended from Korean stock.
Born into an Ainu family in the Nibutani Valley of Hokkaido in 1923,
KAYANO SHIGERU witnessed profound changes among his people as the larger
society attempted to assimilate them. In the 1970s Kayano, a logger, formed
a group to preserve Ainu traditions and to record oral histories and litera-
ture, among them this prayer offered up by woodcutters in the tall Hidaka
Mountains of southern Hokkaido. The prayer, he writes in his memoir Our
Land Was a Forest, *helps avert the ransacking of their toolboxes and sheds*
by foxes, an event called kamuy ipirima, *"gods' whisperings."*

An Ainu I,
in order to raise my children
need what is called money;
so into the tranquil mountain
I have entered to cut standing trees
and harmed the divine mountain-
    dwellers' abode and garden

much to my regret.
But humans and gods alike
raise children.
I, too, have many children.
In order to feed them
and keep them from hunger
I must come to the highest mountains to
    work
Oh god
think of this
and permit an Ainu's deed.

TRANSLATED BY KYOKO SELDEN AND LILI SELDEN

Sakhalin

ANTON CHEKHOV,

MARITIME CHUKCHEE FOLKTALE

*In 1890, the thirty-year-old physician and writer ANTON CHEKHOV
(1860–1904) traveled from Moscow across Siberia to the island of
Sakhalin, where he looked into and reported on the appalling conditions
in the penal colonies there. His published account exposed for a European audience the terrible hardships of convict life on the cold, mountainous island. Here he describes a series of mountain settlements along
the Tatar Strait.*

The river Arkay falls into the Tatar Strait, about eight to ten versts [approx-
imately 5.2 to 6.5 miles] to the north of the Duyka. Not so very long ago it
really was a river, and people went fishing in it for hump-backed salmon, but
now, as a consequence of forest fires and tree-felling, it has grown shallow,
and, towards the summer, dries up completely. However, during heavy periods of rain it overflows its banks as in spring, stormily and noisily, and then
it really makes its presence felt. It has already happened more than once that
the river has washed the vegetable gardens off its banks, and carried the hay

112

and the whole of the exiles' harvests into the sea. It is impossible to guard against such a disaster, since the valley is narrow, and a person can only move away from the river by going up the mountains.

Right by the mouth of the Arkay, where the river curves into the valley, stands the tiny Gilyak village of Arkay-vo, which has given the names to the Arkovo Cordon and the three settlements of Pervoye, Vtoroye and Tretye Arkovo. Two roads lead into the Arkovo Valley from Alexandrovsk—one, through the mountains, which was impassable when I was there, since the bridges along its way had been burned down by forest fires—and the other, a road along the seashore; travel was possible over this latter route only when the tide was out. I set out for the Arkay for the first time at 8 A.M. on 31st July. The tide had begun to go out. It was squalling with rain. The overcast sky, the sea, on which could be seen not a single sail, and the steep clay shoreline had a forbidding air; the waves pounded dull and melancholy. Stunted, sickly trees looked down from high up on the bank; here, out in the open, each of them fights in isolation a cruel battle with the frosts and cold winds, and during the autumn and winter, through long, dreadful nights, each of them sways restlessly from side to side, bends to the ground and creaks in lamentation, and this lamentation is heard by nobody.

The Arkovo Cordon is situated near the Gilyak village. Formerly it had significance, the soldiers who went out hunting escapees lived here, but now an overseer lives here who carries out the duties, it would appear, of Acting Governor of Settlements. Some two versts from the Cordon lies Pervoye Arkovo. It has just one street and owing to the conditions of the place can only grow lengthwise and not in width. When, in time, all three Archives merge, Sakhalin will have a large village consisting of one single street. Pervoye Arkovo was founded in 1883. It has 136 inhabitants. . . . There are 28 householders and they all live in families, except for the convict woman Pavlovskaya, a Catholic, whose cohabitant, the real landlord of the house, died not long ago; she requested me persuasively: "Get me a man appointed to run the house!" Three of them have two houses each. Vtoroye Arkovo was founded in 1884. There are 92 inhabitants—46 men and 46 women. There are 24 householders, all living in families. Of these two have two houses each. Tretye Arkovo was founded at the same time as Vtoroye and it may be seen from this how they rushed to settle the Arkovo Valley. There are 41 inhabitants, 19 men and 22 women, ten of whom are householders, with one co-owner as well. Nine live in families.

All householders in the three Arkovos are shown as having arable land, and the size of the holdings fluctuates between a half and two desyatins [1.3 to 5.4 acres]. One plot has an area of three desyatins. They sow wheat, barley and rye in fairly large quantities and plant potatoes. The majority have potatoes and poultry. Judging from the information compiled by the Governor of Settlements in the Inventory of Landholdings, one might reach the conclusion that, during the short time they have existed, the three Arkovos have enjoyed considerable success in farming; not without reason did one anonymous author write about the working of the land here: "This labor is rewarded with abundance owing to the conditions of the soil of this locality, which are highly favorable to agriculture, as is shown by the vigor of growth of woods and meadows." But in actual fact this is not the case. All three Arkovos belong among the poorest settlements of Northern Sakhalin. There is arable land and there are cattle here, but there has not once been a harvest. Besides the unfavorable conditions common to the whole of Sakhalin, the local householders encounter a further serious enemy in the natural features of the Arkovo Valley, primarily in the soil which is so highly praised by the author I have just quoted. The topsoil here is a two-inch-thick layer of humus, and the subsoil consists of shingle which on hot days heats up so fiercely that it dries out the roots of the plants, and, during a period of rain, does not let the moisture through, since it lies on the clay; because of this the roots rot. Obviously, in such soil, the only plants that can get along without damage to themselves are ones with firm, deep-seated roots, such as, for example, burdocks, and, among cultivated plants, only root crops, swede and potatoes, for all of which into the bargain the soil has to be tilled deeper and more thoroughly than for cereals. I have already spoken of the disasters caused by the river. There are no hay-fields at all; they cut hay on scraps of land in the taiga, or reap it with sickles wherever they come across it, and those who are a little more wealthy buy it in the Tymovsk District. Tales are told of entire families who did not have a single piece of bread during the

winter and lived on nothing else but swede. Not long before my arrival, the
settled-exile Skorin had died of starvation in Vtoroye Arkovo. According to
the stories of the neighbours, he ate only one *funt* of bread every three days,
and he had been doing so for a very long time. "We're all expecting the same
fate," his neighbors, frightened by his death, told me. I recall that, describing their everyday life to me, three women burst into tears. In one cabin,
with no furniture, and with a dark, gloomy stove taking up half the room,
around the female householder children were crying and baby chickens
were cheeping; out she went on to the street and out went the children and
chicks after her. Gazing at them, she laughed and she cried, and apologized
to me for the crying and cheeping; it was from hunger, she said, she could
hardly wait for her husband to get back, he had gone into town to sell
whortleberries to buy bread. She minced up some cabbage leaves and gave
it to the chicks, who threw themselves on it greedily and, finding themselves
deceived raised an even greater squawking. . . .

If a landscape painter should happen to come to Sakhalin, then I recommend the Arkovo Valley to his notice. This spot, besides the beauty of its lo-
cation, is extremely rich in hues and tints, so that it is difficult to get by without
the hackneyed simile of a multicolored carpet or a kaleidoscope. Here there is
dense, sappy verdure with giant burdocks glittering from the rain that has only
just fallen; beside it, in an area no larger than three sazbeils or so, there is the
greenery of rye, then a scrap of land with barley, and then burdocks again, with
a space behind it covered with oats, after that beds of potatoes, two immature
sunflowers with drooping heads, then, forming a little wedge, a deep-green
patch of hemp; here and there plants of the umbelliferous family similar to
candelabras proudly hold up their heads, and this whole diversity of color is
strewn with pink, bright-red and crimson specks of poppies. On the road you
meet peasant women who have covered themselves against the rain with big
burdock leaves, like headscarves, and because of this look like green beetles.
And the sides of the mountains—well, maybe they are not the mountains of
the Caucasus, but they are mountains all the same.

TRANSLATED BY BRIAN REEVE

The MARITIME CHUKCHEE tell this indelicate story about how Big Raven,
in the company of an ancestral human, created the landforms of their
world.

High in the sky, the man pointed down. "There," he said. "There's an empty place." ·

Hearing this, Big Raven let loose some feces; it flew down, it landed, and even as they watched it became a big island, and as they circled, more feces fell and became islands. The continents were born in this way, and there now was plenty of land. Big Raven spun the continents out of his belly.

"I'll do some more, then," Big Raven said.

Big Raven began pissing, but by the time it got to earth it was cleaned up; it became fresh water. So Big Raven was swirling rivers, lakes, and streams out of his belly.

"How about some mountains?" the companion said.

Big Raven strained himself, grunted, grunt, grunt, grunt, down fell hard substances, spun out of Big Raven, and that's how hills, mountains, entire ranges were born. That's how it happened.

TRANSLATED BY HOWARD NORMAN

Storm

(6)

V. K. ARSENIEV

*In 1902, a party of Russian explorers led by the soldier-geographer V. K.
ARSENIEV (1872–1930) entered the unmapped portion of maritime
Siberia bordering Manchuria and Korea. Almost immediately lost in the
high Sihote-Alin Mountains, they were rescued by a Gold trapper named
Dersu, a native of the area who guided the Russians and saved their lives
on several occasions, among them the one Arseniev recounts here. In
1976, Akira Kurosawa translated Arseniev's memoir* Dersu the Trapper
into the prizewinning film Dersu Uzala.

All this time we had been enjoying calm, pleasant weather. It was so warm
that we walked in our summer shirts, and only put on warmer things in the
evening. I revelled in the fine weather but Dersu disagreed with me.

"Look-see, captain," he explained, "how quick all birds eat. Him know
well will be bad."

The barometer stood high. I began to chaff the Gold, but he only answered:
"Birds him know now; me know later."

From the little cabin to the pass over the Sihote-Alin was about five miles. In spite of the weight of our bundles, we stepped out bravely and made good going, with few breathers. About four in the afternoon we reached the Sihote-Alin, and only had to reach the crest. I wanted to push on, but Dersu detained me by the sleeve.

"Wait, captain," he said. "Me think better camp here."

"Why?" I asked.

"Morning, all birds eat quickly; now, look-see, no-can see bird."

And in fact, although birds are usually very lively just before sunset, now in the forest there was a deathly stillness. As though at the word of command, all the birds had hidden themselves.

Dersu advised us to pitch camp and fix the tents particularly firmly and to lay in a good big stock of firewood, not only enough for the night, but for the next day too. I did not argue with him any more, but set out to pick up firewood. A couple of hours later it grew dark. The soldiers had piled up a good lot of firewood, a good deal more than apparently necessary, but they never stopped, and I heard what he said to the Chinamen.

"Lotsa him no know; us must work too."

"Lotsa" is what the Manchurian natives call the Russians.

Again he set to work, so I sent a couple of Cossacks to help him, and it was not till the last glimmer of daylight had faded from the sky that we stopped working.

The moon came out. A clear, calm night looked down on the earth from the sky. The moonlight penetrated deep into the forest, in long pale bands across the dry grass. On the ground, in the sky, and all around, everything was still, and there was no sign of bad weather. Sitting round the fire we drank hot tea and chaffed the Gold.

"You've made a mistake this time, old man," said the Cossacks.

Dersu did not reply, but silently continued strengthening his little tent. He tucked himself under a rock on one side, and on the other rolled up a great big stump and packed it round with stones, filling the holes between them with moss. Over the top he stretched his piece of canvas, and in front he lit a fire. He looked so snug, tucked in like that, that I at once joined him with my things.

Time passed, and all around was as still as before. I too began to think that the Gold had made a mistake, when suddenly round the moon appeared a big dull circle, tinged at the edges with the colours of the rainbow. Then, little by little, the disc of the moon darkened, and its outline became vague and indistinct. The dull circle expanded and enveloped the outer ring. A kind of fog soon veiled the sky, but when it came and whither it was travelling we could not say.

I thought it would end in a shower, and lulled by the thought, fell asleep. How long I slept I do not know, but I was aroused by one of the men. I opened my eyes and saw Murzin standing by me.

"It is snowing," he reported.

I flung off my blanket. All around was pitch dark. The moon had disappeared and a fine snow was falling. The fire was burning brightly and lit up the tents, the sleeping men, and the pile of wood. I roused Dersu. He awoke with a start, looked round in a half-sleepy way, glanced at the sky, and lit his pipe.

Around all was still, but in this very stillness I could now sense a feeling of menace. A few minutes later the snow became thicker, and fell on the ground with a peculiar rustling sound. The rest of the party awoke and began collecting their things.

Suddenly the snow started whirling.

"Now begin," said Dersu.

And as though in answer to his words, in the mountains a distant roar could be heard, and then there fell upon us a violent gust of wind from the side whence least expected. The burning timbers blazed up. Then came a second gust, then a third, followed by a fourth, fifth, and more and more, each more violent and more prolonged than the preceding one. It was a good thing that the tents were firmly pegged down or they would have been carried away.

I glanced at Dersu. He was calmly smoking his pipe, serenely gazing into the fire. The opening of the blizzard did not disturb him. He had in his time seen so many that it had no novelty for him. He seemed to divine my thoughts and said:

"Got much wood; tents well fixed; nothing fear."

In an hour it began to grow light.

The blizzard was what we call a *purga*, during which the temperature can drop well below zero, with the gale so violent that it will lift roofs off houses and uproot trees. Walking during a *purga* is out of the question, and the only hope of safety is to stay where one is. As a rule every blizzard is accompanied by loss of life.

Around us the scene was unbelievable. The wind raged with the utmost violence, smashing off branches of trees, lifting them into the air like feathers. Huge cedars rocked from side to side like saplings. Nothing was visible, neither mountains, nor sky, nor earth, everything enveloped in the roaring whirlwind of snow. For a moment I seemed almost to detect the outline of the nearest tree, just visible through the blinding snow, but only for an instant. Another gust and the misty picture vanished.

We shrank back in our tents and sat in silent awe. Dersu looked round at the sky and muttered something to himself. I reminded him of the blizzard that had caught us on Lake Hanka in 1902.

"Me very much afraid then," he answered. "No firewood; soon all finish."

In the afternoon the storm gave vent to all its fury. Although we were protected by cliffs and the tenting, it was still a wretched shelter. When the wind blew the fire our way, it was hot and smoky as in a house on fire, and when it blew the flame away it was cold.

We had given up going for water and filled the teapot with snow. Luckily there was no lack of that. Towards dusk the blizzard reached the very limit of its violence, and the darker it grew the more terrible it seemed.

We slept little that night. Our attentions were concentrated on keeping warm.

The 21st we spent still sheltering from the storm. Now the wind changed, veering round to the north-east, and the gusts were fiercer than ever. Nothing was visible, even quite near our shelter.

"Why him angry?" said Dersu, in an upset and anxious voice. "When we hurt him?"

"Whom?" asked the Cossacks.

"Me not know how say Russky," answered the Gold. "Him little god, little man, hill all alive, can blow wind, break tree. Us say: Kangu."

"The spirit of the forest or mountain," I thought.

We had great difficulty in keeping the fire alight. The trouble was that every gust blew the burning brands about and covered them with snow piled up in great drifts, and in the afternoon whirlwinds of the utmost violence broke upon us. They raised clouds of snow high into the air and spread a white pall over everything, and then burst out afresh, howling through the forest. Each whirlwind like that left its track marked by a row of fallen trees. Every now and then would come a short pause, and then it would redouble its efforts with intensified ferocity.

Later that afternoon the heavens began to clear slightly, but at the same time the temperature began to fall. Through the thick curtain of snow-cloud a vague, pale glow showed the position of the sun.

It was time to think of more firewood. We crept out and began to amass the fallen timber lying within easiest reach. We worked hard till Dersu said we had enough.

There was no need to try to persuade anybody. We hurried back at once and dived into our tents to warm our benumbed hands by the fire. Thus we passed through yet another night.

Next morning there was a slight improvement. The wind was cutting and fitful. After consultation we decided to make the effort to cross the Sihote-Alin in the hope that it would be easier on the lee of the west flank. The casting vote was given by Dersu.

"Me think him soon finish," he said, and set the example for starting on the road.

It did not take us long. In twenty minutes we had humped our packs and were off once more.

From our camp the ground rose steeply. During those two days a great deal of snow had fallen, and in places it was over a yard in depth. At the top we stopped for a breather. The barometer showed us an altitude of 3000 ft. We called it Patience Pass.

It was a doleful picture we gazed upon on the Sihote-Alin. Here the gale had swept down whole avenues of trees. We were obliged to make a long detour. In the mountains the roots do not strike deep, but spread near the surface, and are often held in position only by a carpet of moss. Many of these had been torn bodily out. The trees rocked and strained and dragged their roots. Black crevices opened and shut in the snowy carpet like great jaws. Kozhevnikov thought he would like to have a swing in one of these, but at that very moment a violent gust burst on us, the tree leant right over, and the Cossack barely had time to jump clear when it crashed to the ground, scattering all round a shower of frozen earth.

TRANSLATED BY MALCOLM BURR

Mountains of China

HAN SHAN, LI PO

HAN SHAN, whose pseudonym means "Cold Mountain," flourished in the mid–eighth century A.D., a contemporary of the great lyric poets Tu Fu, Wang Wei, and Li Po. Unlike his urbane peers, however, he retired to a cliffside cave in the T'ien T'ai Shan of western China, where he devoted himself to religious study and the production of a remarkable body of verse about his circumstances.

> *I've lived on Cold Mountain now*
> *already a few million years*
> *trusting fate I fled to woods and springs*
> *to linger and gaze where I will*
> *no one comes to the cliffs*
> *white clouds keep them shrouded*
> *fine grass serves as a mattress*
> *blue sky does for a quilt*
> *happy with a rock for a pillow*

let Heaven and Earth transform

It's so cold in the mountains
not just now but always
dim ridges eternally suck in snow
dark forests forever spray mist
plants grow after Grain Ears
leaves fall before Autumn Begins
and a long lost traveler here
peers without seeing the sky

Climbing Cold Mountain Road
Cold Mountain Road doesn't end
the streams are long and piled with rocks
the gorges wide and choked with grass
the moss is slick without any rain
the pines sing without the wind
who can get past the tangles of the world
can sit with me in the clouds

Cold Mountain Road is aloof
Cold Gorge Shore is unfriendly
birds chatter away
nobody else it's dead
gusts of wind turn my face
flurries of snow bury me
day after day I don't see the sun
year after year I don't know spring

TRANSLATED BY RED PINE (BILL PORTER)

Li Po (A.D. 701–762) went into self-imposed exile in the mountains of western China. To an urbane friend who asked whether he missed the city, he sent this reply.

If you asked me why I live in these green mountains
I would laugh to myself. My soul is at rest.
Peach blossoms float in the gushing streams;
Another heaven, another earth, lies beyond our own.

Mountains
of Mongolia

NIKOLAI PREJEVALSKY

The Russian naturalist NIKOLAI PREJEVALSKY explored much of Mongolia and western China in the mid–nineteenth century. In this passage from his 1879 memoir From Kulja, Across the Tian Shan to Lob-Nor, *he describes the northern mountains of Mongolia, the scene of much natural beauty.*

Arriving in Yulduz in the middle of May, we found vegetation very backward. The sun had not yet thawed the deep snow, or warmed the frozen ground, and "winter lingering chilled the lap of May." Even in the beginning of June the powers of light and darkness, Ahriman and Ormuz, still strove for mastery. Night frosts, cold westerly and north-westerly winds, even snow at times retarded the early vegetation. But the herbs and flowers of these regions are accustomed to such drawbacks. Give them a few hours' warmth in the daytime, and these children of spring will not long delay in developing their short-lived existence.

It is always thus in the mountains, and in those of Asia in particular. Hardly had one passed through half of May, than with each succeeding day new kinds of flowers showed themselves. On all the moist mountain slopes and in the valleys the wild garlic and the low-growing aconite showed their yellow heads; and, in smaller quantities, Pedicularis and violets began to appear. On the drier ground the blue heads of the Pasque flower (*Pulsatilla*) dotted the surface, and little pink primroses lay scattered over the sides of the hills. Somewhat later, on the dry, stony slopes, saxifrage came into bloom, and last of all, the low, prickly camel's thorn.

In the valleys and by the mountain springs, wherever the sun's rays were hottest by the end of May, appeared forget-me-nots, sun-dew, lady's bed-straw, white and yellow dandelion, wild pea, cinquefoil, stitchwort, and others.

The vegetation of the Yulduz plain is not luxuriant, although its grass is mostly fit for cattle. Flowers only adorned the damper ground by the banks of streams, and this not in abundance. Besides two kinds of vetches, here and there bloomed the blue iris and cuckoo's tears, whilst the dry, clayey ground was studded with the tiny white blossoms of the stonecrop. These complete the list. The lakes and marshes on the Baga-Yulduzgol were worse off still, for here grew no flowering plants of any kind. Animal life was more abundant in Yulduz in spring than we had found it in the preceding autumn. The animals were the same, but the marmots had now awakened from their winter's sleep, and their shrill whistle was unceasingly heard in the higher valleys. The increase in the numbers of birds was even more remarkable, especially of the smaller kinds, which here, as everywhere else, greeted spring with their cheerful melody. Among the stern cliffs of the alpine zone, the lively notes of the hedge-sparrow (*Acceptor altaicus*) mingled now with the cluck and call of the partridge (*Megaloperdix nigellii*); here too mountain swallows (*Chelidon lagopoda*), and flocks of gray-headed finch, still unpaired, disported themselves; and the occasional note of a red-winged wallcreeper might be heard. Lower in the forest belt mountain finch and rock pipit were frequently met with; wagtail (*Budytes citreoleus*) and *Actitis hypaoleucos* nested near the streams, and ruddy sheldrake (*Casarca rutila*) and *Anser indicus* among the rocks. Still lower, at the entrances to the valleys, and on the plain, were field larks, and the stone chat (*Saxicola isabellina*), an exquisite songster. Ducks, storks, sandpipers, gulls and terns were building their nests on the marshes and lakes.

Insects were not numerous in the month of May, humble-bees being the commonest in the alpine meadows. Flies and mosquitoes cannot exist on chilly Yulduz; of snakes and lizards there are none, and only an occasional toad or frog may be caught near a marshy spring.

Early in June we crossed the Narat range, on the southern slopes of which the spring flora was more abundant than in Yulduz, and descended to the headwaters of the Tsanma. Here the climate and vegetation bore a totally different aspect: forests of spruce fir and thick grass two feet high clothed the valley and slopes of the mountains. Rain fell daily; the rich black soil was saturated with moisture like a sponge, and we found the same humidity in the neighbouring valley of the Kunges, only that in the latter, owing to its lower elevation, vegetation was even more advanced, and flowers more profuse.

Our herbarium received considerable accessions. On the other hand, contrary to our expectations, comparatively few nesting birds were found either on the Tsanma or Kunges, the cause probably being the extremely wild nature of the country, avoided by small birds in particular. Now, too, clouds of gnats and fleas made their appearance, from which there was no escape day or night. On our excursions these horrible insects annoyed us mercilessly, and the sudden change of climate from dry and cold to damp and warmth, affected our health unfavourably, particularly on first arriving on the Kunges.

Having completed our researches here, we hastened to Kulja, where we arrived in the beginning of July, tired and ragged, but with a rich store of scientific booty.

Himalayas

❻

SUSAN RIJNHART, ZAHIRUDDIN MUHAMMAD
BĀBUR, SIR MARTIN CONWAY, HINDU MYTH,
SIKKIMESE HYMN, PHOTIUS, MARK TWAIN

*In 1898, the Dutch missionary Petrus Rijnhart, in the company of his
American wife, Susan, and infant son, Charlie, attempted to cross the
Chinese frontier into Tibet to proselytize in the forbidden city of Lhasa.
They encountered ferocious weather, and Charlie soon died of exposure to
the elements, as this dramatic account from* SUSAN RIJNHART's *1901 book*
With the Tibetans in Tent and Temple *relates. Petrus died only days
later, having traveled ahead to seek help for their party, and Susan had
to endure an eight-week journey back to China alone.*

Following the occidental road from the Ts'aidam we had ascended many
passes, and though some of them were over 16,000 feet above the sea, on
none of them did we find old snow, and hence the snowline in that region
cannot be lower than about 17,500 feet. Wild animals abounded in many lo-
calities, yak sometimes being visible from very near. One fine day we surprised a number of the latter which, on seeing us, dashed across a large
stream, their huge tails high in the air, the spray from their headlong rush

into the water rising in clouds, presenting a magnificent sight. Wild mules had been seen in large numbers, especially after we crossed the Mur-ussu river, while bears and antelopes were everyday sights. On August the twenty-first, after we had been ascending for several days, we found ourselves traveling directly south, following up to its source a beautiful stream full of stones, probably one of the Mur-ussu high waters. In front of us were the Dang La mountains, snow-clad and sunkissed, towering in their majesty, and, to us tenfold more interesting because immediately beyond them lay the Lhasa district of Tibet, in which the glad tidings of the gospel were unknown, and in which the Dalai Lama exercises supreme power, temporal and spiritual, over the people. Moreover, as we hoped to obtain permission to reside in that district as long as we did not attempt to enter the Capital, it seemed that our journeyings for the present were almost at an end. This hope, added to the fact that our darling's eight teeth, which had been struggling to get through, were now shining white above the gums, revived our spirits and we all sang for very joy, picking bouquets of bright pink leguminous flowers as we went along.

The morning of the darkest day in our history arose, bright, cheery, and full of promise, bearing no omen of the cloud that was about to fall upon us. Our breakfast was thoroughly enjoyed, Charlie ate more heartily than he had done for some days, and we resumed our journey full of hope. Riding along we talked of the future, its plans, its work, and its unknown successes and failures, of the possibility of going to the Indian border when our stay in the interior was over, and then of going home to America and Holland before we returned to Tankar, or the interior of Tibet again. Fondly our imagination followed the career of our little son; in a moment years were added to his stature and the infant had grown to the frolicking boy full of life and vigor, athirst for knowledge and worthy of the very best instruction we could give him. With what deliberation we decided to give his education our personal supervision, and what books we would procure for him—the very best and most scientific in English, French and German. "He must have a happy childhood," said his father. "He shall have all the blocks, trains, rocking-horses and other things that boys in the homeland have, so that when he shall have grown up he may not feel that because he was a missionary's son, he had missed the joys that brighten other boys' lives." How the tones of his baby voice rang out as we rode onward! I can still hear him shouting lustily at the horses in imitation of his father and Rahim.

Suddenly a herd of yak on the river bank near us tempted Rahim away to try a shot, but the animals, scenting danger, rushed off into the hills to our right; then across the river we saw other yak, apparently some isolated ones, coming towards us, but on closer examination we found they were tame yak driven by four mounted men accompanied by a big, white dog. The men evidently belonged to the locality, and we expected they would come to exchange with us ordinary civilities, but to our surprise when they saw us they quickly crossed our path, and studiously evading us, disappeared in the hills. This strange conduct on their part aroused in our minds suspicions as to their intentions. Carefully we selected a camping-place hidden by little hills; the river flowed in front and the pasture was good.

Though baby's voice had been heard just a few moments previous, Mr Rijnhart said he had fallen asleep; so, as usual, Rahim dismounted and took him from his father's arms in order that he might not be disturbed until the tent was pitched and his food prepared. I had also dismounted and spread on the ground the comforter and pillow I carried on my saddle. Rahim very tenderly laid our lovely boy down, and, while I knelt ready to cover him comfortably, his appearance attracted my attention. I went to move him, and found that he was unconscious. A great fear chilled me and I called out to Mr Rijnhart that I felt anxious for baby, and asked him to quickly get me the hypodermic syringe. Rahim asked me what was the matter, and on my reply a look of pain crossed his face, as he hastened to help my husband procure the hypodermic. In the meantime I loosened baby's garments, chafed his wrists, performed artificial respiration, though feeling almost sure that nothing would avail, but praying to Him who holds all life in His hands, to let us have our darling child. Did He not know how we loved him and could it be possible that the very joy of our life, the only human thing that made life and labor sweet amid the desolation and isolation of Tibet—could it be possible that even this—the child of our love should be snatched from us in that dreary mountain country—by the cold chill hand of Death? What availed our efforts to restore him? What availed our questionings? The blow had already fallen, and we realized that we clasped in our arms only the casket which had held our precious jewel; the jewel itself had been taken for a brighter setting in a brighter world; the little flower blooming on the bleak and barren Dang La had been plucked and transplanted on the Mountains Delectable to bask and bloom forever in the sunshine of God's love. But oh! what a void in our hearts! How empty and desolate our tent, which in the meantime had been pitched and sorrowfully entered! Poor Rahim, who had so dearly loved the child, broke out in loud lamentations, wailing as only orientals can, but with real sorrow, for his life had become so entwined with the child's that he felt the snapping of the heartstrings. And what of the father, now bereft of his only son, his only child, which just a few moments before he had clasped warm to his bosom, knowing not how faint the little heartbeat was growing? We tried to think of it euphemistically, we lifted our hearts in prayer, we tried to be submissive, but it was all so real—the one fact stared us in the face; it was written on the rocks; it reverberated through the mountain silence: Little Charlie was dead.

ZAHIRUDDIN MUHAMMAD BĀBUR (1483–1530) was the first Mughal, or Mongol, emperor of India, and he and his horde ruled over much of Central Asia as well. A devoted warrior, Bābur was also a gifted scholar and ethnographer, and his memoir The Baburnama—*the first autobiography in Islamic literature—paints a fascinating portrait of the lands he conquered. Here, in somewhat breathless prose, he describes the mountains of Kashmir.*

Hindustan . . . is a strange country. Compared to ours, it is another world. Its mountains, rivers, forests, and wildernesses, its villages and provinces, animals and plants, peoples and languages, even its rain and winds are altogether different. . . . Once you cross the Indus, the land, water, trees, stones, people, tribes, manners, and customs are all of the Hindustani fashion. The mountain range in the north that has been mentioned—as soon as the Indus is crossed these mountains are dependent provinces to Kashmir. Although as of this date the provinces in this range, like Pakhli and Shahmang, mostly are not obedient to Kashmir, nonetheless they used to be inside Kashmir. Once past Kashmir there are innumerable peoples, tribes, districts, and provinces in this range. There are people continuously in these mountains all the way to Bengal, even to the ocean. This much has been ascertained and confirmed by the people of Hindustan, but of these groups no one can give any real information. All they say is that the people of the mountains are called Khas. It has occurred to me that since Hindustanis pronounce the sound *sh* as *s*, since the principal city in the mountains is Kashmir, which means "mountains of the Khasis," since *mir* means mountain and the people of this mountain are called Khasia, and since aside from Kashmir no other city has ever been heard of in these mountains, this may be why they call it Kashmir. The products of the people of the mountains are musk, yak-tails, saffron, lead, and copper. The people of India call the range Sivalik Parbat. In the language of India *sava* means a quarter, *lak* means a hundred thousand, and *parbat* means mountain—therefore Sivalik Parbat means "a quarter lak plus a hundred thousand mountains," that is, 125,000 mountains. The snow never melts on these mountains, and the snow covered caps can be seen from some of the provinces of Hindustan, such as Lahore, Sirhind, and Sambhal. In Kabul this mountain range is called the Hindu Kush.

TRANSLATED BY WHEELER M. THACKSTON

In his 1920 account Mountain Memories, *the explorer SIR MARTIN CONWAY remarks on the inaccessibility of Kashmir centuries later.*

The railroad journey of two days from Karachi to Lahor was full of interest and delight—many sights beheld, few comprehended. It was at Lahor that we first really felt India. The impression then received was abiding and is fresh in memory to-day. It was the time of the Holi festival, and the town was thronged with folk in carmine-stained garments and turbans of all colours of the rainbow. Strips of pink and blue cotton waved overhead in the streets. Dust caught the sunlight. The crowd was quiet in its movements, almost silent. Faces were grave, melancholic, yet there was brilliant colour everywhere and thronging life. Where Egypt is black and white, India is red and blue and green. I visited mosques, tombs, and castle-like forts. They were infused with antiquity. The signs of ancient civilization were everywhere displayed. The people evidently belonged to an ancient race. Countless generations were implied in the living. The narrow streets were bordered with houses irregularly planted, planned in picturesque disorder, and often crazy in beautiful decay. Poverty in such surroundings was not sordid nor wealth aggressive. The tombs of princes were often neglected, the houses of the poor well enough cared for. The whole effect left upon my mind was like that of a tangled skein of many-coloured silks. All was pageant—people, streets, mosques palaces, tombs. No one and nothing beheld belonged to my world, or to an ugly world. All floated in a romantic atmosphere in which the impossible might become true and from which the normal was banished.

At Abbottabad, where we spent upwards of a fortnight, our stores and equipment were re-packed into loads, when they had at last been delivered by goods train. We were hospitably entertained in a typical Anglo-Indian community, and we made expeditions into the surrounding hills, which resembled those about the Italian Lakes, but lacked the water. At the end of March we took to the road, and so in due course entered Kashmir and boated up the Jhelam to Srinagar. Nowadays the journey is swiftly accomplished by motor. It took us four days of rough travel in *ekkas* by road and two by boat. Had we travelled faster Kashmir would have burst upon us; by our slow progression it was gradually disclosed. The way lay along rough roads over high hills, then down into a rugged valley and along the side of the gorge till it opened out into the great basin of Kashmir. That was once a hill-surrounded lake, like Geneva's, only the hills are bigger, high enough to be snow-mountains if they stood in the latitude of the Alps. Two small lakes

are now all that remain of the ancient sheet of water. We embarked on one of
them and ascended the river to the other, the Dal Lake, which lies just beyond the city. We also made an expedition farther up still to see Martand and
other ruined temples, monuments of old days when Buddhism prevailed in
the land. Thus the key-note of Kashmir to me was water—the river and the
lakes. We lived on house-boats. Srinagar was a great town of wooden houses
fronting on either bank of the Jhelam. They looked, and in many cases were,
old. A quarter of the town was burnt later in the year, soon after the cholera
epidemic which decimated the crowded population. We felt no presage of
this impending doom. All was gay for us in the springtime. The river fronts
of the city resembled Venice translated into wood, fancifully, even fantasti-
cally, treated; but some of the buildings, notably the Hammadan Mosque,
are dignified and built according to a fine tradition. All over the lands north
of Kashmir, away up to Central Asia, the same type of wooden architecture
for mosques prevails. It is a type more ancient than Persepolis. The builders
of Darius and Xerxes derived from it the forms of the Achaemenian Palaces.
The charm of Kashmir, however, is not in its buildings, but in its waters and
its gardens. There is a gaiety in the air unknown in the pathetic plains of
India. The roofs of the houses and even the graveyards were sheets of blos-
soming iris. The land is everywhere fertile and well-watered. Peasants were
intensively cultivating their little fields. There was life on all hands. Countless villages are dotted about, shaded by splendid chinar trees. Long pro-
cessions of huge poplars line the bank near the city.

The Dal Lake is the heart of Kashmir. Happy indeed were the days we
spent upon it. Its surface for us was always calm, whether we were upon it or
looking down on it from the temple-crowned hill just outside the city—a
viewpoint central to the vale and containing the whole panorama of its bat-
tlemented mountain-walls, with the river winding in seven great silver loops
across the green plain, and the city and lake map spread immediately at
one's feet. On the lake itself are little floating gardens, like carpets, and to its
margin there stretch, down gentle slopes, the fine formal gardens of the great
Mogul. They are built in terraces. Each terrace bears some charming pavil-
ion, or is formally planted with trees and divided by water. Water flows and
races through every garden, leaping into sunlit crystal patterns as it runs

over ribbed marble slabs, or plashing into marble basins, or running in wall-sided channels. The pavilions look down upon the lake across gardened foregrounds. They look, as they in fact once were, fit settings for song and dance and poetry. Here Nur-Alahal charmed back her royal lover with the magic of her voice. Love has nowhere fashioned for itself a more perfect setting, and we were there in serene April weather among a galaxy of flowers. The time and the place were all that could be wished, but alas! the loved ones were far away! Well ahead of the climbing season, we had no need to hasten when each day was more beautiful than the last, but after a fortnight we had been luxurious long enough. One evening in bright moonlight we floated down-stream through the magical city and out into the sleeping vale beyond. Our backs were soon turned to the last of the plains, and the strenuous days of the mountain journey began.

The first pass was easy and low. It was followed by a few marches along pleasant valleys over rough mule-tracks, long since replaced by an excellent motoring road. Thus we came to the foot of the Burzil Pass (13,500 feet), by which the first of the higher parallel ranges, the true Himalaya, must be crossed. You can drive over that also now, but we had to fight our way over it in deep snow and a raging storm. From the plains of India to those of Central Asia the wide intervening tract is ridged and furrowed by parallel ranges and valleys, one beyond another. Rivers, notably the Indus, have cut across these by deep gorges, and some kind of path has generally been fashioned along them, but it often happens that a range can be more easily crossed at some point by a pass than by the gorge. To lead our long caravan of coolies in safety over the deep snow and through the dense fog was no easy task. Snow had been falling heavily for days. Avalanches were tumbling, and larger ones were to be expected. We had been kept stationary for the best part of a week awaiting a chance to force the pass. The way led up a twisting white trough, enveloped in fog. Every step was toilsome. The laden men tried to bolt, or cast themselves on the ground refusing to move. It was a dreary solitude. Every year many lives used to be lost on this route for lack of refuges. To-day it is safe enough. It was past noon before we gained the summit, black night when at length we reached a miserable hut within which the wearied coolies could shelter. Our tents were pitched on the roof.

Everywhere else was mud and slushy snow. A more tiring day I never passed, and it was of necessity foodless. We had to be pushing on all the time. In another hour we must have lost some men from sheer fatigue. Many suffered from snow-blindness. Thus we entered a side-valley of the Indus, and in a few more days reached Astor.

The rain that falls north of the plains of India comes from the south-west. As the damp air meets the hills it is precipitated upon them. Thus the north-eastward moving flood of air becomes dried to successively higher levels as it passes over successively higher ridges. By the time it has been carried beyond the main Himalayan range (which we had just crossed) it is dried up to a great height. Thenceforward only the highest snow-peaks reach up far enough to cause further precipitation, which falls in snow upon them and them alone. North of the Burzil Pass rain falls in rapidly decreasing amounts into the valleys. Thus every day's march now took us through a region of diminishing fertility. At Astor the wild vegetation is sparse and hardy; fields to produce crops must be irrigated. A march or two beyond Astor the valleys become deserts of sand, stones, and rock, where nothing grows that is not watered by a running stream, natural or artificial.

The river of the Astor valley joins the Indus through a deep gorge, along which no path runs. I know not by what route the new high-road has been engineered. In our time one had to climb over a shoulder 10,000 feet high, whence a rapid descent led down to the main valley. This shoulder is called the Hatu Pir. The view from it, to one coming into the world of the great mountains for the first time, was an overwhelming revelation. It would be easy here to quote the description written on the spot, but I am now concerned with subjective emotions as memory holds them, not with objective facts. The Hatu Pir was one of the culminating stations in my Pilgrimage of Romance. There, as in Egypt, as at Lahor, a new world of wonder was opened for me. I looked in at the gate through which the onward way was to lead, and the sight beheld was astounding and glorious. The desert and the mountains I already loved were here united, and on a scale visibly stupendous. Thus far the mountains we had passed had been seen with eyes that did not comprehend their scale, but here the enormity of things was unmistakable. If Nanga Parbat be thought of as a giant kneeling in prayer, with head on the ground, my platform was upon his heel and the great mass of him rose behind me. Turning round to the left I could look into the Indus gorge of Chilas, the deepest cañon in the world, 24,000 feet in depth from the crest of Nanga Parbat to the river-bank, one steep, unbroken incline of snow and rock. Not this way, however, was the eye caught and riveted, but straight ahead northward, where the Indus valley came toward me end-on. It was like looking lengthways into the empty hold of a tremendous ship. Below was the flat desert with the Indus' mighty torrent looking from here like a little rill, cutting through the flood. Gigantic cliffs rose on one hand, buttress beyond buttress of sloping rock on the other. Miles and miles away the valley bent out of sight and great mountains closed it. Two tiny patches of irrigated green demonstrated the barrenness of all else. It was an overwhelming view, and I had come upon it suddenly round a corner. The world has seemed to me a more majestic place ever since. Moreover, this was no landscape of the moon, but one long associated with man. The track we had been following is of extreme antiquity. It must have been traversed by ancient invaders coming down from the north time after time, by Buddhist pilgrims, by followers of Islam with faces set toward Mecca, by merchants and travellers from earliest days. This they also had beheld. In wonder and reverence I drank in the vision. Of all the sights beheld in Asia this comes back oftenest to me and remains most vivid.

The MAHABHARATA, *an epic encyclopedia of Hindu mythology, records that the gods used the Himalayas to obtain immortality.*

There is a shining mountain named Meru, an unsurpassed mass of energy; its blazing golden peaks outshine even the light of the sun. The gods and Gandharvas frequent its glittering, gold-adorned slopes, but men who abound in *adharma* cannot approach that immeasurable mountain. Dreadful beasts of prey wander over it and divine herbs illuminate it. The great mountain stands piercing the firmament with its peak, and it is graced by trees and streams. It resounds with the charming songs of various flocks of birds, but others cannot approach it even in thought. Its magnificent slopes are studded with many gems, and an infinity of magic wishing-trees grow there. The gods, who dwell in heaven and are of great vigour, rich in ascetic powers, came together, mounted its plateau, and sat there to take counsel in order to obtain the ambrosia. While the gods were thinking and conferring together, the god Narayana said to Brahma, "Let the gods and demons churn the ocean which is like a churning pot, and when the great ocean is churned there will be ambrosia, and you will also obtain all the herbs and gems. Churn the ocean, O gods, and you will find ambrosia in it."

The tremendous mountain named Mandara is adorned with mountain peaks like pointed clouds; it is covered with a net of vines, it rings with the song of many birds, and it is crowded with tusked animals. Celestial nymphs and gods and demons and Kinnaras frequent it, and it extends for eleven thousand leagues above the earth and as many leagues below. All the band of gods were unable to uproot it, and so they came to Vishnu and Brahma and said, "Think of some perfect and effective plan to uproot Mount Mandara for our welfare." Vishnu and Brahma agreed, and the potent serpent Ananta forcibly uprooted that king of mountains with all its forests and forest-dwellers, and the gods went with the mountain to the ocean and said to him, "We will churn your water to obtain ambrosia." The lord of waters said, "Let me also have a share of it. I will bear the intense agitation from the whirling of Mandara." The gods and demons then said to the king of tortoises, the supreme tortoise, "You are the one suited to be the resting-place for this mountain." The tortoise agreed, and Indra placed the tip of the mountain on his back, fastening it tightly. They made Mandara the churning-stick and the serpent Vasuki the cord, and they began to churn the ocean, the treasure of waters, for ambrosia. The gods acted together with the demons, for they all wished for the ambrosia.

The great demons grasped one end of the king of serpents, and all the gods held him by the tail. Ananta and the blessed god Narayana would lift the head of the serpent first from one side and then from the other and throw it down again and again. As the gods vigorously hurled the snake Vasuki about, winds full of smoke and flame came out of his mouth repeatedly, and these masses of smoke became clusters of clouds with lightning, and they rained down upon the bands of gods who were exhausted and over-heated from their exertions. Showers of flowers fell down from the tip of the mountain peak, strewing garlands everywhere on the gods and demons. Then a great roar, like the thunder of a great cloud, came forth from the ocean as it was churned by the gods and demons with Mount Mandara; for various water creatures, crushed by the great mountain, were dying by the hundreds in the salt water, and the mountain destroyed many kinds of aquatic beings living in the subterranean levels of hell. The mountain whirled about so that great trees filled with birds spun off and fell from the mountain peak. As the trees were crushed against one another, a fire born of their friction blazed forth into flames and enveloped Mount Mandara, which looked like a dark cloud charged with lightning. The fire burnt the elephants and lions who were driven out, and all the various creatures there lost their life's breath. Then Indra, the best of immortals, put out that burning fire everywhere with water from his clouds. But the various saps exuded from the great trees and the juices from many herbs flowed into the water from the ocean. And from these juices, which had the essence of ambrosia, and from the exudation of liquid gold mixed with the water, the gods obtained immortality.

According to Sikkimese Buddhist legend, NYEN-CHEN TANG-LA, the embodiment of the trans-Himalaya range of northern Tibet, was once an enemy of Buddhism. The missionary Padma Sambhava converted him only after Nyen-chen Tang-la tried to bar his entrance into the region with snowstorms and sleet. The missionary won by singing this song of praise.

> *I invoke thy father*
> *The mountain god Ode Gunggyel,*

I invoke thy mother,
The Turquoise Bird with One Wing.
Full of reverence I name thy dwelling,
The Long Marsh of the low-lying Land.
Turquoise green eagles flutter about there.
Joy-arousing is this place,
Which even in winter bears the green of spring.
Happy is the land in which this god dwells.
I name the name by which the gods know thee:
King of the Scent-Eaters, Five Locks of Hair.
I name thy secret name:
Flaming Thunderbolt.
What wearest thou on thy body?
Thou wearest white silk and white woollen garments.
What dost thou ride upon?
Thou ridest a divine horse with white hooves.
Thou wanderest through the Three Worlds,
Thy white color is of radiant holiness,
Thy right hand raiseth a bamboo staff,
And with thy left hand thou countest the beads of a crystal rosary.

TRANSLATED BY RENÉ VON NEBESKY-WOJKOWITZ

PHOTIUS, *the third-century Greek author of the speculative* Indika, *had this strange news to report of the people of the Himalayas.*

There is a river that passes through India; it is not very long, but it is approximately two stadia wide. The name of this river is Hyparchos in Indian, and in Greek "bearer of all goods." Thirty days each year, this river carries amber; in effect, the Indians say that, in the mountains, there are trees that hang over its waters, and there is a season in which tears fall from the trees. . . . These tears fall into the river and harden. This tree is called in Indian "siptachoras," which, in Greek means sweet, pleasant. So it is that the Indians gather amber. . . .

It is said that there live in these mountains dog-headed men; they wear clothes made from animal skins, and speak no language but bark like dogs and recognize one another by these sounds. Their teeth are stronger than those of dogs, and their nails the same as theirs, but are longer and more curved. They inhabit the mountains down to the Indus; black is their skin and great their sense of justice, as with the other Indians with whom they have dealings; they understand the Indians' language but cannot speak with them; it is by means of cries and hand and finger signs that they make themselves understood, after the fashion of deaf mutes; the Indians call them Kalustrioi, which in Greek means Kynokephaloi [dogheads]. This people are numbered up to 120,000. . . .

The Kynokephaloi living in the mountains do no work; they live by hunting, and when they have killed their game, they bake it in the sun; they also raise sheep, goats and asses. They drink the milk and sour milk of their sheep; they also eat the fruit of the siptachoras. . . . They dry fruits and make fruit baskets, as do the Greeks with raisins. The Kynokephaloi make a raft on which they place a load of dried fruits, purple dye and amber worth one thousand talents; all of this is brought each year to the king of the Indians. They also bring other products which they exchange with the Indians for bread, flour and cotton clothing; they also buy swords which they use to hunt wild beasts, as well as bows and javelins. . . . They are invincible in battle because they live in the high mountains which are difficult of access. Every five years, the king makes them a present of 300,000 bows, 300,000 javelins, 120,000 light shields and 50,000 swords.

These Kynokephaloi have no houses, but live in caves. . . . The women bathe once a month, when they have their periods, and never at any other time. As for the men, they never bathe, but do wash their hands.

They wear a light dress of trimmed hides, as thin as possible, men and women alike. . . . They have no beds, but make pallets of leaves. . . . All of these, both men and women, have a tail that hangs down from their hips like those of dogs, but longer and furrier.

They couple with their women on all fours like dogs; to unite otherwise is a shameful thing for them. They are just and the most long-lived of any human race, for they live for 170 years, and some of them for two hundred.

MARK TWAIN (1835–1910), who visited India in 1892, found the vistas of the Himalayas to be less than inspiring.

After lecturing [in Darjeeling] I went to the Club that night, and that was a comfortable place. It is loftily situated, and looks out over a vast spread of scenery: from it you can see where the boundaries of three countries come together, some thirty miles away; Thibet is one of them, Nepaul another, and I think Herzegovina was the other. Apparently, in every town and city in India the gentlemen of the British civil and military service have a club; sometimes it is a palatial one, always it is pleasant and homelike. The hotels are not always as good as they might be, and then the stranger who has access to the Club is grateful for his privilege and knows how to value it.

Next day was Sunday. Friends came in the gray dawn with horses, and my party rode away to a distant point where Kinchinjunga and Mount Everest show up best, but I stayed at home for a private view; for it was very cold, and I was not acquainted with the horses, any way. I got a pipe and a few blankets and sat for two hours at the window, and saw the sun drive away the veiling gray and touch up the snow-peaks one after another with pale pink splashes and delicate washes of gold, and finally flood the whole convulsion of snow-mountains with a deluge of rich splendors.

Kinchinjunga's peak was but fitfully visible, but in the between times it was vividly clear against the sky—away up there in the blue dome more than 28,000 feet above sea level—the loftiest land I had ever seen, by 12,000 feet or more. It was 45 miles away. Mount Everest is a thousand feet higher, but it was not a part of that sea of mountains piled up there before me, so I did not see it; but I did not care, because I think that mountains that are as high as that are disagreeable.

Frontiers

RICHARD FRANCIS BURTON,
T. E. LAWRENCE

He called himself an "amateur barbarian," but his fellow British Army officers called him "that devil Burton." RICHARD FRANCIS BURTON (1821–1890) had no time for petty indignation, for he was too busy playing out the life of a hero in what Rudyard Kipling called "the Great Game," conquering the world on England's behalf. This passage from Goa and the Blue Mountains *(1851) is vintage Burton, full of the pride of empire and of keen observation, despite its sometimes sounding like a realtor's brochure in praise of Ootacamund, an officers' rest camp in the 8,700-foot Neilgherry Mountains of India.*

Now we fall into the main road at the foot of the zigzag, which climbs the steep skirt of Giant Dodabetta. Our nags, snorting and panting, breast the hill—we reach the summit—we descend a few hundred yards—catch sight of some detached bungalows—a lake—a church—a bazaar—a station.

The cantonment of Ootacamund, or, as it is familiarly and affectionately termed by the abbreviating Saxon, "Ooty," is built in a punch bowl, formed by the range of hills which composes the central crest of the Neilgherries. But first for the "Windermere."

The long narrow winding tarn which occupies the bottom of Ooty's happy vale, is an artificial affair, intended, saith an enthusiastic describer, "like that of Como, to combine utility with beauty." It was made by means of a dam, which, uniting the converging extremities of two hills, intercepted the waters of a mountain rivulet, and formed an "expansive and delightful serpentine lake," about two miles in length, upon an average six hundred yards broad, in many places forty feet deep, generally very muddy, and about as far from Windermere or Como as a London Colosseum or a Parisian Tivoli might be from its Italian prototype. Two roads, the upper and the lower, wind round the piece of water, and it is crossed by three embankments; the Willow Bund, as the central one is called, with its thick trees and apologies for arches, is rather a pretty and picturesque object. The best houses, you may remark, are built as close to the margin of the lake as possible. Turn your eyes away from the northern bank; that dirty, irregular bazaar is the very reverse of romantic. The beauties of the view lie dispersed above and afar. On both sides of the water, turfy peaks and woody eminences, here sinking into shallow valleys, there falling into steep ravines, the whole covered with a tapestry of brilliant green, delight your eye, after the card-table plain of Guzerat, the bleak and barren Maharatta hills, or the howling wastes of sun-burnt Scinde. The background of distant hill and mountain, borrowing from the intervening atmosphere the blue and hazy tint for which these regions are celebrated, contrasts well with the emerald hue around. In a word, there is a rich variety of form and colour, and a graceful blending of the different features that combine to make a beautiful *coup d'oeil,* which, when the gloss of novelty is still upon them, are infinitely attractive.

The sun is sinking in the splendour of an Indian May, behind the high horizon, and yet, marvellous to relate, the air feels cool and comfortable. The monotonous gruntings of the frequent palanquin-bearers—a sound which, like the swift's scream, is harsh and grating enough, yet teems in this region with pleasant associations—inform us that the fair ones of Ootacamund are actually engaged in taking exercise. We will follow their example, beginning at "Charing Cross,"—the unappropriate name conferred upon those few square yards of level and gravelled ground, with the stunted tree boxed in the centre. Our path traverses the half-drained swamp that bounds this end of the Neilgherry Windermere, and you observe with pain that those authors who assert the hills to be "entirely free from the morasses and the vast collection of decayed vegetables that generate miasma," have notably deceived you. In 1847, there is a small swamp, formed by the soaking of some arrested stream, at the bottom of almost every declivity. We presume the same was the case in 1826. Indeed, were the Neilgherries seven or eight hundred feet, instead of as many thousands, above the level of the sea, even the Pontine marshes would be better adopted for the accommodation of Quartana and Malaria. Before you have been long in the hills, you will witness many amusing accidents occurring to new comers, who attempt to urge their steeds through the shaking bogs of black mud, treacherously lurking under a glossy green coating of grassy turf. . . .

Two things strike your eye as novel, in India.

There is a freshness in the complexion of the Sanitarians that shows wonderfully to advantage when compared with the cadaverous waxy hue which the European epidermis loves to assume in the tropics. Most brilliant look the ladies; the gentlemen are sunburnt and robust; and the juveniles appear fresh and chubby, quite a different creation from the pallid, puny, meagre, sickly, irritable little wretches that do nothing but cry and perspire in the plains. Another mighty pleasant thing, after a few years of purely camp existence, is the nonmilitary appearance and sound of Ootacamund. Uniform has been banished by one consent from society, except at balls and parties. The cotton and linen jackets, the turbaned felt "wide-awake," and the white jockey's cap, with its diminutive apron, intended to protect the back of the head from the broiling sun, are here exchanged for cloth coats and black hats. Morning bugles and mid-day guns, orderlies, and order-books, the "Officers' call" and "No parade to-day," are things unknown. Vestiges of the "shop" will, it is true, occasionally peep out in the shape of a regimental cap, brass spurs, and black pantaloons, denuded of the red stripe. But such traces rather add to our gratification than otherwise, by reminding us of A.M. drills, meridian sword exercises, and P.M. reviews in days gone by. . . .

We will conclude our ciceronic task with calling your attention to one fact, namely, that the capital of the Neilgherries is growing up with maizelike rapidity. Houses are rising in all directions; and if fickle fortune will only favour it, Ooty promises fair to become in a few years one of the largest European settlements in India. But its fate is at present precarious. Should the Court of Directors be induced to revise the old Furlough and Sick-Leave Regulations, then will poor Ooty speedily revert to the Todas and jackals—its old inhabitants. On the contrary, if the status quo endure, and European regiments are regularly stationed on the hills, officers will flock to Ootacamund, the settlers, retired servants of Government, not Eurasian colonists, will increase in number, schools will flourish and prosperity steadily progress. The "to be or not to be" thus depends upon the turn of a die.

The chilly shades of evening are closing rapidly upon us, and we know by experience that some care is necessary, especially for the newly arrived health-hunter. So we wend our way homewards, remarking, as night advances, the unusual brilliancy of the heavenly bodies. Venus shines almost as brightly as an average English moon in winter; her light with that of the lesser stars is quite sufficient to point out to us the direction of "Subaltern Hill."

In 1928, T. E. LAWRENCE (1888–1935), famous as "Lawrence of Arabia," was posted to a Royal Air Force outpost on the high-plateau frontier of Afghanistan. He wrote of the place to a fellow airman.

You can hardly conceive the quiet of the tiny place. At night they shut it all up with barbed wire, and by day we are not allowed to go out beyond the edge of the aerodrome without an escort; not that the tribes are now unfriendly, but it is an old tradition that they ought to be, and so strict precautions are the rule in all these forts. Even by day, when the fort gates are open, there is an unbroken peace over us. We are in a plain, some miles wide, and are ringed by a wall of mountains, sharp mountains, quite clear and clean in line; and these seem to keep off wind and access. I feel as though I had slipped over the edge of the world a little way, and landed on some ledge a few feet down the far side. We get few posts, and slow ones; have no shops or visitors or news; in fact it is like a little bit of Heaven; a perfect home from home. I have been looking for a place like this for years, with little hope that such a thing existed.

Central Asia

⑥

KIRGHIZ EPIC, SVEN HEDIN

In the Kirghiz national epic can be found a sacred geography of the mountains of Central Asia. Here, the KHAN orders his retainers to gather the peoples of the world so that he can delineate his realm. Er Manas, from another Kirghiz tribe, is a rival for the Khan's throne.

When Bok-murun's young friends heard their Khan's command, they mounted and rode out. Together they circled all four corners of the earth, one like the other, summoning guests to the feast.

Kökötöy's son Bok-murun shouted from his throne and summoned his companions: "How shall I conduct this feast? How shall I race the horses? How shall I win a part in the next world? Where shall I entertain these infidels and Muslims?

"I will move on," he said, "and camp in Sairam. I will move on and camp in Chimkent! I will go over Sari-Bulak, cross the Kara-buura, descend to the broad Talas! I will move on and pass over Karakul to the open country. I will camp there, fattening my animals! I will hang wood for frames and repair my yurts! I will move again and cross over the Karabalta Pass and go to the Kajindi River! I will travel along the Korogotu River and ford the Chüi River at It-keçüü, then travel down the Ak-jar Valley and camp at Ak-bulun, shear the sheep and cover the yurts! I will move on from that place and cross the Irgyati River and go to Kopu! I will go along the Karkara River there, and camp, and meet with the Kalday people, and boil salt! Then I will cross the Temirilik Mountains, cross the Kuuluk Mountains, cross the Bakti-kuuray, cross the Kusmurun Mountains and camp at the confluence of the Great and Little Kulja rivers! When seven months pass, I will build firepits, and when ten months pass, I will gather wood! I will win a place in the next world, will hold a feast for every infidel and Muslim! Summon them from my throne! Bring them all, every one of them!"

The heralds heard their lord Bok-murun and rode away. They circled the four corners of the earth and invited all the infidels and Muslims to the feast.

When he invited Er Manas, one herald received no reply. The herald said, "The arrow when released does not turn from its target. The herald when ordered does not turn from his journey. What answer will I give my lord Bok-murun?"

Manas lay playing chess on the summit of Uluu-kamir with Almambet, his chancellor, who had captured three pieces, much to Manas's anger, and he flew into a rage when he saw the herald. The chancellor said, "Manas, my lord, when you are happy it is like the sun, but when your brows are knit it is as if the snow is falling on the mountains!"

Then Er Manas spoke. "Ah, my companions! Bright Moonlight! Radiant Sunshine! I have gathered you from all the lands. Have you seen this herald? Take him to a cleft in the wild mountains and spreadeagle him!"

At a cleft in the wild mountains they spreadeagled the herald, and when they had driven in the stakes, they rode their horses over him.

Then Er-Manas went on his horse down the mountains to battle Bok-murun. Will ever another such son of the people be born?

TRANSLATED BY WILHELM RADLOFF

*In the mid-1890s, the Swedish explorer SVEN HEDIN (1865–1952) under-
took a series of mapping expeditions throughout Central Asia. These
brought him no end of adventures, including this difficult passage
through the mountains of western China.*

Leaving Kopa on July 30th, we directed our march towards the east-
southeast, and crossed over a series of ravines, called *chapps,* deeply excavated in the conglomerates, but dry, except after rain. At the Mitt, an affluent
of the Kara-muran, the landscape became picturesque. The river emerged
from between the granite cliffs through a gateway less than fifty yards wide.
But immediately after it emerged, it spread itself out in a broad channel
which it had carved through the conglomerates, and was joined from the
right by the Yakkachapp, at that season a mere dry ravine with a stony bottom. Like those of the Mitt, its sides were almost vertical, and flung back the
rattle of the caravan with a sharp echo. By means of this ravine we ascended
to a series of loess hills, soft in outline and overgrown with grass. Then the
track swung off to the southeast, towards the entrance of a transverse valley,
traversed by a little brook on its way down to the plain. The district was
called Dalai-kurgan, and was inhabited by eighteen families of Taghliks,
who owned among them some 6000 sheep. They lived in small huts partly
excavated out of the loess terraces. We encamped on the left bank of the
stream, in the entrance to the valley, and let all our animals run free on the
luxuriant grass.

Immediately south of us towered up the mighty mountain-chain which
the Chinese call Kwen-lun (Kuen-lun); the Taghliks, however, had no general name for it. The secondary range, which was pierced by the Dalai-
kurgan stream, was called the Tokkuz-davan (the Nine Passes) east of the
Kara-muran; though at Dalai-kurgan itself that name was not in use. The
Taghliks maintained there was only one pass giving access to the high
plateau of Tibet—namely, the pass of Chokkalik; but they would not under-
take to say that we could get through with our camels. I decided, therefore,
to reconnoitre the pass before sending on the whole of the caravan.

Accordingly, on August 1st, accompanied by Fong Shi, Islam Akhun, Roslakh, and two Taghliks, I rode up the valley of the Dalai-kurgan to the pass of the same name (14,330 feet in altitude), and on the following day pushed on eastward to the principal pass (16,180 feet). Thence I obtained a magnificent view of the ocean of tumbling mountain-peaks. The ascent was certainly steep; still we thought the camels could manage it. But the descent on the other side was very much worse, owing to the sharp, jagged rocks which protruded through the almost precipitous gravelly slope. After carefully considering the matter in counsel together, we decided to make the attempt. The baggage could be lowered down the gravel slope; the horses and donkeys would be able to take care of themselves; and if the camels could not manage it, we could roll them up in felt carpets, and so haul them down. Having come to this decision, we returned to Dalai-kurgan over the pass of Sarik-kol (13,720 feet), arriving there on the evening of August 3d.

The caravan was given another day's rest, and then the long string of animals started for the aghil of Sarik-kol (the Village of the Yellow Valley), and there they got their last bite of fresh, sappy grass.

On August 6th, the caravan, divided into several separate groups, each in charge of a specially appointed leader, and the whole making an imposing appearance, wound slowly up the glen towards the pass of Sarik-kol. The pasturage continued to diminish in extent as we climbed higher; what there was clung for the most part to the banks of the little stream. The bed of the torrent wound mostly through soft earth, but sometimes through conglomerate strata, and its bottom was littered with pieces of bright gray and green granite. In the highest part of the glen the naked granite rocks hung right over the stream, although in places they were still crowned with patches of grass. Meanwhile the glen gradually contracted, and grew steeper and steeper. Slowly, painfully, the animals clambered up the gravelly talus, which choked the trumpet-shaped gap cut through the crest of the range, and over which the beds of the torrents radiated, like the ribs of a fan, upon the head of the glen below. The camels toiled cautiously up the loose gravel slope. Every minute one or other of the horses or donkeys fell, and lost ground while they were being unloaded and loaded again; then they would push on at a quicker pace in the endeavor to catch up with the caravan. I usually rode in the rear, so as to have an eye upon them all; and it was with a feeling of real relief that I saw the last of the animals disappear behind the summit of the pass.

The southern side of the pass was much less steep, and led down into a wide glen with plenty of loose soil but rather scanty yeylaks (pasture). On both sides it was shut in by imposing mountain-spurs, like those which overhung the Sarik-kol on the north. In consequence of the inconsiderable fall and the relatively feeble erosive power of the water, the solid rock was not eaten away, although the crest of the main range presented very fantastic outlines.

We kept beside the rivulet which babbled down the middle of the glen until we reached the broad main valley of Lamachimin, and were just turning to the left—i.e., eastward—towards the pass of Chokkalik, when the aksakal, or chief of the Taghliks, who was to guide us over it, blurted out that there was a more convenient pass, called Yappkaklik, in the upper valley of the Mitt. When, therefore, he told me that Chokkalik was the only pass across the range, he told me a deliberate lie. The fact was, he was afraid to show us a hitherto unknown path into Tibet through fear of the Chinese. But, having brought us so far on the road, he plucked up courage a little, and gave me fuller and more definite information. I reprimanded him smartly for having deceived me, and taken us under false pretenses all the way over the passes of Dalai-kurgan, Chokkalik, and Sarik-kol. All the same, I was not sorry to have had the opportunity of making a reconnaissance of the district.

We therefore turned and directed our course southwest, and then due south, crossed the brook that came down from the pass of Chokkalik, left the lower extremity of the glen of Dalai-kurgan on the right, and so threaded the transverse glen of Mitt, considerably farther to the west. This glen, too, was pretty wide, and so level that to us, accustomed as we were to the steep slopes, it appeared to incline towards the south; but the course of the torrent, flowing in the opposite direction, convinced us that we were the victims of an ocular delusion. The stream issued from between two lofty granite spurs, which formed a sort of gateway, and meandered in a broad, shallow, silent current across an almost absolutely level plain. Its bed was lined with soft mud, into which the horses sank over the fetlocks; there was

not a pebble or a splinter of stone to be seen in it. At intervals the stream
spread out into lakelike expansions, and the shore lines showed that when in
full flood it very nearly stretched from one side of the glen to the other.
There were several very sharp turns in its course, and in places it was divided by low islands of mud. Its volume was augmented by rivulets from two
or three springs, situated at the foot of the mountains on the left, and the
water in them was perfectly clear and fresh, although there were thin white
lines along their edges, indicative of saline evaporations.

We pitched our camp at the foot of a conglomerate terrace on the right
bank of the stream, commanding a magnificent view to the south. The valley
continued to widen out, and finally ended in an extensive plain, upon which
several side-glens debouched, and which was crossed by the river Mitt, split
into a great number of arms, many of them containing water. In the far, far
distance, still to the south, I perceived a line of snowy peaks, imperfectly distinguishable through the hazy atmosphere, peeping up over the tops of the
intervening ranges, which abutted upon the plain *en echelon*.

Our camp was the scene of much life and bustle, notwithstanding that
there was but a scanty supply of pasturage, and that much poorer in quality
than it was at Lamachimin. In the middle of the camp were the two white
tents, with the provision-bags, boxes, saddles, and other impedimenta piled
up between them. The horses were coupled two and two together to prevent
them from straying too far away, but the donkeys and camels were allowed to
run freely at large, and tugged greedily at the grass.

Anatolia

FREDERICK BURNABY, BOB SHACOCHIS

In the winter of 1876, CAPTAIN FREDERICK BURNABY (1835–1902) undertook a dangerous crossing of what was then Asia Minor to monitor the designs of the Russian crown on Turkey. Along the way, crossing great mountain ranges and fording wide rivers, he took notes on the customs of the Turkish people, notes he later collected in his best-selling book On Horseback Through Asia Minor. *Here, high above the region of Lake Van, he remarks on the often subtle ways of the mountain people.*

"My brother will be on horseback all the day. He will look well down the precipices," said Mohammed with a chuckle.

He had observed that the Englishman did not relish riding a few inches from a chasm, and Mohammed was rather amused to learn that his fellow-servant would now no longer have the chance of walking by the precipices. He himself, though not particularly brave in other respects, never seemed to value his neck when on horseback. No matter how steep the slopes might be, Mohammed seldom or ever took the trouble to dismount from his animal, which, under the influence of two good feeds of barley every day, had improved considerably since the march from Tokat.

"Why should I dismount?" Mohammed would say. "If I am to slip and be killed, it will happen, and I cannot prevent it."

The fellow had been accustomed to a mountainous country all his life, and had previously been employed as a *Zaptieh* [freighter]. This may account for his coolness on horseback. But, at a later period of the journey, and when it was necessary for us to descend some rapids in a boat, Mohammed showed unmistakable signs of fear, and was not at all to be consoled by Radford's remark that, if he (Mohammed) were to be drowned, it would be his fate, and so would not signify.

We reached the crest of a lofty height. A wide stream appeared below our feet.

"What is the name of that river?" I inquired. The welcome announcement, "The Frat," made me aware that at last I had arrived on the banks of the Euphrates—here a broad stream about 120 yards wide and nine or ten feet deep. Numerous boulders half choked up the river's channel. The waves splashed high in the air as they bounded over these obstacles; the sound of the troubled waters could be distinctly heard even at our elevation.

We continued the march alongside the bank of the world-renowned river. The path was cut out of the solid rock. In some places the track was not above four feet wide. No balustrade or wall had been made to keep a horse or rider from slipping down the chasm. Presently the road wound still higher amidst the mountains. The river beneath us seemed no broader than a silver thread.

On we went. The sound of bells made us aware that there was a caravan approaching. Our guide rode first. A few moments later, about 100 mules, all laden with merchandise, could be seen coming towards our party. We should have to pass them; how to do so seemed a difficult problem to solve. The track was not wider than an average dinner-table.

The guide soon settled the matter. Taking a whip, he struck the leading mule; the latter, to avoid punishment, ran with his load up a steep slope along the side of the path. The rest of the animals followed. There seemed to be scarcely foothold for a goat, but the mules found one. They were removed from the path on which we stood; my people could advance in safety.

Numbers of vines clad the lower part of the mountain slopes. Here and there a few chalets made of white stone could be seen. These, I was informed, belong to the wealthier Turks of Egin, who come to reside here during the grape season.

Below us some fishermen were seated in a boat apparently made of basket-work. It looked like a Welsh coracle, but was of much larger dimensions. They were engaged in fishing with a sort of drag-net; one of them was busily employed in mending a smaller one of the same kind.

"Beautiful fish are caught here," said the guide. "Some are 100 okes in weight (about 260 lbs.). The people salt, and eat them in the winter."

We met some sick soldiers lying across the path. They had fallen out of the ranks and were basking themselves in the sun, utterly regardless of the fact that their battalion was, ere this, a two hours' march ahead of them.

"What is the matter with you?" I inquired of one man.

"Footsore," was his reply, at the same time pointing to his frost-bitten feet.

"And with you?" to another.

"I, Effendi, am weak and hungry."

"What! have you had no breakfast?"

"No."

I then discovered that these soldiers had been twenty-four hours without food! There was no grumbling at this breakdown in the commissariat department. The men were solacing themselves with a cigarette, the property of one of the party, and which he was sharing with his comrades.

Our route leads us by some high rocks. They are broken into strange and fantastic forms; they rear themselves up on each bank of the Euphrates, and frown down on the waters below. Here domes and pinnacles stand out in bold relief; there, the figure of a man, shaped as if from the hands of a sculptor, is balanced on a projecting stone, and totters on the brink of the abyss.

Mulberry and apple-trees grow in wild profusion along the banks. We leave them behind. The track steadily ascends. We are more than 1200 feet from the waters. I gaze down on the mighty river; it winds its serpent-like coils at our feet. They twist and foam and lose themselves behind the crags. Higher we go.

Vegetation disappears, we are in the realms of snow; continuing for some miles over the waste, the path descends into a valley. Egin lies before us.

It is a long, straggling town, with a population of 10,000 souls, and much resembles Arabkir. We rode over the roofs of many houses ere we reached our destination—the house of an Armenian merchant, who had ridden out himself to place it at our disposal. The following day I called upon the Caimacan—a little man, who spoke Italian very fairly. He had been only seven months at his present post. The Cadi was seated at his side. After the governor had announced that the Conference was a failure—a piece of news which I had heard before—the Cadi observed that he should like to tell me a story.

"He relates a story very well," said the Caimacan.

"We all like his stories," said the rest of the company.

"By all means," I said; and the Cadi, thus encouraged, began,—

"Many thousand years ago there was a prophet—he was a great man, he was a marvel—his name was Daniel!"

This last word was duly repeated by the assembled guests; and the Caimacan gave a little cough.

"I have heard this story before," he observed; "but it is a good one. Go on."

"Well," continued the Cadi, "Daniel had a dream. In his dream he saw a young man, Samson was his name. Samson was beautifully dressed; his clothes alone would have cost all the gold and caime that have ever been circulated at Constantinople. The rings on his fingers were encrusted with precious stones—beautiful stones—each one more bright and lovely than the eye of the most beautiful woman whom mortal man has ever seen.

"But, Samson himself was pale, his features were wasted away; he was very thin, and, on carefully looking at him, Daniel discovered that he was dead. There was a large scroll of paper lying at his feet. No other man could have deciphered the letters on it; but the Prophet read them at once, and he galloped his eye over the scroll with the same rapidity as a hunter in pursuit of a hare—"

"He read very quickly!" interrupted the Caimacan.

"Daniel was a Hodja" [learned man], observed the Cadi indignantly; "of course he did!

"Samson had conquered almost the whole world," continued the speaker; "but there was one very poor and mountainous country which did not acknowledge him as its lord.

"Samson had 10,000 wives, all of them fat and lovely. The keys of his treasure-chests were in themselves a load for 10,000 camels. He was all vigorous and able to enjoy every blessing which Allah had bestowed upon him—"

"Was he not satisfied with 10,000 wives?" remarked one of the audience.

"No," said the Cadi. "Some men are never satisfied; Samson was one of them. He wanted more. His heart was not full, he wished to conquer the poor country, and take a few wives from the lovely daughters of the mountaineers. He came with an enormous army. The people fled. The troops ate up everything. There were no more provisions. There was nothing left even for the king. Samson offered 10,000 sacks of gold for a handful of millet-seed. It could not be purchased. The soldiers died; the sergeants died; the officers died; the Pachas died; and, last of all, Samson died.

"Let this be the fate of the Russians if they come here," added the Cadi. "The Tzar has much land—he is rich—he has many more soldiers than we have, he has everything to make life happy. Yet he is not content; he wishes to take from his poor neighbour the pittance which he possesses. Let Allah judge between him and us," continued the speaker. "And God alone knows who will be victorious!"

"We shall beat them!" said the Caimacan.

Soon afterwards my visit came to an end.

Bob Shacochis chose the occasion of his thirty-ninth birthday both to quit smoking and to climb 16,945-foot Mount Ararat, known to alpinists as

*the "Big Doggie" after a play on its Turkish name, Agri Dagi. He didn't
quite succeed at either, but his account of his attempts, published in* Outside *magazine, makes for first-class adventure writing.*

The next day dawned cold and clear—9/9/90, my birthday, and I fully expected to die, choking either on chemical gas or Nicorette gum or both. As
I understood the plan, our objective for the day was to acclimatize to the altitude, promenade up to 13,800 feet, where the high camp was situated, eat
lunch, exclaim about how damn high and cold it really was, retreat back
down the slope to our feathered nests, and rejoice, each according to his
abilities. My own version of the plan was more ambitious: I had vowed to
forsake smoking the entire day and night, breaking a twenty-year record.

When Ahmet saw me at breakfast, he beamed, all bright and cheering
rays. "Bob! We go! No problem!" He shook a cigarette from his pack, tempting me back into the brotherhood. I had no alternative but to flee, slipping
in with Halis's veterans. Hands-on, the first and lasting impression of Ararat
was of a volcanic dreamscape where a wanderer was forbidden to ask for for-
giveness. Massive basalt bombs peppered its flanks in all directions, fanned
out like black huts at the lower altitudes but increasing in density the higher
we went, until we were picking our way through huge tumbled galleries, the
rocks sharply edged like broken lumps of glass. Where there were no rocks,
there were baked meadows of field grass, rasping in the wind. The mountain
was overgrazed, not by livestock, but by the macrocosm. Instead of the expected bears and wolves and wild boars, I could do no better than a ladybug
and a half-dozen honeybees. Ararat was theirs.

I began to falter, and soon drifted back among Sandwich and his duck-
lings, all in a row, stabbing one another with their ski poles. I pulled over to
let them pass. "Good day," I bowed. "Lovely morning, eh? *Auf Wiedersehen.*"
Those who spoke English pecked at me, vicious health harpies, and those
who didn't made do with cold neglect. I had not announced my birthday because being celebrated, I feared, would interfere with my growing dignity as
a scapegoat. Accordingly, I fell back some more, and there was Ahmet.

"Ahmet, are you following me? I can feel you breathing down my neck."

"Bob! Bob! Bob! We go. No problem. We smoke. It's good."

My conversations with Ahmet were intensely soothing. When I looked up from my feet to speak again, though, there was Rudi glowering at me, and when I looked up the next time, I was alone on Ararat, tracking footprints through an illicit solitude. I had never seen silence of such uncompromised scope, the altitude abstracting the valley and composing the panorama of the horizon into a Euclidean sampler, all swooping, slanting masses, planispheres and primary shapes, glimmering in the thermals. It was as fine a birthday present as I'd ever received.

I stayed with the trail until midafternoon, when I caught sight of high camp, still, at my speed, an hour ahead, and then turned back down. To my surprise, Ahmet was waiting for me, clearly set at ease to see he wouldn't have to go and fetch me. He clapped me on the back and we descended, dropping into another twisty, close-walled gully, so steep our strides grew longer and longer as gravity put the idea into our heads to race. Ahmet whooped and accelerated out of sight. I braked to a stop, red lights blinking. I had thought prudence and good judgment and flexibility would keep me out of hot water, but no one had told me going up was easy, compared with going down. All the unpaid bills started coming due. My return took hours, and it infused weariness right into my marrow. I fell four times, controlled slides through the gravel that sucked out from under me, my legs too weak to fight.

Back in camp, off-duty soldiers were cooling out in the community tent, paying rapt attention to a broadcast from a transistor radio. From our quartermaster, I purchased a bottle of water and joined them at the table. We shook hands, and I asked them to aim high if they should see me sleepwalking. Erol was there, so I had asked him for the news from Iraq and Saudi Arabia—were they still on the map? The soldiers said screw the news, screw Iraq; they were listening to a soccer game. I finished the water and begged for hot tea. My flesh throbbed in its cells.

I asked Erol to tell Ahmet I wanted to discuss a few things with him. It was done. Ahmet peered keenly into my face, without expression, then spoke rapidly to Erol, who translated. "He says, 'What do you want to know?' "

"I want to find out the history of the Kurds."

Ahmet studied me and gave me the most piercing look of betrayal I have ever received. And yet I didn't get it. He spoke again to Erol, waited for the translation, and left. Now even Erol seemed oddly without humor.

"Ahmet says he is sorry, but he knows nothing about the history of the Kurds."

What a damn vacant fool I was. The Kurds had been gassed in Iraq, massacred in Iran; Turkey was the one relatively safe haven they occupied in the world, and even here they were under the thumb, however lightly it pressed. The inviolable mountains near the Iraqi border were a Kurdish stronghold and in fact supported an armed (but largely inactive) independence movement. And although Kurds held elected seats in parliament, the Kurdish language remained banned in all public forms. Essentially, at an expense I had no ability to calculate, I had just asked Ahmet to jeopardize his employment and maybe make a tour of his own in the police stations.

Erol, no dummy, shrugged it off. Nobody wanted the camp contaminated by politics, where it had no place, no use, no point. I felt wretched, then infinitely worse as Erol explained they had summoned another guide up the mountain from Dogubayazit. He spoke English and would be assigned to me alone. Oh, the ignominy, to be coddled with my own guide! And, as my composure failed, he introduced himself—Bulent, a Turk from the Sea of Marmara—and as he talked on, I impolitely cradled my head on the table, with no desire whatsoever for palaver. He gave up on me and walked away.

I had not smoked yesterday, nor would I today, and I was swaggering a bit after breakfast, because I knew I had high camp nailed. Bulent quickly asserted his own approach to the way things were done. While the Kurdish guides folded their hands over the small of their backs, lending a preoccupied, professorial stoop to their walking posture, Bulent favored ski poles to assist his footing. At the gorge above camp, where Halis veered his squad to the right, Bulent led me to the left, politely suggesting I not step on the fragile grass. For the most part, we spoke little but pegged along, Bulent monitoring my progress and condition. When the party halted for lunch, we were right there.

But then I ruined myself again by clambering into the rocks, my stomach churning. After a particularly long pause to catch my wind, I pivoted summitward to discover Bulent asleep on his feet, bent over his poles. The afternoon turned late. On the perimeter of high camp, I lowered myself down onto the rubble, hypnotized by the Dog. Finally I was here, on the threshold of the summit of the beast. Beneath its white mass, the high camp was like a grotto, cloud-shadowed and mysterious, quarried out from the glacier, its palisades of ice streaked with dirt and volcanic debris. Stones plinked out of the frozen face and rolled musically onto the moraine.

As soon as the tent was pitched, a blizzard raged down on us, stretching prodigiously to the valley two miles below. Rob and I scuttled inside. I could not unzip my sleeping bag. I could not manage the zipper on my daypack or my duffel bag. If anybody had inquired about me, I would have to tell them I had keeled over dead. I lay on my sleeping bag, booted and jacketed. It had grown terrifically cold. Dinner was called, but I could not respond. Bulent brought me a cup of macaroni soup, a thermos of tea. Falling through layer after layer of stupefying aches, I landed on a brittle layer of sleep. Bulent was back at 2 A.M., rousing us for the summit.

There were stars above the silvered dome, but not many—no omens good or bad. Rob had defected from Halis's group, and together with Bulent we groped our way forward, Bulent's headlamp dabbing into the unknown. On Ararat, I had not made the acquaintance of steep until now.

Executing a tight back-and-forth traverse, we made a zigzag stitch right up over the rocks. If you've humped up the Washington Monument with your throat swollen shut and a clothespin on your nose and a chest cold, that's about what it was like on the first section, at least for me.

We constituted a provisional vanguard. Below, the embers of Halis's raiders bobbed out from camp and formed a beautiful jeweled snake, slithering upward. A crag obscured them, and when they came into view again, they were halfway to us, we could hear their dull clank and puff, and Sandwich was coming on. By the time Ahmet waded into the invisible stream of night, Halis had overtaken us, and we halted to let his company pass. The imagery was powerful, militaristic—the solemn clandestine movement under cover of night, the lowered heads and muffled thuds of footsteps, the circumspect cones of dim light preceding each individual, the intense sense of mission that prohibited talk or comment, the implicit glory. The operation was pure war-game and uplifting drama, and since we had no sons to give to it, we gave up Rob, who fastened himself like a burr on the tail of a wolf and was gone.

Sandwich filed by. No one exchanged a word. Ahmet filed by and I thought I recognized a radiance from a visible fragment of Ahmet's smile, wishing me well. Twenty minutes later, when we craned our necks, we could see the almost imperceptible backwash of light from the procession above us, then it flicked its tail for the last time, and vanished.

"Bub?"

"Bulent?"

Bulent's English was better than he gave himself credit for, but clogged and submerged in the deep bass vowels and glottal stops, irrefutably male, of Turkish.

"Uh . . . how do you feel? Are you sick? Does your head ache? Do you want to stop?"

This discourse became the refrain of our ascent, an Araratian call-and-response: Are you . . . ? No, boss. Do you . . . ? No, boss. Bulent was my Moses, leading me to an elusive promised land, and I hearkened to his command. In the growing light he seemed more trusting of me, permitting himself to ascend out of view. Ten minutes ahead, I'd find him sagged over his poles, dozing.

To tell the truth, I felt like the most persecuted man on the planet, and I had ceased joking with myself about my prospects or the risks. I traveled only in twelve-foot sections or less, my lungs extended to full volume with each breath, but the wash of oxygen was missing, and I could not be satisfied. Extended beyond my limits, past ordinary recklessness, I had put myself in a position where anything could happen. I was aware that altitude sickness buried mountaineers no matter their level of experience, that it was most lethal to climbers with a stubborn streak, and that I was a prime but untested candidate for it. I was suffering as I had never suffered, and yet there was an absorbing momentum, an onward press so inexorable that it never crossed my mind to dig in my foot and make it stop, a perpetual motion aspiring onward, but all the while descending within, unseen, like a deep-sea diver.

I pushed on alone for a few minutes. A storm had enveloped the summit, but the first trekkers would be dancing on it by now. I gazed up from my labor and saw Rudi, picking his way down toward me, on the verge of panic. He shouted in my face, thumping the left side of his chest. I understood the words "heart attack." I nodded with lethargic stupidness and he pushed wildly past, bent forward into an invisible gale.

Bulent and I reunited without mention of Rudi; he simply asked if I would be happier back in camp.

"Bulent, do you want me to go back?"

It wasn't a fair question at all, and I knew he shouldn't answer it. On his deadpan face his own weariness showed from this frustrating trial of his patience. But the question seemed to make him reconsider the unspoken nature of our pact, and he grinned. We rested for a half-hour, replenished ourselves with liquids, and pressed on.

After this, everything was different between us. Bulent's brow unfurrowed; a bit of excitement married his eyes. For eight and a half hours we'd been clawing the slope together, and now he suddenly had faith in my perseverance. We had become partners. He looked at his wristwatch. There was still time to reach the summit, he said, if I could increase my pace.

He encouraged one more surge from me, which placed me gasping on a ledge. Before I could catch my wind and move, Halis and his partisans blocked the path in front of me, fattened with self-esteem, and I spent three unnecessary steps climbing off to let them pass. I offered congratulations, but no one looked over at me.

I convinced myself to make the next four steps. I made forty or fifty, at glacial speed, before the next group pushed me aside. Sandwich hailed me on the wing; the others glanced sideways, with no fellowship to spare, as though I might jump in their way. This cold shoulder for such hot effort! To hell with false modesty—I'd earned a salute, a nod, something. They have slain the Big Doggie, I cried out in righteousness, emulating Noah in that regard. They have bagged their trophy, and must make room on the shelf.

I trudged ahead and came even with Bulent. From here, the seamless bleak roll of the summit was at hand, and we saw Ahmet's company hiking down its curve. Two hundred feet above us the rockscape terminated for good upon a knoll, with nothing beyond but the glacier. Rob appeared on its crest and bounded down to where we stood. . . . "You didn't miss anything," he said, downplaying it for my benefit.

This was too much. I narrowed my eyes down the mountain, down toward the valley where all human endeavor had been rendered microscopic—furious, *furious.* "I put a curse on all of them," I snarled. I condemned them to roam endlessly in search of fatuous triumph, stumbling to keep up with a merciless cigar-smoking guide, spraining their ankles on the bones of sinners that cluttered the trails to Paradise.

"What?" Rob said, his eyes opening wide. "Look, don't worry about them." He told me I was doing great; he was proud of me.

"Great?" I snapped. "Phooey. Anyone who wants to climb this mountain can, except for fascist relics in cardiac arrest and diarrhetic junkies." I couldn't help but wonder if tantrums were a little-known symptom of altitude sickness. Noah's sole recorded utterance in the Bible was a curse and a blessing, so there was the mountaineer's precedent.

Bulent and I pressed ahead, atoning for my peccadilloes. I struggled now with a mild headache. Bulent took six more steps and turned to see if I had followed. I hadn't. My pulse roared, I waited for it to calm itself, and we moved on. Ahmet appeared above us on the crest. He threw his arms up when he spotted me and came hopping joyously down the slope as fast as his legs would carry him. From the beginning he had measured me by my own standards. He had studied them as he studied everything, an avid student of all that came his way out here in the remote core of eastern Turkey, and he had not found them wanting—he understood what the mountain was for me. Whatever the price of his tribute and compassion, it was worth it; worth, in fact, more—an Everest or two. He crowed, he embraced me, his face stuck in mine, his eyes glistening, nodding emotionally and with exhiliration. "Bob! Bravo! Bravo, Bob!" And then he let me go and was gone to tend his flock.

It was the greatest inducement to endure and do well that a person could expect from heaven or earth, but that was it for me. I have been undermined by Ahmet's goodness. We pressed on, slowly conquering the knoll, and tagged the glacier—16,200 feet. Bulent was very happy. "One hour more. We can do it, we can," he said. "You are so pigheaded. We can."

"Bulent," I said, "I can't." The hour would split slowly and divide into two. There was no chance he could urge me back down before nightfall. I had seen what I could do, and this was it.

Zion

HEBREW TEXT

With Sinai, Mount Zion—whose name means something like "stony ground"—is the holiest of the Bible's many sacred mountains; although small at 2,500 feet, it commands a view of Jerusalem, and in ancient times was the repository of the Ark of the Covenant. Psalm 48 invites its celebration as God's holy mountain.

Great is the Lord, and greatly to be praised in the city of our God, in the mountain of his holiness.

Beautiful for situation, the joy of the whole earth, is mount Zion, on the sides of the north, the city of the great King.

God is known in her palaces for a refuge.

For, lo, the kings were assembled, they passed by together.

They saw it, and so they marvelled; they were troubled, and hasted away.

Fear took hold upon them there, and pain, as of a woman in travail.

Thou breakest the ships of Tarshish with an east wind.

As we have heard, so have we seen in the city of the Lord of hosts, in the city of our God: God will establish it for ever. Selah.

We have thought of thy loving kindness, O God, in the midst of thy temple.

According to thy name, O God, so is thy praise unto the ends of the earth: thy right hand is full of righteousness.

Let mount Zion rejoice, let the daughters of Judah be glad, because of thy judgments.

Walk about Zion, and go round about her: tell the towers thereof.

Mark ye well her bulwarks, consider her palaces; that ye may tell it to the generation following.

For this God is our God for ever and ever: he will be our guide even unto death.

EUROPE

If you ask me where I am

Well I live here beyond the mountains

It is far but I am near

I live in another world

But you live in it too

GUNNAR EKELÖF

Hellas

ARCHILOCHOS, SAPPHO,
ALKMAN, PAUSANIAS

The ANCIENT GREEKS *regarded the mountains that surrounded them as the sanctuaries of the gods and the domain of wild animals. Their literature, however, looks far more to the sea than to the highlands, and references to mountains are rare. Here are a few surviving lyric fragments.*

> *Until*
> *then*
> *mountaintops*

ARCHILOCHOS

> *the road to towering Olympos*
> ....
> *Desire rattles my brain*

as the mountain wind
tears through the trees

SAPPHO

The valleys sleep
and the mountaintops,
the sea cliffs,
the mountain streams
Rhipa, mountain covered with trees,
up top it's black as night

ALKMAN

The Greek geographer PAUSANIAS, *writing in the second century* A.D., *describes sights that have since disappeared from the flanks of Mount Helikon, in Boeotia.*

They say that Otos and Ephialtes were the first humans to offer sacrifices to the Muses on Mount Helikon and to dedicate the summit to them. They founded the city of Askre there too. Hegesinous writes about this in Atthis:

Askre and Poseidon
the earthshaker lay together.
The seasons turned and she bore him a son,
Oioklos. With the sons of Alokos
he laid the foundations for Askre
under Helikon of the many streams.

I have not read this poem myself, inasmuch as it perished well before I was born. But Kallipos of Corinth, writing about Orchomenos, quotes from it, and, following Kallipos, I do likewise.

Early on, people believed that there were three Muses, and they called them Study, Memory, and Song. Later, it is said, Pieros, for whom the mountain in Macedonia is named, established nine Muses at Thespiai and gave them their present names. Pieros probably thought this was a wise thing to do, or he may have been told to do it by an oracle, or a Thracian may have taught him, inasmuch as the Thracians in those days were so much more advanced than the Macedonians. . . .

On Helikon, as you approach the Grove of the Muses, you will see the spring called Aganippe on your left. Aganippe is a daughter of the stream Termessos, which also flows on Helikon. Up there is a portrait of Eupheme, the Muses' nurse, carved on mountain rock. Her portrait, with the demigod Linos behind her, makes a kind of little cave. Linos, the son of Urania and Amphimaros—himself a son of Poseidon—was the greatest musician of his time, because of which Apollo jealously murdered him. All the barbarians, along with the Greeks, know his story, and even the Egyptians have a song about Linos, although they call him Maneros. . . .

At the very crest of Helikon is the stream called Lamos, and a place called the Reedbed. There is Narkissos's spring, where Narkissos looked and, seeing his reflection in the water, fell in love with himself, and died there pining for his own touch. This is truly stupid. Imagine, a boy old enough to fall in love not knowing himself from a reflection! There is another story, which I think to be true, that is much less well known. It is this: Narkissos had a twin sister, who dressed exactly like him. He was in love with her. When she died, he used to visit the spring; he knew that he was looking at his reflection, but he imagined that he was seeing her visage there in the water. That must have made him feel better. Whatever the case, I believe that the earth produced the flower we call *narkissos* long before this boy came along. Mount Helikon is carpeted with this flower for most of the year.

Mountains of Water
and Mystery

⟲

RUSSIAN FOLK POEMS, ROMANIAN

AND BULGARIAN FOLKTALES

The Russian futurist poet VELEMIR KHLEBNIKOV *(1885–1922) took great
interest in the folk poetry of his native country, seeing in it the possibilities
for an incantatory esthetic that would restore a long-forgotten, natural
music. He was fond of scouring old books of folklore, like the 1836
Skazanija russkogo naroda ("Popular Russian Legends") for models,
among them this pair of northern Russian "bald mountain poems," magical songs sung in the arctic highlands. He notes, "The magic in a word remains magic even if it is not understood and loses none of its power." These
words are surely magical, and just as surely not understandable to us.*

I

Kumara
Nich, nich, pasalam, bada.
Eschochomo, lawassa, schibboda.
Kumara

A.a.o. -o.o.o. -i.i.i. -e.e.e. -u.u.u. -ye.ye.ye.
Aa, la ssob, li li ssob lu lu ssob.
Schunschan
Wichoda, kssara, gujatun, gujatun, etc.

I I

io, ia,-o-io, ia, zok, io, ia,
pazzo! io, ia, pipazzo!
Sookatjema, soossuoma, nikam, nissam, scholda.
Paz, paz, paz, paz, paz, paz, paz, paz!
Pinzo, pinzo, pinzo, dynsa.
Schono, tschikodam, wikgasa, mejda.
Bouopo, chondyryamo, bouopo, galpi.
Ruachado, rassado, ryssado, zalyemo.
io, ia, o, io, ia, zolk. io nye zolk, io ia zolk.

A large body of Romanian legend centers on a hero, FLORIA, who undertakes
all sorts of wonderful adventures in the service of kings, damsels, and other
worthies. In this story, Floria has shown kindness to the king of the storks
and has been promised a kindness in return, a marker he calls when the
king of Romania demands that Floria bring him the magical water of life
and death. The story winningly combines Floria's legend with that of
"clanging mountains"—a common motif in mountain stories around the
world—and, along the way, an etiological tale of why storks have no tails.

Returning to his palace, the stork, who was the king of the storks, called all
the storks together, and asked them whether they had seen or heard or been
near the mountains that knock against one another, at the bottom of which
are the fountains of the water of life and death.

All the young and strong looked at one another, and not even the oldest one ventured to reply. He asked them again, and then they said they had never heard or seen anything of the waters of life and death. At last there came from the rear a stork, lame on one foot, blind in one eye, and with a shriveled-up body, and with half of his feathers plucked out. And he said, "May it please your majesty, I have been there where the mountains knock one against the other, and the proofs of it are my blinded eye and my crooked leg." When the king saw him in the state in which he was, he did not even take any notice of him.

Turning to the other storks, he said: "Is there any one among you who, for my sake, will run the risk and go to these mountains and bring the water?" Not one of the young and strong, and not even any of the older ones who were still strong replied. They all kept silence. But the lame stork said to the king, "For your sake, O Master King, I will again put my life in danger and go." The king again did not look at him, and turning to the others repeated his question; but when he saw that they all kept silence, he at last turned to the stork and said to him: "Dost thou really believe, crippled and broken as thou art, that thou wilt be able to carry out my command?"

"I will certainly try," he said.

"Wilt thou put me to shame?" the king again said.

"I hope not; but thou must bind on my wings some meat for my food, and tie the two bottles for the water to my legs."

The other storks, on hearing his words, laughed at what they thought his conceit, but he took no notice of it. The king was very pleased, and did as the stork had asked. He tied on his wings a quantity of fresh meat, which would last him for his journey, and the two bottles were fastened to his legs. He said to him, "A pleasant journey." The stork, thus prepared for his journey, rose up into the heavens, and away he went straight to the place where the mountains were knocking against one another and prevented any one approaching the fountains of life and death. It was when the sun had risen as high as a lance that he espied in the distance those huge mountains which, when they knocked against one another, shook the earth and made a noise that struck fear and terror into the hearts of those who were a long distance away.

When the mountains had moved back a little before knocking against one another, the stork wanted to plunge into the depths and get the water. But there came suddenly to him a swallow from the heart of the mountain, and said to him, "Do not go a step further, for thou art surely lost."

"Who art thou who stops me in my way?" asked the stork angrily.

"I am the guardian spirit of these mountains, appointed to save every living creature that has the misfortune to come near them."

"What am I to do then to be safe?"

"Hast thou come to fetch water of life and death?"

"Yes."

"If that be so, then thou must wait till noon, when the mountains rest for half an hour. As soon as thou seest that a short time has passed and they do not move, then rise up as high as possible into the air, and drop down straight to the bottom of the mountain. There, standing on the ledge of the stone between the two waters, dip thy bottles into the fountains and wait until they are filled. Then rise as thou hast got down, but beware lest thou touchest the walls of the mountain or even a pebble, or thou art lost."

The stork did as the swallow had told him; he waited till noontide, and when he saw that the mountains had gone to sleep, he rose up into the air, and, plunging down into the depth, he settled on the ledge of the stone and filled his bottles. Feeling that they had been filled, he rose with them as he had got down, but when he had reached almost the top of the mountains, he touched a pebble. No sooner had he done so, when the two mountains closed furiously upon him; but they did not catch any part of him, except the tail, which remained locked up fast between the two peaks of the mountains.

With a strong movement he tore himself away, happy that he had saved his life and the two bottles with the waters of life and death, not caring for the loss of his tail.

And he returned the way he had come, and reached the palace of the king of the storks in time for the delivery of the bottles. When he reached the palace, all the storks were assembled before the king, waiting to see what would happen to the lame and blind one who had tried to put them to shame. When they saw him coming back, they noticed that he had lost his tail, and they began jeering at him and laughing, for he looked all the more ungainly, from having already been so ugly before.

But the king was overjoyed with the exploit of his faithful messenger; and he turned angrily on the storks and said, "Why are you jeering and mocking? Just look round and see where are your tails. And you have not lost them in so honorable a manner as this my faithful messenger." On hearing this they turned round, and lo! one and all of them had lost their tails.

And this is the reason why they have remained without a tail to this very day.

TRANSLATED BY M. GASTER

The mountains are full of mysteries, as this Bulgarian legend of the culture hero DEMIR BABA, ruler of the high Balkan region of Khorosan, suggests.

All wise men come from Khorosan.

Demir Baba was not only a spiritual leader but a warlike man, with martial skills. He could stand on a horse and throw a lance. When he threw one and it fell someplace, that place would become a shrine, and people would pray there. He and his followers would set up towns.

Demir Baba once lived atop the Shipka mountain, the mountain that separates north and south. It is the highest mountain in the Balkans. People said to him, "Wherever you say, we will build a town." Demir Baba threw a lance to the top of the Shipka mountain. "Who," he said, "would come here to honor me?" The people said, "Wherever, believe us. People will come." He threw his javelin to the same place. "Then that is where I will go. If I get up at six in the morning, it is not until twelve that I can reach that spot."

Once he said, "Go here!" They said, "Why here? There is nothing, it's deserted." But they go, and they sleep the night, and in the morning they see that everything is green.

And Elmali Baba. He does gardening. Demir Baba approaches him and says, "Why don't you bring us watermelons and cantaloupes?" Elmali Baba says, "But I just planted them yesterday!"

"Go and see." And Elmali Baba brings back watermelons and cantaloupes.

"Why don't you bring us some apples?"

"But they are very young; they are not ready to eat!"

"Go and look." And Elmali Baba brings back apples.

"From now on you will be known as Elmali Baba [*elma*, "apple"], and when you reach forty years, you will be as wise as us."

All wise men come from Khorosan.

TRANSLATED BY SCOTT L. MALCOLMSON

Highlands

DOROTHY WORDSWORTH,

WILLIAM BUTLER YEATS, SCOTTISH FOLK

SONGS, ALASTAIR BORTHWICK

Dorothy Wordsworth (1771–1855), sister of William and friend of Samuel Taylor Coleridge, was, in the words of her editor Aubrey de Sélincourt, "probably the most distinguished of English writers who never wrote a line for the general public." In this excerpt from her Alfoxden Journal *(1798), only a small portion of which survives, she captures the moods of the northern English mountains in a strangely clement season.*

Alfoxden, 20th January 1798

The green paths down the hillsides are channels for streams. The young wheat is streaked by silver lines of water running between the ridges, the sheep are gathered together on the slopes. After the wet dark days, the country seems more populous. It peoples itself in the sunbeams. The garden, mimic of spring, is gay with flowers. The purple-starred hepatica spreads itself in the sun, and the clustering snow-drops put forth their white heads, at first upright, ribbed with green, and like a rosebud; when completely opened, hanging their heads downwards, but slowly lengthening their slender stems. The slanting woods of an unvarying brown, showing the light through the thin net-work of their upper boughs. Upon the highest ridge of that round hill covered with planted oaks, the shafts of the trees show in the light like the columns of a ruin.

21st Walked on the hill-tops—a warm day. Sat under the firs in the park. The tops of the beeches of a brown-red, or crimson. Those oaks, fanned by the sea breeze, thick with feathery sea-green moss, as a grove not stripped of its leaves. Moss cups more proper than acorns for fairy goblets.

22nd Walked through the wood to Holford. The ivy twisting round the oaks like bristled serpents. The day cold—a warm shelter in the hollies, capriciously bearing berries. Query: Are the male and female flowers on separate trees?

23rd Bright sunshine, went out at 3 o'clock. The sea perfectly calm blue, streaked with deeper colour by the clouds, and tongues or points of sand, on our return of a gloomy red. The sun gone down. The crescent moon, Jupiter, and Venus. The sound of the sea distinctly heard on the tops of the hills, which we could never hear in summer. We attribute this partly to the bareness of the trees, but chiefly to the absence of the singing of birds, the hum of insects, that noiseless noise which lives in the summer air. The villages marked out by beautiful beds of smoke. The turf fading into the mountain road. The scarlet flowers of the moss.

24th Walked between half-past three and half-past five. The evening cold and clear. The sea of a sober grey, streaked by the deeper grey clouds. The half dead sound of the near sheep-bell, in the hollow of the sloping coombe, exquisitely soothing.

25th Went to Poole's after tea. The sky spread over with one continuous cloud, whitened by the light of the moon, which, though her dim shape was seen, did not throw forth so strong a light as to chequer the earth with shadows. At once the clouds seemed to cleave asunder, and left her in the centre of a black-blue vault. She sailed along, followed by multitudes of stars, small, and bright, and sharp. Their brightness seemed concentrated, (half-moon).

26th Walked upon the hill-tops; followed the sheep tracks till we overlooked the larger coombe. Sat in the sunshine. The distant sheepbells, the sound of the stream; the woodman winding along the halfmarked road with his laden pony; locks of wool still spangled with the dewdrops; the bluegrey sea, shaded with immense masses of cloud, not streaked; the sheep glittering in the sunshine. Returned through the wood. The trees skirting the wood, being exposed more directly to the action of the sea breeze, stripped of the net-work of their upper boughs which are stiff and erect, like black skeletons, the ground strewed with the red berries of the holly. Set forward before two o'clock. Returned a little after four.

28th A very stormy day. William walked to the top of the hill to see the sea. Nothing distinguishable but a heavy blackness. An immense bough riven from one of the fir trees.

30th William called me into the garden to observe a singular appearance about the moon. A perfect rainbow, within the bow one star, only of colours more vivid. The semi-circle soon became a complete circle and in the course of three or four minutes the whole faded away. Walked to the blacksmith's and the baker's; an uninteresting evening.

31st Set forward to Stowey at half-past five. A violent storm in the wood; sheltered under the hollies. When we left home the moon immensely large, the sky scattered over with clouds. These soon closed in contracting the dimensions of the moon without concealing her. The sound of the pattering shower, and the gusts of wind, very grand. Left the wood when nothing remained of the storm but the driving wind, and a few scattering drops of rain. Presently all clear, Venus first showing herself between the struggling clouds; afterwards Jupiter appeared. The hawthorn hedges, black and pointed, glittering with millions of diamond drops; the hollies shining with broader patches of light. The road to the village of Holford glittered like another stream. On our return, the wind high—a violent storm of hail and rain at the Castle of Comfort. All the Heavens seemed in one perpetual motion when the rain ceased; the moon appearing, now half veiled, and now retired behind heavy clouds, the stars still moving, the roads very dirty.

1st February About two hours before dinner, set forward towards Mr Bartholemew's. The wind blew so keen in our faces that we felt ourselves inclined to seek the covert of the wood. There we had a warm shelter, gathered a burthen of large rotten boughs blown down by the wind of the preceding night. The sun shone clear, but all at once a heavy blackness hung over the sea. The trees almost roared, and the ground seemed in motion with the multitudes of dancing leaves, which made a rustling sound, distinct from that of the trees. Still the asses pastured in quietness under the hollies, undisturbed by these forerunners of the storm. The wind beat furiously against us as we returned. Full moon. She rose in uncommon majesty over the sea, slowly ascending through the clouds. Sat with the window open an hour in the moonlight.

2nd Walked through the wood, and on to the Downs before dinner; a warm pleasant air. The sun shone, but was often obscured by straggling clouds. The redbreasts made a ceaseless song in the woods. The wind rose very high in the evening. The room smoked so that we were obliged to quit it. Young lambs in a green pasture in the coombe, thick legs, large heads, black staring eyes.

3rd A mild morning, the windows open at breakfast, the redbreasts singing in the garden. Walked with Coleridge over the hills. The sea at first obscured by vapour; that vapour afterwards slid in one mighty mass along the sea-shore; the islands and one point of land clear beyond it. The distant country (which was purple in the clear dull air), overhung by straggling clouds that sailed over it, appeared like the darker clouds, which are often seen at a great distance apparently motionless, while the nearer ones pass quickly over them, driven by the lower winds. I never saw such a union of earth, sky, and sea. The clouds beneath our feet spread themselves to the water, and the clouds of the sky almost joined them. Gathered sticks in the wood; a perfect stillness. The redbreasts sang upon the leafless boughs. Of a great number of sheep in the field, only one standing. Returned to dinner at five o'clock. The moonlight still and warm as a summer's night at nine o'clock.

4th Walked a great part of the way to Stowey with Coleridge. The morning warm and sunny. The young lasses seen on the hill-tops, in the villages and roads, in their summer holiday clothes—pink petticoats and blue. Mothers with their children in arms, and the little ones that could just walk, tottering by their side. Midges or small flies spinning in the sunshine; the songs of the lark and redbreast; daisies upon the turf; the hazels in blossom; honeysuckles budding. I saw one solitary strawberry flower under a hedge. The furze gay with blossom. The moss rubbed from the pairings by the sheep, that leave locks of wool, and the red marks with which they are spotted, upon the wood.

A mountain on the road to Dublin serves as a touchstone for revivifying the world through the creation of art in WILLIAM BUTLER YEATS' famous poem "The Peacock."

> *What's riches to him*
> *That has made a great peacock*
> *With the pride of his eye?*
> *The wind-beaten, stone-grey,*
> *And desolate Three Rock*
> *Would nourish his whim.*
> *Live he or die*
> *Amid wet rocks and heather,*
> *His ghost will be gay*
> *Adding feather to feather*
> *For the pride of his eye.*

In his Popular Ballads of England and Scotland, *FRANCIS CHILD (1882–1898) writes, with evident sadness, that this is a "romantic ballad of which, unfortunately, one stanza only has been preserved." The tra-*

dition has it that the song concerns a young lady who was carried away by the fairies into the mountains, and that she sings for her home, invisible to and unheard by the friends that search the hills for her. This is what she sings:

O Alva hills is bonny
Dalycountry hills is fair,
But to think on the braes of Menstrie
It maks my heart fu sair.

The rugged highlands are a dangerous place for cattle, the ancient Celtic measure of wealth. This ancient song, recorded by folklorist Alexander Carmichael in the mid–nineteenth century, was sung to protect the herds.

Pastures smooth, long, and spreading,
Grassy meads aneath your feet,
The friendship of God the Son to bring you home
To the field of the fountains,
    Field of the fountains.

Closed be every pit to you,
Smoothed be every knoll to you,
Cosy every exposure to you,
Beside the cold mountains,
    Beside the cold mountains.

*Ben MacDhui, one of the Scottish Highlands' tall peaks, is said to harbor
a cousin of the Himalayan yeti, as mountaineer* Alastair Borthwick
writes in his 1947 memoir Always a Little Further.

The Great Grey Man of Ben MacDhui, or Ferlas Mor as he is called in the
Gaelic, is Scotland's Abominable Snowman and the only mountain ghost I
have heard of in this part of the world. He ranks high in the supernatural
Debrett, for he has been seen by responsible people who have reputations to
lose, most of them expert mountaineers accustomed to hills at night and not
given to imagining things.

He first reached print about twenty-five years ago, when Professor J.
Norman Collie, a mountaineer of international repute who not only made
first ascents of most of Scotland's major cliffs (a peak in the Cuillin is named
after him), but climbed extensively in the Alps and was with Mummery on
Nanga Parbat in the Himalaya, admitted that strange things had happened
to him on Ben MacDhui. He had been alone on the summit at midnight; and
so peculiar were the things he saw there that he did not stop running until
he was halfway down to the Rothiemurchus.

He related this experience at a dinner of the Cairngorm Club; and immediately others, equally reputable, came forward and admitted that they,
too, had seen queer things on MacDhui. According to their descriptions the
Great Grey Man is a tremendous shadowy creature, and his height is vari-
ously reported to be anything from ten to forty feet. He appears generally at
night; and one's natural reaction is to run as fast as possible in the opposite
direction.

There are two interesting points about the circumstances under which
he has appeared. First, several men claim that they saw him before they
knew of his existence: only when Collie gave the lead did they admit that
they had seen something too, so they did not hear the tale and then imagine
themselves into meeting Ferlas Mor. And second, there is no known mountain phenomenon which could account for him. If the sun is shining, it fre-

quently happens that a climber's shadow is cast on a screen of mist some distance away, so that he can march along a ridge with a huge shadow stalking along in space beside him. But this is a common trick of mist and sun which would scare no one. I have seen it half a dozen times. It is interesting, but not in the least eerie. Any one who makes a habit of climbing knows what causes it; and, instead of running away, whoops with delight, rakes his rucksack for a camera, and tries to photograph it. It is known as the Brocken spectre, after the peak in the Harz Mountains where it commonly occurs. But Brocken spectres cannot live without sunlight: the moon is not sufficiently bright. And the Great Grey Man walks at night.

I know two men who claim to have heard Ferlas Mor. The first was alone, heading over MacDhui for Corrour on a night when the snow had a hard, crisp crust through which his boots broke at every step. He reached the summit, and it was while he was descending the slopes which fall towards the Larig that he heard footsteps behind him, footsteps not in the rhythm of his own, but occurring only once for every three steps he took.

"I felt a queer, crinkly feeling on the back of my neck," he told me, "but I said to myself, 'This is silly. There must be a reason for it.' So I stopped and the footsteps stopped, and I sat down and tried to reason it out. I could see nothing. There was a moon about somewhere, but the mist was fairly thick. The only thing I could make of it was that when my boots broke through the snow-crust they made some sort of echo. But then every step should have echoed, and not just this regular one-in-three. I was scared stiff. I got up, and walked on, trying hard not to look behind me. I got down all right—the footsteps stopped a thousand feet above the Larig—and I didn't run. But, man, if anything had as much as said 'Boo' behind me, I'd have run down to Corrour like a streak of lightning!"

The second man's experience was roughly similar. He was on MacDhui, and alone. He heard footsteps. He was climbing in daylight, in summer; but so dense was the mist that he was working by compass, and visibility was almost as poor as it would have been by night. The footsteps he heard were made by something or some one trudging up the fine screes which decorate the upper parts of the mountain, a thing not extraordinary in itself, though the steps were only a few yards behind him, but exceedingly odd when the mist suddenly cleared and he could see no living thing on the mountain, at that point devoid of cover of any kind.

"Did the steps follow yours exactly?" I asked him.

"No," he said. "That was the funny thing. They didn't. They were regular all right; but the queer thing was that they seemed to come once for every two and a half steps I took."

He thought it queerer still when I told him the other man's story. You see, he was long-legged and six feet tall, and the first was only five-feet-seven!

Once I was out with a search-party on MacDhui; and on the way down after an unsuccessful day I asked some of the gamekeepers and stalkers who were with us what they thought of it all. They worked on MacDhui, so they should know. Had they seen Ferlas Mor? Did he exist or was it just a silly story?

They looked at me for a few seconds, and then one said:

"We do not talk about that."

Mountains
of Europe

JOHN RUSKIN

The esthetic theorist and social critic JOHN RUSKIN *(1819–1900)*
grounded many of his ideas of art in the rural and natural worlds. This
excerpt from his Modern Painters of Truth *offers Ruskin's thoughts on*
mountains after a continental tour.

Mountains are, to the rest of the body of the earth, what violent muscular action is to the body of man. The muscles and tendons of its anatomy are, in
the mountain, brought out with fierce and convulsive energy, full of expression, passion, and strength; the plains and the lower hills are the repose and
the effortless motion of the frame, when its muscles lie dormant and concealed beneath the lines of its beauty, yet ruling those lines in their every un-
dulation. This, then, is the first grand principle of the truth of the earth. The
spirit of the hills is action; that of the lowlands, repose; and between these
there is to be found every variety of motion and of rest; from the inactive
plain, sleeping like the firmament, with cities for stars, to the fiery peaks,
which, with heaving bosoms and exulting limbs, with the clouds drifting

like hair from their bright foreheads, lift up their Titan hands to Heaven, saying, "I live forever!"

But there is this difference between the action of the earth, and that of a living creature, that while the exerted limb marks its bones and tendons through the flesh, the excited earth casts off the flesh altogether, and its bones come out from beneath. Mountains are the bones of the earth, their highest peaks are invariably those parts of its anatomy which in the plains lie buried under five and twenty thousand feet of solid thickness of superincumbent soil, and which spring up in the mountain ranges in vast pyramids or wedges, flinging their garment of earth away from them on each side. The masses of the lower hills are laid over and against their sides, like the masses of lateral masonry against the skeleton arch of an unfinished bridge, except that they slope up to and lean against the central ridge: and finally, upon the slopes of these lower hills are strewed the level beds of sprinkled gravel, sand, and clay, which form the extent of the champaign. Here then is another grand principle of the truth of earth, that the mountains must come from under all, and be the support of all; and that everything also must be laid in their arms, heap above heap, the plains being the uppermost. Opposed to this truth is every appearance of the hills being laid upon the plains, or built upon them. Nor is this a truth only of the earth on a large scale, for every minor rock (in position) comes out from the soil about it as an island out of the sea, lifting the earth near it like waves beating on its sides.

Volcano

JON THORLAKSSON

JON THORLAKSSON, a Lutheran minister of Sandfell, Iceland, was conducting a service when the long-dormant volcano Lounagrupr erupted. Here he describes the event in an account that W. H. Auden thought worthy of preserving almost whole in his 1937 book Letters from Iceland, *a collaboration with fellow poet Louis MacNeice.*

In the year 1727, on the 7th of August, which was the tenth Sunday after Trinity, after the commencement of divine service in the church of Sandfell, as I stood before the altar, I was sensible of a gentle concussion under my feet, which I did not mind at first; but, during the delivery of the sermon, the rocking continued to increase, so as to alarm the whole congregation; yet they remarked that the like had often happened before. One of them, a very aged man, repaired to a spring, a little below the house, where he prostrated himself on the ground, and was laughed at by the rest for his pains; but, on his return, I asked him what it was he wished to ascertain, to which he replied, "Be on your guard, Sir; the earth is on fire!" Turning, at the same moment, towards the church door, it appeared to me, and all who were present, as if the house contracted and drew itself together. I now left the church, necessarily ruminating on what the old man had said; and as I came opposite to Mount Flega, and looked up towards the summit, it appeared alternately to expand and be heaved up, and fall again to its former state. Nor was I mistaken in this, as the event shewed; for on the morning of the 8th, we not only felt frequent and violent earthquakes, but also heard dreadful reports, in no respect inferior to thunder. Everything that was standing in the houses was thrown down by these shocks; and there was reason to apprehend, that mountains as well as houses would be overturned in the catastrophe. What most augmented the terror of the people was, that nobody could divine in what place the disaster would originate, or where it would end.

After nine o'clock, three particularly loud reports were heard, which were almost instantaneously followed by several eruptions of water that gushed out, the last of which was the greatest, and completely carried away the horses and other animals that it overtook in its course. When these exudations were over, the ice mountain itself ran down into the plain, just like melted metal poured out of a crucible; and on settling, filled it to such a height, that I could not discover more of the well-known mountain Lounagrupr than about the size of a bird. The water now rushed down the east side without intermission, and totally destroyed what little of the pasturegrounds remained. It was a most pitiable sight to behold the females crying, and my neighbours destitute both of counsel and courage: however, as I observed that the current directed its course towards my house, I removed my family up to the top of a high rock, on the side of the mountain, called Dalskardstorfa, where I caused a tent to be pitched, and all the church utensils, together with our food, clothes and other things that were most necessary, to be conveyed thither; drawing the conclusion, that should the eruption break forth at some other place, this height would escape the longest, if it were the will of God, to whom we committed ourselves, and remained there.

Things now assumed quite a different appearance. The Jökull itself exploded, and precipitated masses of ice, many of which were hurled out to the sea; but the thickest remained on the plain, at a short distance from the foot of the mountain. The noise and reports continuing, the atmosphere was so completely filled with fire and ashes, that day could scarcely be distinguished from night, by reason of the darkness which followed, and which was barely rendered visible by the light of the fire that had broken through five or six cracks in the mountain. In this manner the parish of Oraefa was tormented for three days together; yet it is not easy to describe the disaster as it was in reality; for the surface of the ground was entirely covered with pumice-sand, and it was impossible to go out in the open air with safety, on account of the red-hot stones that fell from the atmosphere. Any who did venture out, had to cover their heads with buckets, and such other wooden utensils as could afford them some protection.

On the 11th it cleared up a little in the neighbourhood; but the ice-mountain still continued to send forth smoke and flames. The same day I rode, in company with three others, to see how matters stood with the parsonage, as it was most exposed, but we could only proceed with the utmost danger, as there was no other way except between the ice-mountain and the Jökull which had been precipitated into the plain, where the water was so hot that the horses, almost got unmanageable: and, just as we entertained the hope of getting through by this passage, I happened to look behind me, when I descried a fresh deluge of hot water directly above me, which, had it reached us, must inevitably have swept us before it. Contriving, of a sudden, to get on the ice, I called to my companions to make the utmost expedition in following me; and by this means, we reached Sandfell in safety. The whole of the farm, together with the cottages of two tenants, had been destroyed; only the dwelling houses remained, and a few spots of the tuns. The people stood crying in the church. The cows which, contrary to all expectation, both here and elsewhere, had escaped the disaster, were lowing beside a few hay-stacks that had been damaged during the eruption. At the time the exudation of the Jökull broke forth, the half of the people belonging to the parsonage were in four nearly-constructed sheep-cotes, where two women and a boy took refuge on the roof of the highest; but they had hardly reached it when, being unable to resist the force of the thick mud that was borne against it, it was carried away by the deluge of hot water and, as far as the eye could reach, the three unfortunate persons were seen clinging to the roof. One of the women was afterwards found among the substances that had proceeded from the Jökull, but burnt and, as it were, parboiled; her body was so soft that it could scarcely be touched. Everything was in the most deplorable condition. The sheep were lost; some of which were washed up dead from the sea in the third parish from Oraefa. The hay that was saved was found insufficient for the cows so that a fifth part of them had to be killed; and most of the horses which had not been swept into the ocean were afterwards found completely mangled. The eastern part of the parish of Sida was also destroyed by the pumice and sand; and the inhabitants were on that account obliged to kill many of their cattle.

The mountain continued to burn night and day from the 8th of August, as already mentioned, till the beginning of Summer in the month of April the following year, at which time the stones were still so hot that they could not be touched; and it did not cease to emit smoke till near the end of the Summer. Some of them had been completely calcined; some were black and full of holes; and others were so loose in their contexture that one could blow through them. On the first day of Summer 1728, I went in company with a person of quality to examine the cracks in the mountain, most of which were so large that we could creep into them. I found here a quantity of saltpetre and could have collected it, but did not choose to stay long in the excessive heat. At one place a heavy calcined stone lay across a large aperture; and as it rested on a small basis, we easily dislodged it into the chasm but could not observe the least sign of its having reached the bottom. These are the more remarkable particulars that have occurred to me with respect to this mountain; and thus God hath led me through fire and water, and brought me through much trouble and adversity to my eightieth year. To Him be the honour, the praise, and the glory for ever.

Vesuvius, Etna,
and the Apennines

⑥

PLINY THE YOUNGER, CARLO LEVI,

FRANCISCAN TEXT

Pliny the Elder was a naturalist of voracious appetites, physical and in-
tellectual, whose curiosity got the better of him when Mount Vesuvius
erupted in A.D. 79. His nephew PLINY THE YOUNGER, *writing to the histo-*
rian Tacitus, describes Pliny's last days.

My uncle was at that time with the fleet under his command at Misenum. On
the 14th of August, about one in the afternoon, my mother excitedly pointed
out to him a cloud that appeared in the sky, one of a very unusual size and
shape. He had just taken a turn in the sun, and, after bathing himself in cold
water, and making a light lunch, gone back to his books: he immediately
arose and went out upon a rising ground from where he might get a better
sight of it. A cloud, from which mountain was uncertain, at this distance (but
it was found afterwards to come from Mount Vesuvius), was ascending, the
appearance of which I cannot give you a more exact description of than by
likening it to that of a pine tree, for it shot up to a great height in the form of
a very tall trunk, which spread itself out at the top into a sort of branches; oc-

casioned, I imagine, either by a sudden gust of air that impelled it, the force of which decreased as it advanced upward, or the cloud itself being pressed back again by its own weight, expanded in the manner I have mentioned; it appeared sometimes bright and sometimes dark and spotted, as it was either more or less impregnated with earth and cinders.

This phenomenon seemed to a man of such learning and research as my uncle extraordinary and worth further looking into. He ordered a light vessel to be readied, and told me, if I liked, to accompany him. I said I would rather continue my work, as he had earlier given me something to write out. As he was coming out of the house, he received a note from Rectina, the wife of Bassus, who was in the utmost alarm at the imminent danger which threatened her; for her villa lay at the foot of Mount Vesuvius, and there was no way of escape but by sea. She begged him to come to her aid. What he had begun from a philosophical, he now carried out in a noble and generous spirit. He ordered the galleys to put to sea, and went himself on board with an intention of assisting not only Rectina, but the many towns that lay strewn along that beautiful coast. Hastening then to the place from where others had fled in utmost terror, he steered his course direct to the point of danger, and with so much calmness and presence of mind as to be able to make and dictate his observations on the motion and all the phenomena of that dreadful scene.

He was now so close to the mountain that the cinders, which grew thicker and hotter the nearer he approached, fell into the ships, together with pumice stones, and black pieces of burning rock: they were in danger too not only of being run aground by the sudden retreat of the sea, but also from the vast fragments that rolled down from the mountain, and obstructed all the shore. Here he stopped to consider whether he should turn back again; to which the pilot advising him, "Fortune," said he, "favors the brave; steer to where Pomponianus is."

Pomponianus was then at Stabiae, separated by a bay, which the sea, after several insensible windings, forms with the shore. He had already sent his baggage on board; for though he was not at that time in actual danger, yet being within sight of it, and indeed extremely near, if it should in the least increase, he was determined to put to sea as soon as the wind, which was

blowing dead in-shore, should go down. It was favorable, however, for carrying my uncle to Pomponianus, whom he found in the greatest consterna-
tion: he embraced him tenderly, encouraging and urging him to keep up his
spirits, and, the more effectively to soothe his fears by seeming unconcerned
himself, ordered a bath to be got ready, and then, after having bathed, sat
down to supper with great cheerfulness, or at least (what is just as heroic)
with every appearance of it. Meanwhile broad flames shone out in several
places from Mount Vesuvius, which the darkness of the night contributed to
render still brighter and clearer. But my uncle, in order to soothe the appre-
hensions of his friend, assured him it was only the burning of the villages,
which the country people had abandoned to the flames: after this he retired
to rest, and it is most certain he was so little disquieted as to fall into a sound
sleep: for his breathing, which, on account of his corpulence, was rather
heavy and sonorous, was heard by the attendants outside. The court which
led to his apartment being now almost filled with stones and ashes, if he had
continued there any time longer, it would have been impossible for him to
have made his way out. So he was awakened and got up, and went to Pomponianus and the rest of his company, who were feeling too anxious to think
of going to bed. They consulted together whether it would be most prudent
to trust to the houses, which now rocked from side to side with frequent and
violent concussions as though shaken from their very foundations; or fly to
the open fields, where the calcined stones and cinders, though light indeed,
yet fell in large showers, and threatened destruction. In this choice of dangers they resolved for the fields: a resolution which, while the rest of the
company were hurried into by their fears, my uncle embraced upon cool
and deliberate consideration. They went out then, having pillows tied upon
their heads with napkins; and this was their whole defense against the storm
of stones that fell round them.

It was now day everywhere else, but there a deeper darkness prevailed
than in the thickest night; which however was in some degree alleviated by
torches and other lights of various kinds. They thought proper to go farther
down upon the shore to see if they might safely put out to sea, but found the
waves still running extremely high, and boisterous. There my uncle, laying
himself down upon a sail-cloth, which was spread for him, called twice for

some cold water, which he drank, when immediately the flames, preceded by a strong whiff of sulfur, dispersed the rest of the party, and obliged him to rise. He raised himself up with the assistance of two of his servants, and instantly fell down dead, suffocated, as I conjecture, by some gross and noxious vapor, having always had a weak throat, which was often inflamed. As soon as it was light again, which was not until the third day after this melancholy accident, his body was found entire, and without any marks of violence upon it, in the dress in which he fell, and looking more like a man asleep than dead.

In his memoir Words Are Stones, *the noted Italian writer* Carlo Levi *(1902–1975) records a postwar tour of the mountains of Sicily, an area that to him seemed still part of the nineteenth century.*

Coming out of Catania, the road at once crosses the *sciara* [lava flow] of Curia. It is a wonderful and terrible landscape black and purple and gray, of bare or lichen-covered lava blown by some prehistoric wind into strange, wrinkled waves. In the midst of the lava there is a new working-class quarter of white houses, like a city in the desert. We drove right across the *sciara* through different kinds of lava, some of it still unchanged after centuries, some of it crumbled and transformed: it is the plants which slowly make the stone into fertile soil. First come the fungi and mosses and lichens, red, green or gray, encrusting the purple basalt and breaking it up to the point where cardamom and then broom can take root, and another kind of broom called, in dialect, *cichiciaca*. Not until after the broom does the prickly pear make its appearance—plant of resurrection, the tree of the lava, tenderly green on the stony slopes. After the prickly pear come the other plants—the fig tree, the pistachio tree, the almond, the olive, and, lastly, the vine. Thus the stone which has flowed from the volcano can be dated from the plants which grow upon it, until the moment when another flow submerges the last vines and the olives and the prickly pears and the broom bushes and the lichens, and the stone desert comes back again.

Leaving the *sciara* behind, the road brought us to Misterbianco, into the midst of the ducal estates memories of De Felice and the peasant risings. Further on another *sciara,* that of the year 1760, comes down from the Monti Rossi, the outposts of Etna. Through the most splendid orange groves we reached Paternò. Beyond the Simeto River appeare the mountain country of Centuripe, the naked interior of Sicily. The town had a festive look, and was full of garlands and lamps; preparations were going on for the feast of Saint Barbara during the next few days. We crossed the Via Fallica; but my companions assured me this was merely the name of a person. There was a crowd of people in front of the church: they were getting ready the car of Saint Barbara, sister saint of Saint Agatha, and the *cannelori,* the great wax candles, carved and engraved and painted, which were to be carried by hand in the procession. We went into the storehouse where the candles are kept, and the peasants who were there showed them to me. There was a candle for the carters and carriers, a candle for the laborers, a candle for the farmers, a candle for the bakers, a candle for the shopkeepers with great big pink angels on it ("This," the peasants told me, "is the drunkards' candle"). They were very proud of their own candle, the peasants' candle. All around it there were carved scenes of the saint's martyrdom. First of all, the tearing off of her breasts (for Saint Barbara, too—in the same way as, and perhaps even more than, Saint Agatha—is an Earth saint, a Mount Etna saint, sacred to fire and volcanic eruptions); then, Saint Barbara carried naked to her "shame," Saint Barbara in front of Christ, and, finally, her father, the Saracen king, cutting off her head.

Through herds of long-horned goats and extremely elegant cemeteries we went on to Santa Maria di Licodia. "This is a quiet place," said the *contadino* who was one of my traveling companions. "Here Communists, Christian Democrats and Fascists all play cards together." Here, in far-off days, when Santa Maria di Licodia was called Etna Inessa, stood the famous temple of Vulcan or possibly of the more ancient local god of fire, Adrano, surrounded by a sacred wood which was guarded by a thousand dogs which were able, by divine instinct, to distinguish the good from the wicked.

Farther on, on the mountainside, like a gray military fortress, stands the feudal castle of Baron Spitalieri. Beyond Biancavilla and its cemetery we arrived at Adrano, formerly Aderno, sacred, as its name implies, to lava and the gods of fire. In front of the Saracen castle opens out the valley of the Simeto, which every year has tremendous floods; and opposite, like a desolate and fantastic theatrical scene, are the mountains of Enna with towns and villages perched on top of their bare summits—Centuripe, Regalbuto, Troina, and the feudal estates of Baron Spitalieri, Baron Solima and others. The Simeto is in truth a boundary line. On the near side Etna, visible high against the sky like some unattainable god, and Etna's realm, snowy wastes and basalt above, and then, as you come down, thickets of chestnut and bracken, and, lower still, vineyards and gardens and citrus groves and villages and green plantations, on a soil which is always crumbling and fortuitous but full of salts and abundantly fertile, life-giving juices. On the far side, beyond the Simeto, lie desolate, bare feudal estates, corn country, but destitute, yellow, treeless, uninhabited, sun-smitten, mysterious in its nakedness, a far, remote world where the shining gods of the volcano have never set foot. We stopped only for a moment at Adrano, an illustrious town, full of history, rich in brigand enterprise (the brigands were once in league with the feudal lord but more recently have become isolated and independent), a center, both in former and in recent times, of working-class struggle, where only last year the laborer Girolamo Rosano was killed in a demonstration in the piazza. Farther on, far away on the mountains, Enna and Calascibetta appeared, and on the other side Cesaro and the bare mountains of the province of Messina. After another *sciara,* the Sciara Nova, one of the hundred that flow down like streams from Etna, we came into Bronte.

TRANSLATED BY ANGUS DAVIDSON

Mountains are the abodes of angels. They are the haunt of devils, too, as
Saint Francis of Assisi *(1182–1226) found when he went high into the*
Apennines to prepare for the Feast of the Assumption.

When the Feast of the Assumption of Our Lady drew close, Francis sought
to find a fitting spot, more secret and remote, where he could keep in solitude
the forty days' fast of St. Michael the Archangel, which begins that feast.

He called Friar Leo and said to him, "Go stand at the doorway of the oratory of the Place of the Friars. When I call you, return to me."

Friar Leo went and stood in the doorway; and Francis walked away a
distance and called to him. Friar Leo, hearing him call, returned to him, and
St. Francis said, "Son, let us search out another, more secret spot from
which you will not be able to hear me when I call."

As they searched, they saw, on the southern side of the mountain, a
lonely place quite well fitted to his purpose; but it was impossible to reach
it, because there was in front of it a deep rocky chasm, horrible and fearful.

With much labor, they laid a fallen tree over the chasm to make a bridge,
and crossed over to the other side. Then Francis sent for the other friars and
told them that he intended to keep the forty days' fast of St. Michael in that
solitary place. They made a little cell there, so deep in the rock that they
could hear no cry he might utter.

When they finished making the cell, he said to them: "Go back to the
Place of the Friars and leave me here alone; for, with the help of God, I mean
to keep this fast in this place without any trouble or distraction. Please, let
no one of you come to me, nor allow any layperson to come to me for counsel. Friar Leo, you come to me once a day, alone, with a little bread and
water, and at night once again, at the hour of matins. Come in silence. When
you are at the foot of the bridge, say to me: *'Lord, open my lips.'* If I answer
you, cross the bridge and come to my cell, and we will say matins together.
But if I do not answer you, leave at once." Francis said this because he was
sometimes so enraptured in the spirit of God that he did not hear or perceive anything with the senses.

Then Francis gave them his blessing; and the friars returned to the monastery.

The Feast of the Assumption arrived, and Francis began the holy fast with ascetic severity, mortifying his body and praying. In his prayers, which attained ever greater virtue with the passing days, he prepared his mind to receive the divine mysteries and splendors, and his body to withstand the assaults of the devils against whom he fought.

One day, Francis came forth from his cell to pray in the cavity of a hollow rock, from which point to the ground is a very great height, a terrible and fearful precipice. Suddenly the devil came in a terrible form, with much noise, and struck Francis, trying to make him fall into the chasm. Francis, having nowhere to run, and being unable to endure the cruel vision of the demon, turned around and pressed his hands and face and body against the rock, commending himself to God while trying to find a handhold. Now, God does not allow His servants to be tempted beyond what they can endure, and so, suddenly, the rock miraculously hollowed itself to the exact shape of Francis's body, and received him as if he had immersed himself in liquid wax. The face and hands of St. Francis are imprinted on that rock today.

The devil could not cast Francis down from there, but long afterward, when Francis was dead, he did just that to a dear and devout friar who was building a real bridge so that the faithful could travel safely to the place of the miracle. The friar was balancing a thick log on his head, and he fell into the chasm log and all. God, who had saved Francis from falling, also saved the devout friar, who, as he fell, loudly commended himself to Francis, who in turn immediately appeared and set him on the rocks below, unharmed.

The other friars, who heard his cry as he fell, believed that he had been dashed to pieces because of the great height from which he had fallen. With much sorrow and weeping they took a bier and went around to the other side of the mountain to search for his remains. When they descended from the mountain, the friar who had fallen met them, still balancing the log on his head and loudly singing the *Te Deum laudamus*. He told the friars how the blessed Francis had rescued him, and then they all traveled to the little cell, singing the *Te Deum laudamus* all together, and praising and thanking God together with Francis for the miracle he had performed.

Sierra

ANTONIO MACHADO

*A<small>NTONIO</small> M<small>ACHADO</small> (1875–1939), a native of Seville, wrote many hymns
of love to the Sierra Nevada, which overlooks the city.*

> *In the white mountains . . .*
> *Minute snow*
> *and wind in the face.*
> *Within the pines*
> *the white snow*
> *erases the road.*
> *A fierce wind blows*
> *from Urbión to Moncayo.*
> *Highlands of Soria!*

> ....

> *It is the grayness of oaks*

and the barrenness of stones.
When the sun sets
the river awakens.
          Oh, faraway mountains,
mauve and violet!
In the shadowy air
only the river makes a sound.
          Purple moon
of an ancient evening,
in a cold field
more lunar than earthly!

....

          Soria of blue mountains
and of violet barrens,
how many times I've dreamed
of this flowery valley
where the Guadalquivir flows
past golden orange trees
to the sea.

AIps

SAMUEL TAYLOR COLERIDGE,

JOHANN WOLFGANG VON GOETHE,

SIR LESLIE STEPHEN, MRS. H. W. COLE,

CHARLES DICKENS, ERNEST HEMINGWAY

In his poem "Hymn Before Sunrise, in the Vale of Chamouni," SAMUEL TAYLOR COLERIDGE (1772–1834) commemorates a view of 15,771-foot Mont Blanc.

O dread and silent Mount! I gazed upon thee,
Till thou, still present to the bodily sense,
Didst vanish from my thought: entranced in prayer,
I worshipped the invisible alone.

Thou too again, stupendous Mountain! thou,
That as I raise my head, awhile bowed low
In adoration, upward from thy base
Slow travelling with dim eyes suffused with tears,
Solemnly seemest, like a vapoury cloud,
To rise before me.—Rise, O ever rise,
Rise like a cloud of incense from the Earth!

Thou kingly Spirit throned among the hills,
Thou dread ambassador from Earth to Heaven,
Great Hierarch! tell thou the silent sky,
And tell the stars, and tell yon rising Sun,
Earth, with her thousand voices, praises God.

JOHANN WOLFGANG VON GOETHE (1749–1832) had a similarly ethereal view of Mont Blanc, as he reports in his Travels in Switzerland and Italy *(1779).*

It grew darker and darker as we approached the valley of Chamonix, and when at last we entered it, only the big massive features were discernible. The stars came out one by one, and above the summits in front of us a light whose origin we could not explain. It was clear, but like the Milky Way without sharpness and brilliance, and seemed closer, like the Pleiades. We could not take our eyes away from it, and as our position changed we saw it tower above the tops of all the mountains round us in a pyramid which seemed to have a light concealed within it, gleaming out of the dark as a glow-worm might, and at last we realized that this must be the peak of Mont Blanc itself. It was strangely, surpassingly beautiful. It shone down on us, with the stars that clustered round it, not indeed with their twinkling light, but with that of a broad radiant body, belonging to a higher sphere; it was difficult to believe it had its roots in earth.

SIR LESLIE STEPHEN (1832–1904) was a freethinking writer whose work in such publications as Cornhill Magazine *and* Pall Mall Gazette *helped*

raise English journalism to heights it has not since attained. His lives of Jonathan Swift, Alexander Pope, Samuel Johnson, George Eliot, and other writers are still standard references. He was also largely responsible for introducing mountaineering to England, and served as president of the Alpine Club for several years, writing essays for its journal that he later collected in The Playground of Europe *(1871).*

Virginia Woolf, Stephen's daughter, considered "Sunset on Mont Blanc," a powerful study in mountain moods, the best work her father ever wrote.

The ordinary view from Mont Blanc is not specially picturesque—and for a sufficient reason. The architect has concentrated his whole energies in producing a single impression. Everything has been so arranged as to intensify the sense of vast height and an illimitable horizon. In a good old guidebook I have read, on the authority (I think) of Pliny, that the highest mountain in the world is 300,000 feet above the sea; and one is apt to fancy, on ascending Mont Blanc, that the guess is not so far out. The effect is perfectly unique in the Alps; but it is produced at a certain sacrifice. All dangerous rivals have been removed to such a distance as to become apparently insignificant. No grand mass can be admitted into the foreground; for the sense of vast size is gradually forced upon you by the infinite multiplicity of detail.

Mont Blanc must be like an Asiatic despot, alone and supreme, with all inferior peaks reverently couched at his feet. If a man, previously as ignorant of geography as a boy who has just left a public school, could be transported for a moment to the summit, his impression would be that the Alps resembled a village of a hundred hovels grouped round a stupendous cathedral. Fully to appreciate this effect requires a certain familiarity with Alpine scenery, for otherwise the effect produced is a dwarfing of the inferior mountains into pettiness instead of an exaltation of Mont Blanc into almost portentous magnificence. Grouped around you at unequal distances lie innumerable white patches, looking like the tented encampments of scattered army corps. Hold up a glove at arm's length, and it will cover the whole of such a group. On the boundless plain beneath (I say "plain," for the greatest mountain system of Europe appears to have subsided into a rather uneven plain) it is a mere spot, a trifling dent upon the huge shield on whose central boss you are placed. But you know, though at first you can hardly realise the knowledge, that that insignificant discoloration represents a whole mountain district. One spot, for example, represents the clustered peaks of the Bernese Oberland; a block, as big as a pebble, is the soaring Jungfrau, the terrible mother of avalanches; a barely distinguishable wrinkle is the reverse of those snowy wastes of the Blumlisalp, which seem to be suspended above the terrace of Berne, thirty miles away; and that little whitish stream represents the greatest icestream of the Alps, the huge Aletsch Glacier, whose monstrous proportions have been impressed upon you by hours of laborious plodding. One patch contains the main sources from which the Rhine descends to the German ocean, two or three more overlook the Italian plains and encircle the basin of the Po; from a more distant group flows the Danube, and from your feet the snows melt to supply the Rhône. You feel that you are in some sense looking down upon Europe from Rotterdam to Venice and from Varna to Marseilles. The vividness of the impression depends entirely upon the degree to which you can realise the immense size of all these immeasurable details.

Now, in the morning, the usual time for an ascent, the details are necessarily vague, because the noblest part of the view lies between the sun and the spectator. But in the evening light each ridge, and peak, and glacier stands out with startling distinctness, and each, therefore, is laden with its weight of old association. There, for example, was the grim Matterhorn: its angular dimensions were of infinitesimal minuteness; it would puzzle a mathematician to say how small a space its image would occupy on his retina; but, within that small space, its form was defined with exquisite accuracy; and we could recognise the precise configuration of the wild labyrinth of rocky ridges up which the earlier adventurers forced their way from the Italian side. And thus we not only knew, but felt that at our feet was lying a vast slice of the map of Europe. The effect was to exaggerate the apparent height, till the view had about it something portentous and unnatural: it seemed to be such a view as could be granted not even to mountaineers of earthly mould, but rather to some genie from the *Arabian Nights,* flying high above a world tinted with the magical pouring of old romance.

Thus distinctly drawn, though upon so minute a scale, every rock and slope preserved its true value, and the impression of stupendous height became almost oppressive as it was forced upon the imagination that a whole world of mountains, each of them a mighty mass in itself, lay couched far beneath our feet, reaching across the whole diameter of the vast panorama. And now, whilst occupied in drinking in that strange sensation, and allowing our minds to recover their equilibrium from the first staggering shock of astonishment, began the strange spectacle of which we were the sole witnesses. One long, delicate cloud, suspended in mid-air just below the sun, was gradually adorning itself with prismatic colouring. Round the limitless horizon ran a faint fog-bank, unfortunately not quite thick enough to produce that depth of colouring which sometimes makes an Alpine sunset inexpressibly gorgeous.

The weather—it was the only complaint we had to make—erred on the side of fineness. But the colouring was brilliant enough to prevent any thoughts of serious disappointment. The long series of western ranges melted into a uniform hue as the sun declined in their rear. Amidst their folds the Lake of Geneva became suddenly lighted up in a faint yellow gleam. To the east a blue gauze seemed to cover valley by valley as they sank into night and the intervening ridges rose with increasing distinctness, or rather it seemed that some fluid of exquisite delicacy of colour and substance was flooding all the lower country beneath the great mountains. Peak by peak the high snowfields caught the rosy glow and shone like signal-fires across the dim breadths of delicate twilight. Like Xerxes, we looked over the countless host sinking into rest, but with the rather different reflection, that a hundred years hence they would probably be doing much the same things, whilst we should have long ceased to take any interest in the performance.

And suddenly began a more startling phenomenon. A vast cone, with its apex pointing away from us, seemed to be suddenly cut out from the world beneath; night was within its borders and the twilight still all round; the blue mists were quenched where it fell, and for the instant we could scarcely tell what was the origin of this strange appearance. Some unexpected change seemed to have taken place in the programme; as though a great fold in the curtain had suddenly given way, and dropped on to part of the scenery. Of course a moment's reflection explained the meaning of this uncanny intruder; it was the giant shadow of Mont Blanc, testifying to his supremacy over all meaner eminences. It is difficult to say how sharply marked was the outline, and how startling was the contrast between this pyramid of darkness and the faintly-lighted spaces beyond its influence; a huge inky blot seemed to have suddenly fallen upon the landscape. As we gazed we could see it move. It swallowed up ridge by ridge, and its sharp point crept steadily from one landmark to another down the broad Valley of Aosta. We were standing, in fact, on the point of the gnomon of a gigantic sundial, the face of which was formed by thousands of square miles of mountain and valley. So clear was the outline that, if figures had been scrawled upon glaciers and ridges, we could have told the time to a second; indeed, we were half-inclined to look for our own shadows at a distance so great that the whole villages would be represented by a scarcely distinguishable speck of colouring.

The huge shadow, looking ever more strange and magical, struck the distant Becca di Nona, and then climbed into the dark region where the broader shadow of the world was rising into the eastern sky. By some singular effect of perspective, rays of darkness seemed to be converging from above our heads to a point immediately above the apex of the shadowy cone. For a time it seemed that there was a kind of anti-sun in the east, pouring out not light, but deep shadow as it rose. The apex soon reached the horizon, and then to our surprise began climbing the distant sky. Would it never stop, and was Mont Blanc capable of overshadowing not only the earth but the sky? For a minute or two I fancied, in a bewildered way, that this unearthly object would fairly rise from the ground and climb upwards to the zenith. But rapidly the lights went out upon the great army of mountains; the snow all round took the livid hue which immediately succeeds an Alpine sunset, and almost at a blow the shadow of Mont Blanc was swallowed up in the general shade of night.

The display had ceased suddenly at its culminating point, and it was highly expedient for the spectators to retire. We had no time to lose if we would get off the summit before the grip of the frost should harden the snows into an ice-crust; and in a minute we were running and sliding downwards at our best pace towards the familiar Corridor. Yet as we went the sombre magnificence of the scenery seemed for a time to increase. We were between the day and the night. The western heavens were of the most brilliant blue with spaces of transparent green, whilst a few scattered cloudlets gloated as if with internal fire. To the east the night rushed up furiously, and it was difficult to imagine that the dark purple sky was really cloud less and not blackened by the rising of some portentous storm. That it was, in fact, cloudless, appeared from the unbroken disc of the full moon, which, if I may venture to say so, had a kind of silly expression as though it were a bad imitation of the sun, totally unable to keep the darkness in order.

With how sad steps, oh moon, thou climb'st the sky,
How silently and with how wan a face!

as Sidney exclaims. And truly, set in that strange gloom the moon looked wan and miserable enough; the lingering sunlight showed by contrast that she was but a feeble source of illumination; and, but for her half-comic look of helplessness, we might have sympathised with the astronomers who tell us that she is nothing but a vast perambulating tombstone, proclaiming to all mankind in the words of the familiar epitaph, "As I am now, you soon shall be!" To speak after the fashion of early mythologies, one might fancy that some supernatural cuttlefish was shedding his ink through the heavens to distract her, and that the poor moon had but a bad chance of escaping his clutches.

Hurrying downwards with occasional glances at the sky, we had soon reached the Grand Plateau, whence our further retreat was secure, and from that wildest of mountain fastnesses we saw the last striking spectacle of the evening. In some sense it was perhaps the most impressive of all. As all Alpine travellers know, the Grand Plateau is a level space of evil omen, embraced by a vast semicircle of icy slopes. The avalanches, which occasionally descend across it, and which have caused more than one catastrophe, give it a bad reputation; and at night the icy jaws of the great mountain seem to be enclosing you in a fatal embrace. At this moment there was something half grotesque in its sternness. Light and shade were contrasted in a manner so bold as to be almost bizarre. One half of the cirque was of a pallid white against the night, which was rushing up still blacker and thicker, except that a few daring stars shone out like fiery sparks against a pitchy canopy; the other half, reflecting the black night, was relieved against the last gleams of daylight; in front a vivid band of blood-red light burnt along the horizon, beneath which seemed to lie an abyss of mysterious darkness. It was the last struggle between night and day, and the night seemed to assume a more ghastly ferocity as the day sank, pale and cold, before its antagonist. The Grand Plateau, indeed, is a fit scene for such contrasts; for there in mid-day you may feel the reflection of the blinding snows like the blast of a furnace, where a few hours before you were realising the keenest pangs of frost-bite. The cold and the night were now the conquerors, and the angry sunset-glow seemed to grudge the victory. The light rapidly faded, and the darkness, no longer seen in the strange contrast, subsided to its ordinary tones. The magic was gone; and it was in a commonplace though lovely summer night that we reached our resting-place at the Grands Mulets.

We felt that we had learnt some new secrets as to the beauty of mountain scenery, but the secrets were of that kind which not even the initiated can reveal. A great poet might interpret the sentiment of the mountains into song; but no poet could pack into any definite proposition or series of propositions the strange thoughts that rise in different spectators of such a scene. All that I at last can say is that some indefinable mixture of exhilaration and melancholy pervades one's mind; one feels like a kind of cheerful Tithonus "at the quiet limit of the world," looking down from a magic elevation upon the

dim fields about the homes
Of happy men that have the power to die.

One is still of the earth, earthy; for freezing toes and snow-parched noses are lively reminders that one has not become an immortal. Even on the top of Mont Blanc one may be a very long way from heaven. And yet the mere physical elevation of a league above the sea-level seems to raise one by moments into a sphere above the petty interests of everyday life. Why that should be so, and by what strange threads of association the reds and blues of a gorgeous sunset, the fantastic shapes of clouds and shadows at that dizzy height, and the dramatic changes that sweep over the boundless region beneath your feet, should stir you like mysterious music, or, indeed, why music itself should have such power, I leave to philosophers to explain. This only I know, that even the memory of that summer evening on the top of Mont Blanc has power to plunge me into strange reveries not to be analysed by any capacity, and still less capable of expression by the help of a few black marks on white paper.

MRS. H. W. COLE, a proper Victorian lady, offered this advice for women tourists to the Alps in her book A Lady's Tour Round Monte Rosa *(1859).*

Of course every lady engaged on an Alpine journey will wear a broad-brimmed hat, which will relieve her from the encumbrance of a parasol. She should also have a dress of some light woollen material, such as carmelite or alpaca, which, in case of bad weather, does not look utterly forlorn when it has once been wetted and dried. Small rings should be sewn inside the seams of the dress, and a cord passed through them, the ends of which should be knotted together in such a way that the whole dress may be drawn up at a moment's notice to the requisite height. If the dress is too long, it catches the stones, especially when coming down hill, and sends them rolling on those below. I have heard more than one gentleman complain of painful blows suffered from such accidents.

Such good advice as Mrs. Cole's was not always heeded, as CHARLES DICK-ENS (1812–1870) writes in his 1857 novel Little Dorrit, *in a passage describing the arrival of a group of travelers to the then-remote Swiss monastery of Saint Bernard.*

Seen from those solitudes, and from the pass of the Great Saint Bernard, which was one of them, the ascending Night came up the mountain like a rising water. When it at last rose to the walls of the convent of the Great Saint Bernard, it was as if that weather-beaten structure were another Ark, and floated away upon the shadowy waves.

Darkness, outstripping some visitors on mules, had risen thus to the rough convent walls, when those travelers were yet climbing the mountain. As the heat of the glowing day, when they had stopped to drink at the streams of melted ice and snow, was changed to the searching cold of the frosty rarefied night air at a great height, so the fresh beauty of the lower journey had yielded to barrenness and desolation. A craggy track, up which the mules, in single file, scrambled and turned from block to block, as though they were ascending the broken staircase of a gigantic ruin, was their way now. No trees were to be seen, nor any vegetable growth, save a poor brown scrubby moss, freezing in the chinks of rock. Blackened skeleton arms of wood by the wayside pointed upward to the convent, as if the ghosts of former travelers, overwhelmed by the snow, haunted the scene of their distress. Icicle-hung caves and cellars built for refuges from sudden storms, were like so many whispers of the perils of the place; never-resting wreaths and mazes of mist wandered about, hunted by a moaning wind; and snow, the besetting danger of the mountain, against which all its defenses were taken, drifted sharply down.

The file of mules, jaded by their day's work, turned and wound slowly up the steep ascent; the foremost led by a guide on foot, in his broad-brimmed hat and round jacket, carrying a mountain staff or two upon his shoulder, with whom another guide conversed. There was no speaking among the string of riders. The sharp cold, the fatigue of the journey, and a new sensation of a catching in the breath, partly as if they had just emerged from very clear crisp water, and partly as if they had been sobbing, kept them silent.

At length, a light on the summit of the rocky staircase gleamed through the snow and mist. The guides called to the mules, the mules pricked up their drooping heads, the travelers' tongues were loosened, and in a sudden burst of slipping, climbing, jingling, clinking, and talking, they arrived at the convent door.

Other mules had arrived not long before, some with peasant-riders and some with goods, and had trodden the snow about the door into a pool of mud. Riding saddles and bridles, packsaddles and strings of bells, mules and men, lanterns, torches, sacks, provender, barrels, cheeses, kegs of honey and butter, straw bundles and packages of many shapes, were crowded confusedly together in this thawed quagmire, and about the steps. Up here in the clouds, every thing was seen through cloud, and seemed dissolving into cloud. The breath of the men was cloud, the breath of the mules was cloud, the lights were encircled by cloud, speakers close at hand were not seen for cloud, though their voices and all other sounds were surprisingly clear. Of the cloudy line of mules hastily tied to rings in the wall, one would bite another, or kick another, and then the whole mist would be disturbed with men diving into it, and cries of men and beasts coming out of it, and no bystander discerning what was wrong. In the midst of this, the great stable of the convent, occupying the basement story, and entered by the basement door, outside which all the disorder was, poured forth its contribution of cloud, as if the whole rugged edifice were filled with nothing else, and would collapse as soon as it had emptied itself, leaving the snow to fall upon the bare mountain summit.

While all this noise and hurry were rife among the living travelers, there, too, silently assembled in a grated house, half a dozen paces removed, with the same cloud enfolding them, and the same snow flakes drifting in upon them, were the dead travelers found upon the mountain. The mother, storm-belated many winters ago, still standing in the corner with her baby at her breast; the man who had frozen with his arm raised to his mouth in fear of hunger, still pressing it with his dry lips after years and years. An awful company, mysteriously come together! A wild destiny for that mother to have foreseen. "Surrounded by so many, and such companions, upon whom I never looked and never shall look; I and my child will dwell together inseparable, on the Great Saint Bernard, outlasting generations who will come to see us, and will never know our name, or one word of our story but the end."

The living travelers thought little or nothing of the dead just then. They thought much more of alighting at the convent door, and warming themselves at the convent fire. Disengaged from the turmoil, which was already calming down as the crowd of mules began to be bestowed in the stable, they hurried shivering up the steps and into the building. There was a smell within, coming up from the floor of tethered beasts, like the smell of a menagerie of wild animals. There were strong arched galleries within, huge stone piers, great staircases, and thick walls pierced with small sunken windows—fortifications against the mountain storms, as if they had been human enemies. There were gloomy vaulted sleeping rooms within, intensely cold, but clean and hospitably prepared for guests. Finally, there was a parlor for guests to sit in and to sup in, where a table was already laid, and where a blazing fire shone red and high.

In this room, after having had their quarters for the night allotted to them by two young Fathers, the travelers presently drew round the hearth. They were in three parties; of whom the first, as the most numerous and important, was the slowest, and had been overtaken by one of the others on the way up. It consisted of an elderly lady, two gray-haired gentlemen, two young ladies, and their brother. These were attended (not to mention four guides) by a courier, two footmen, and two waiting-maids: which strong body of inconvenience was accommodated elsewhere under the same roof. The party that had overtaken them, and followed in their train, consisted of only three members: one lady and two gentlemen. The third party, which had ascended from the valley on the Italian side of the Pass, and had arrived first, were four in number: a plethoric, hungry, and silent German tutor in spectacles, on a tour with three young men, his pupils, all plethoric, hungry, and silent, and all in spectacles.

These three groups sat round the fire eyeing each other dryly, and waiting for supper. Only one among them, one of the gentlemen belonging to the party of three, made advances toward conversation. Throwing out his lines for the Chief of the important tribe, while addressing himself to his own companions, he remarked, in a tone of voice which included all the company, if they chose to be included, that it had been a long day, and that he felt for the ladies. That he feared one of the young ladies was not a strong or accustomed traveler, and had been over fatigued two or three hours ago. That he had observed, from his station in the rear, that she sat her mule as if she were exhausted. That he had, twice or thrice afterward, done himself the honor of inquiring of one of the guides, when he fell behind, how the young lady did. That he had been enchanted to learn that she had recovered her spirits, and that it had been but a passing discomfort. That he trusted (by this time he had secured the eyes of the Chief, and addressed him) he might be permitted to express his hope that she was now none the worse, and that she would not regret having made the journey.

"My daughter, I am obliged to you, sir," returned the Chief, "is quite restored, and has been greatly interested."

"New to mountains, perhaps?" said the insinuating traveler.

"New to—ha—to mountains," said the Chief.

"But you are familiar with them, sir?" the insinuating traveler assumed.

"I am—hum—tolerably familiar. Not of late years. Not of late years," replied the Chief, with a flourish of his hand.

The insinuating traveler, acknowledging the flourish with an inclination of his head, passed from the Chief to the second young lady, who had not yet been referred to, otherwise than as one of the ladies in whose behalf he felt so sensitive an interest.

He hoped she was not incommoded by the fatigues of the day.

"Incommoded certainly," returned the young lady, "but not tired."

The insinuating traveler complimented her on the justice of the distinction. It was what he had meant to say. Every lady must doubtless be incommoded, by having to do with that proverbially unaccommodating animal, the mule.

"We have had, of course," said the young lady, who was rather reserved and haughty, "to leave the carriages and fourgon at Martigny. And the impossibility of bringing any thing that one wants to this inaccessible place, and the necessity of leaving every comfort behind, is not convenient."

"A savage place, indeed," said the insinuating traveler.

The elderly lady, who was a model of accurate dressing, and whose manner was perfect, considered as a piece of machinery, here interposed a remark in a low soft voice.

"But, like other inconvenient places," she observed, "it must be seen. As a place much spoken of, it is necessary to see it."

"Oh! I have not the least objection to seeing it, I assure you, Mrs. General," returned the other, carelessly.

"You, madam," said the insinuating traveler, "have visited this spot before?"

"Yes," returned Mrs. General. "I have been here before. Let me recommend you, my dear," to the former young lady, "to shade your face from the hot wood, after exposure to the mountain air and snow. You too, my dear," to the other and younger lady, who immediately did so; while the former merely said, "Thank you, Mrs. General, I am perfectly comfortable, and prefer remaining as I am."

Famed as an outdoor writer and journalist long before his novels and short stories achieved wide circulation, ERNEST HEMINGWAY *(1899–1961) filed this report from the mountains of Switzerland for the* Toronto Star Weekly *of December 22, 1923.*

While it was still dark, Ida, the little German maid, came in and lit the fire in the big porcelain stove, and the burning pine wood roared up the chimney.

Out the window the lake lay steel gray far down below, with the snow-covered mountains bulking jagged beyond it, and far away beyond it the massive tooth of the Dent du Midi beginning to lighten with the first touch of morning.

It was so cold outside. The air felt like something alive as I drew a deep breath. You could swallow the air like a drink of cold water.

I reached up with a boot and banged on the ceiling.

"Hey, Chink. It's Christmas!"

"Hooray!" came Chink's voice down from the little room under the roof of the chalet.

Herself was up in a warm, woolen dressing-robe, with the heavy goat's wool skiing socks.

Chink knocked at the door.

"Merry Christmas, mes enfants," he grinned. He wore the early morning garb of big, woolly dressing-robe and thick socks that made us all look like some monastic order.

In the breakfast-room we could hear the stove roaring and crackling. Herself opened the door.

Against the tall, white porcelain stove hung the three long skiing stockings, bulging and swollen with strange lumps and bulges. Around the foot of the stove were piled boxes. Two new shiny pairs of ash skis lay alongside the stove, too tall to stand in the low-ceilinged chalet room.

For a week we had each been making mysterious trips to the Swiss town below on the lake. Hadley and I, Chink and I, and Hadley and Chink, returning after dark with strange boxes and bundles that were concealed in various parts of the chalet. Finally we each had to make a trip alone. That was yesterday. Then last night we had taken turns on the stockings, each pledged not to sleuth.

Chink had spent every Christmas since 1914 in the army. He was our best friend. For the first time in years it seemed like Christmas to all of us.

We ate breakfast in the old, untasting, gulping, early morning Christmas way, unpacked the stockings, down to the candy mouse in the toe, each made a pile of our things for future gloating.

From breakfast we rushed into our clothes and tore down the icy road in the glory of the blue-white glistening alpine morning. The train was just pulling out. Chink and I shot the skis into the baggage car, and we all three swung aboard.

All Switzerland was on the move. Skiing parties, men, women, boys and girls, taking the train up the mountain, wearing their tight-fitting blue caps, the girls all in riding-breeches and puttees, and shouting and calling out to one another. Platforms jammed.

Everybody travels third class in Switzerland, and on a big day like Christmas the third class overflows and the overflow is crowded into the sacred red plush first class compartments.

Shouting and cheering the train crawled alongside the mountain, climbing up towards the top of the world.

There was no big Christmas dinner at noon in Switzerland. Everybody was out in the mountain air with a lunch in the rucksack and the prospect of the dinner at night.

When the train reached the highest point it made in the mountains, everybody piled out, the stacks of skis were unsorted from the baggage-car and transferred to an open flat car hooked on to a jerky little train that ran straight up the side of the mountain on cog wheels.

At the top we could look over the whole world, white, glistening in the powder snow, and ranges of mountains stretching off in every direction.

It was the top of a bob sled run that looped and turned in icy windings far below. A bob shot past, all the crew moving in time, and as it rushed at express train speed for the first turn, the crew all cried, "Ga-a-a-a-r!" and the bob roared in an icy smother around the curve and dropped off down the glassy run below.

No matter how high you are in the mountains there is always a slope going up.

There were long strips of seal-skin harnessed on our skis, running back from the tip to the base in a straight strip with the grain of the hair pointing back, so that you pushed right ahead through the snow going up hill. If your skis had a tendency to slide back the slipping movement would be checked by the seal-skin hairs. They would slide smoothly forward, but hold fast at the end of each thrusting stride.

Soon the three of us were high above the shoulder of the mountain that had seemed the top of the world. We kept going up in single file, sliding smoothly up through the snow in a long upward zig-zag.

We passed through the last of the pines and came out on a shelving plateau. Here came the first run-down—a half-mile sweep ahead. At the brow the skis seemed to drop out from under and in a hissing rush we all three swooped down the slope like birds.

On the other side it was thrusting, uphill, steady climbing again. The sun was hot and the sweat poured off us in the steady up-hill drive. There is no place you get so tanned as in the mountains in winter. Nor so hungry. Nor so thirsty.

Finally we hit the lunching place, a snowed-under old log cattle barn where the peasant's cattle would shelter in the summer when this mountain was green with pasture. Everything seemed to drop off sheer below us.

The air at that height, about 6,200 feet, is like wine. We put on our sweaters that had been in our ruck-sacks coming up, unpacked the lunch and the bottle of white wine, and lay back on our ruck-sacks and soaked in the sun. Coming up we had been wearing sun glasses against the glare of the snowfields, and now we took off the amber shaded goggles and looked out on a bright, new world.

"I'm really too hot," Herself said. Her face had burned coming up, even through the last crop of freckles and tan.

"You ought to use lampblack on your face," Chink suggested.

But there is no record of any woman that has ever yet been willing to use that famous mountaineer's specific against snowblindness and sun-burn.

It was no time after lunch and Herself's daily nap, while Chink and I practiced turns and stops on the slope, before the heat was gone out of the sun and it was time to start down. We took off the seal skins and waxed our skis.

Then in one long, dropping, swooping, heart-plucking rush we were off. A seven-mile run down and no sensation in the world that can compare with it. You do not make the seven miles in one run. You go as fast as you believe possible, then you go a good deal faster, then you give up all hope, then you don't know what happened, but the earth came up and over and over and you sat up and untangled yourself from your skis and looked around. Usually all three had spilled together. Sometimes there was no one in sight.

But there is no place to go except down. Down in a rushing, swooping, flying, plunging rush of fast ash blades through the powder snow.

Finally, in a rush we came out on to the road on the shoulder of the mountain where the cog-wheel railway had stopped coming up. Now we were all a shooting stream of skiers. All the Swiss were coming down, too. Shooting along the road in a seemingly endless stream.

It was too steep and slippery to stop. There was nothing to do but plunge along down the road as helpless as though you were in a mill race. So we went down. Herself was way ahead somewhere. We could see her blue beret occasionally before it got too dark. Down, down, down the road we went in the dusk, past chalets that were a burst of lights and Christmas merriment in the dark.

Then the long line of skiers shot into the black woods, swung to one side to avoid a team and sledge coming up the road, passed more chalets, their windows alight with the candles from the Christmas trees. As we dropped past a chalet, watching nothing but the icy road and the man ahead, we heard a shout from the lighted doorway.

"Captain! Captain! Stop here!"

It was the German-Swiss landlord of our chalet. We were running past it in the dark.

Ahead of us, spilled at the turn, we found Herself and we stopped in a sliding slither, knocked loose our skis, and the three of us hiked up the hill towards the lights of the chalet. The lights looked very cheerful against the dark pines of the hill, and inside was a big Christmas tree and a real Christmas turkey dinner, the table shiny with silver, the glasses tall and thin stemmed, the bottles narrow-necked, the turkey large and brown and beautiful, the side dishes all present, and Ida serving in a new crisp apron.

It was the kind of a Christmas you can only get on top of the world.

OCEANIA AND EREWHON

This snow mountain is the navel of the world,

where snow leopards dance. . . .

There is no place more wonderful than this.

THE HUNDRED THOUSAND

SONGS OF MILAREPA

Mountain Dreaming

AUSTRALIAN ABORIGINAL MYTHS

The WARAMUNGGUWI PEOPLE of Arnhem Land tell this story about a low mountain range that borders their territory. "To come into dreaming" means something like to be made part of the creation.

Namarudu, lightning spirit, was going along looking for a place to live in when he saw an old man in the jungle, on his way to find fish. The old man looked around, and seeing Namarudu coming said to himself, "Oh! he's coming up to me, that dangerous fellow! He'll kill me—I can't do anything about it." He ran to hide in the densest part of the jungle. But Namarudu came closer and closer, and at last saw him. "Why are you afraid of me?" he asked the old man, "I won't hurt you, let's go and look for fish together." The old man said, "No, I won't go with you, because I'm afraid. I'm looking for people, many people living together. They are the same as I am; but you're Namarudu, you might kill me." He left him, went off to where those people were camped among the rocks; they were eating fish and meat and wild honey, killing goanna and watersnake. Afterward the old man went hunting again. But he heard Namarudu coming, running, making a noise like wind. "Maybe he's coming after me again!" Well, Namarudu came chasing him, he came running to where that man was standing. The man fled, saying, "Go away! I don't like you to come running up to me, I don't want you!" He went back, that Namarudu. And that man went back too, back to the others, where they were camping among the rocks.

Namarudu said to himself, "Shall I go and shut them up, where they're sleeping in the caves? Then they'll come into Dreaming for ever!" He was alone. But that man was back with the others eating meat and vegetable foods; and afterward they slept. In the night, Namarudu came up to where they were sleeping. He heard a little boy calling out, crying and crying, and he said, "That's their little boy crying! I'll go and look at them!" He went, he looked at the place, where they were all asleep. Well, he closed them in the caves, sealing them up. They couldn't do anything about getting out; he shut them in for ever. They slept, they tried to get up, they looked about—no, there was no hole anywhere, where before they used to leave the cave, because Namarudu had sealed them in. They got up, and one man called out: but they just came into Dreaming. They stand there in spirit, turned into stone. They remain there for ever, among the rocks where before Namarudu shut them in, at Mandjawaindjau, just west of Cannon Hill, not far from the East Alligator River. There they came into Dreaming for ever.

The YANKUNTJATJARA *relate this story about Ayers Rock, or Uluru, which lies in nearly the dead center of Australia.*

Uluru was created by two boys who were playing in the mud after a heavy rain. When they had finished they traveled south to Wiputa, in the Musgrave Ranges, and killed and ate a euro. Near Mount Conner, one of the boys threw a spear at a wallaby, but the club fell to the ground and created a freshwater spring. He refused to tell the other boy where this spring was, and the other boy nearly died of thirst. They began to fight, and they fought all the way up to the summit of Mount Conner, where their bodies became giant boulders.

Mount Cook

FREDA DU FAUR

A native Australian, FREDA DU FAUR moved with her family to New Zealand. She found that she was drawn more to mountaineering than to the family's ranching business, however, and in 1914 she scaled 12,349-foot Mount Cook, the first Anglo woman to do so. In this passage from her 1915 book The Conquest of Mount Cook, *she describes her first travels in the New Zealand mountains.*

People who live amongst the mountains all their lives, who have watched them at sunrise and sunset, in midday heat or moonlight glow, love them, I believe, as they love the sun and flowers, and take them as much for granted. They have no conception how the first sight of them strikes to the very heart-strings of that less fortunate individual, the hill-lover who lives in a mountainless country. From the moment my eyes rested on the snow-clad alps I worshipped their beauty and was filled with a passionate longing to touch those shining snows, to climb to their heights of silence and solitude, and feel myself one with the mighty forces around me. The great peaks towering into the sky before me touched a chord that all the wonders of my own land had never set vibrating, and filled a blank of whose very existence I had been unconscious. Many people realize the grandeur and beauty of the mountains, who are quite content to admire them from a distance, if strenuous physical exertion is the price they must pay for a nearer acquaintance. My chief desire as I gazed at them was to reach the snow and bury my hands in its wonderful whiteness, and dig and dig till my snow-starved Australian soul was satisfied that all this wonder of white was real and would not vanish at the touch.

To a restless, imaginative nature the fascination of the unknown is very great; from my childhood I never saw a distant range without longing to know what lay on the other side. So in the mountains the mere fact of a few thousand feet of rock and snow impeding my view was a direct challenge to climb and see what lay behind it. It is as natural to me to wish to climb as it is for the average New Zealander to be satisfied with peaceful contemplation from a distance.

The night of my arrival at the Hermitage the chief guide, Peter Graham, was introduced to me. Knowing his reputation as a fine and enthusiastic mountaineer, I felt sure that he, at least, would understand my craving for a nearer acquaintance with the mountains. I asked him what it was possible for a novice to attempt. After a few questions as to my walking capabilities, he suggested that I should accompany a party he was taking up the Sealy Range. Only an incident here and there remains of that climb. Firstly, I remember fulfilling my desire to dig in the snow (at the expense of a pair of very sunburnt hands) and joyously playing with it while the wiser members of the party looked on. Likewise I remember a long, long snow slope, up which we toiled in a burning sun, never seeming to get any nearer to the top. At length, when the summit came in sight, the others were so slow I could not contain my curiosity; so I struck out for myself instead of following in Graham's footsteps. Soon I stood alone on the crest of the range, and felt for the first time that wonderful thrill of happiness and triumph which repays the mountaineer in one moment for hours of toil and hardship. On the descent I experienced my first glissade; it was rather a steep slope, and I arrived at the bottom wrong side up, and inconveniently filled with snow. These facts, however, did not deter me from tramping back to the top just for the pleasure of doing the same thing all over again.

Mount Kare

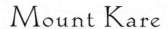

ISABELLA TREE

The highlands of New Guinea are the scene of the world's greatest current gold rush. As British journalist ISABELLA TREE recounts in Islands in the Clouds *(1994), she went to have a look for herself, a quest that involved hazardous travel.*

Before us, the power lines dictated a vertical track up the ridge dividing Porgera from the high plateaux of Kare and beyond. Dan approached the ridge with a look of grim determination.

"We've got to get this old heap of metal up the hill," he said, as if we were a train that might run out of steam. Then added, superstitiously perhaps, "Don't worry, old girl, you'll make it.

"People always think helicopters can hop over anything," he explained, sending flickers of alarm through my stomach. "They can't just take off on a vertical indefinitely, particularly at this altitude. I have a lot of respect for this ridge."

Our ascent was, indeed, alarmingly sluggish—like a lift that threatens to stop short of the top floor. When we cleared the summit, skimming the topmost trees, it was with a bare six feet to spare.

"Close one," said Dan.

We emerged onto a bald scape of waterlogged land. It was too high for trees—only eagles and kites patrolled the skies up here.

"Now this is Gold Country," said Dan as we descended with a flourish over the marshland. "There's so much gold here it's painful. Sometimes when the sun's at the right angle, you can see it glinting at you from the rivers."

He turned the chopper over a muddy yellow waterway wriggling across the valley floor.

"This river's a gold mine in itself. It's supplied by run-off from all these mountains around us. It's positively bulging with gold. That little lake at the end there is causing excitement at the moment. But I doubt it will come to much. For the time being anyway it's proving logistically impossible to excavate."

The lake was actually a sinkhole, disappearing two thousand feet into an underground shaft. The river tumbled down in a great waterfall which, over the millennia, had carved out a basin in the rock like a giant soup ladle. All the gold particles suspended in the water were being caught in this ladle, while the river itself ran on over the top and continued down towards the Sepik. Earlier in the year, geologists using the latest South African technology had sent a scoop down into the ladle and pulled up pure gold. So far, however, they had found no economical way of retrieving the rest. It was hardly surprising that earlier prospectors had returned verdicts of no interest when they panned the lowland rivers; the Highlands had retained their wealth in a geographical gold pan.

We swung round towards Mt Kare and Dan pointed to a patch of ground littered with plastic and wooden stakes. The earth had been torn and chewed and spat aside.

"That's the old Mt Kare camp site," he shouted, "and those are the holes where the villagers dug for gold with their bare hands. I used to come here myself in the rush, along with every other weathercock in the business. At one point, they said the area above Mt Kare was the most congested airspace in the world. It's a wonder, without any traffic control, not one chopper went down.

"We used to hover over the holes to see if any of the diggers wanted a ride. See, they couldn't walk out 'cos they'd get mugged by rascals waiting for 'em in the mountains. So they'd hold up a nugget and I'd come down for a look. If it didn't look big enough I'd shake my head and sure enough, this guy—muddier than a pig in a feeding trough some of 'em—would reach into his pockets and pull out a bigger one. Then I'd lower the chopper and he'd climb onto the skids and up into the cockpit. Got myself a piece weighing ten ounces once.

"Sounds a bit out of order doesn't it? But that's what PNG [Papua New Guinea] is all about. Some guys used to chopper their gold right out to Australia—tax free. There's no telling how much of Mt Kare left the country in '88. Those were crazy days.

"Now that's the old lady herself—Mt Kare," he said spinning to one side. "You can see the CRA mine site next to the original landslide. It's all fenced off now to keep out the villagers. They're pumping up water from the river below to help them wash the remaining ore out of the mountain."

The landslide was a bitter disappointment after the fantastic tales we'd been hearing. The sad little mud slide down one side of a small hill seemed an unlikely instigator of the biggest local gold rush in history. It belied the havoc it had caused.

Beyond the mountain, by the Gewa River, which had thronged with panners only three years before, were two tiny camp sites: the last of the illegal prospectors who made their living scratching for gold in the surrounding country or breaking into the mine site at night.

Our detour to Mt Kare had taken us away from the power lines, so we circled the mountain and turned into a southerly wind to catch up with them. Strung out with orange warning balls like ships' buoys, they led us nearer the Indonesian border. Every half-mile or so, even over the most difficult terrain, the line was punctuated by wooden helicopter platforms for service access. They were set ingeniously into bare rock or secured by deep foundations in the wet ground.

With a fractional drop in altitude dense forest resumed, and in the treetops giant cobwebs glistened in the sunlight. The power lines were leading
us into a descent from a belt of mountains that had averaged 11,500 feet to
the gas drill site amongst the limestone karst of the Karius Range which
peaked at around 8200 feet. With the heat of mid-morning, cloud had risen
from the valleys and now lay like a thick sponge below us. We circled dizzily,
clutching the arm rests and searching for a break in the cloud. When we
found it we plummeted through the shreds of condensation to a gloomier,
sun-deprived world below. It took seconds to recover from the nausea of
several negative G's.

"Sorry about that," said Dan, "those holes can close up fast as you find
them. You've got to take your chance soon as you see it."

Then he added, with some satisfaction, "But that's what we're looking
for. There's Hides."

Before us rose the forest-covered mountain of Tumbudu and, perched
on its pinnacle, the new Hides gas operation, no more than a single drill hole
in a meagre acre of cleared trees. From it, down a precipitous cliff, ran the
pipeline pumping liquid gas to the power station four miles away on the valley floor. Just below the discovery site, a secondary well was being drilled.
"They're going to be pumping ten million cubic feet of gas a day from those
things," shouted Dan. "But the plant's not finished so nothing's running
yet. You can see the station down there, on the Tagari River. It covers about
twenty acres, but they've also got a camp further downriver and a forward
base at Kobalu, only twelve miles from Tari."

Even with gold and oil discoveries on its doorstep, the Tari Basin had remained a haven from the chaotic development in the rest of PNG. It remained geographically isolated, culturally self-confident and fiercely
independent. It was inhabited by some of the most ferocious of all the High-
land tribes, the Hull Wigmen, who were the last large valley population to
be contacted in the explorations of the 1930s. . . .

We flew along the eastern side of the valley, which was bordered by the
same massive range of mountains that we had crossed to enter Tari from the
north. The range here reached 11,500 feet once again, with the Doma Peaks
rising spectacularly to 11,700 feet. This was the barrier which separated

Tari and the Southern Highlands from Enga and which, even now, presented a terrifying obstacle to pilots. The lowest pass was the Tari Gap—one
of the most notorious piloting black spots in PNG and subject to momen-
tary eclipses of cloud. Strangely, perhaps, it had an appetite for mission
planes. Pilots flying for MAF—the Mission Aviation Fellowship—had the
worst crash record. They had a reputation, it must be said, for flying on a
wing and a prayer. Some had stickers on their flight bags saying "God is my
copilot." Others boasted of flying with a Bible for a flight manual. All of
them seemed to push themselves just that little bit further than good sense
alone would allow. The Huli Wigmen had another explanation: they said it
was simply Tari claiming rightful payback for the intrusions of the outside
world.

"Dozens of pilots have met their Maker here," said Dan. "I've said a few
Hail Marys here myself on some occasions."

As if on cue the Tari Gap flaunted itself through the drifting cloud
ahead. Dan's casual and almost continuous banter was abruptly suspended
as he applied all his concentration to the challenge ahead. Around us in the
forest great waterfalls crashed noiselessly and white cockatoos and multicolored parrots were flushed from the treetops. We broke blindly through
the gap and out into the miracle of life ever after. The Erave River meandered lazily in the sunshine as if nothing had happened.

Pele

HAWAIIAN MYTH

Hawaiian mythology includes manifold stories of the goddess Pele, who, spurned and raped, assembled a cohort of fire gods in the heart of Kilauea, once a tall mountain but now a crater 3,646 feet deep, to visit volcanic destruction on the land. NATHANIEL EMERSON collected several versions in the early 1900s.

> Wild the sea-mist at Kohala-loa,
> Sea roughed by the breeze from the upper hills,
> Sea that peeps o'er the cliffs of Kupehau,
> Invading the groves of pandamus;
> It reaches the lowlands of Maui—
> The sea of this Goddess, this Queen.
> The lehuas are twisted like garlands
> At the touch of this sea of god Pele;
> For Pele, indeed, is my god.
> Wonder and awe possess me!

Thou mountain wall all swathed in mist,
Now groans the mountain-apple tree;
I see a fire of blazing rocks;
I see an aged dame, who snores
On lava plate, now hot, now cold;
Now 'tis canoe in shape, well propped,
A chock 'neath bow, midships, astern;
Needs bail the waist where drains the bilge,
Else salt will crust like staring eye—
Gray roving eye of lawless Niheu.
Wonder and awe possess me!

On famed Moloka'i of Hina,
At the pall of Unu-ohua,
Where burn the lamps of Haupu,
Assemble the throng of little gods.
Then comes forth Pele, a great god,
Haumea and Hiiaka,
And Kukuena and Okaoka:
If the small fire burns, let it burn!
'Tis the beaming of Pele's eye,
The flashing of heavenly fire.
Wonder and awe possess me!

Now to Nanati of Ka-ula-hea;
At Mauna-lei Pele plaits her a wreath;
She plaits it of i-e-ie;
Hiiaka pelts head with ginger cone;
Haumea anoints her body;
And Pele eats with zest the flesh
From the turtle of Poli-hua—
A young thing, short in the neck,
Backed like a crab from the sea,

Like a sea-turtle plated and patterned—
Turned into meat for Pele,
Food for the heavenly flame.
Wonder and awe possess me!

From the ether above Kaua'i
To the blossoms afloat at Wailua
Ranges the flight of Pele's gaze.
She sees Oahu floating afar;
Feels thirst for the watery mirage;
Inhales the scent of mokihana—
The bath-water of Hiiaka.
She once had a contest there;
She had no tenant to guard the place.
Pele spurns with her feet the long waves;
They give back a flash like her eye,
A flash that's repeated on high.
Wonder and awe possess me!

When Pele came voyaging from the east
And landed at Mo'o-kini—
The rain poured down at Ku-malae—
Her people set up an image,
And there they made their abode,
With the workmen who carve the canoe;
And they offered prayers and gave thanks;
Then Pele led them in journey
To the cape of Lele-iwi,
Where they breathed the incense of hala.
With Mokau-lele's rich lehua
Goddess Pele weaved her a wreath.
They built a village at Pu'u-lena,
Her bedroom at Papa-lau-ahi,

A mighty hall at Kilauea.
Wonder and awe possess me!

When Pele fell through from Kahiki
Bitter the rain, lightning and quaking—
The big-dropped rain that shatters the leaves
Of the women folk in Mau-kele's wilds.
Pele came in the dusk of the night,
With toss and sway of the long-backed waves.
The ocean heaved at Pele's rush;
The great god thundered in heaven;
The strata of earth were uptorn;
The reef-plates broken, crushed; and rent
Was the surf-plank of Kane at Maui.
What a piling of portents by the Sun-god
Over the Green Lake Ka-hala-loa!
Wonder and awe possess me!

It was Wa'a gazed on the fishing fleet,
His watch-tower the cliffs of Kohala,
While the witch-ruler, O Pu'u-loa,
Entreated the wayfaring one,
And the goddess who gilds the lehua
Set aglow Maka-noni's sunlit verge.
One day for gathering and choosing
The flowers devoted to worship,
The next day in upland frosty Huoi.
The earth-creatures glimmer and glow
While the eastern sun tops Kumu-kahi.
Sidewise the black crab springs from his hole
And Kohala spreads out 'neath the orb
That fails to give warmth to the night,
And the Sun hangs low in the sky,

And the clouds, they canopy heaven.
Wonder and awe possess me!

Aua'a-hea meets death, spite of
Steam-bath,—a boar unpurged of bristles—
And poultice hot of aheahea,
An herb that serves as a dish for the gods,
A tidbit for the king's table.
Thunder resounds in the heavens; rain falls,
Bitter as tears of Ka-ula-hea;
Clouds, torn and ragged, fill the sky,
A piled-up ominous cloud-pillar,
A fabric reared by heaven's rain-god—
A collect of evils was that.
The gods were aghast at the scandal:
For once Pele found herself duped;
For once Pele shifted in bed;
For once Pele drank to the dregs—
The cup was the brew of her consort;
Her bed the spikes of a-a.
Stone-armored, passion had slaked.
Where then was her armor of stone?
The prophets, in congress assembled,
Consult on the rape of the goddess—
Red-headed Kane, Ku of the Trade-wind,
Compeers of Pele, consumers of trees,
The women of eight-fold incantations.
Wonder and awe possess me!

They stamp out the fire in the Pit;
"Stand shoulder to shoulder," their cry;
"Shoulder to shoulder," echoes the throng
On the heights of Mauli-ola,—

Where the green leaf distills the water,
Men search for like hovering owls.
Chew thou the herb with thy friend,
I will offer mine to my god.
The fault of Pele's condoned;
She lifts herself from her huddle in bed
A couch far down in the Pit—
It now becomes plates of smooth lava,
How like the flight of a swift canoe
Is the flow of the pahoehoe,
As the mountain melts and rolls away!
Hiiaka, the darling of Pele,
Then soars aloft to the realms of light,
As the crab climbs up Kau-wiki—
The crab retreats from man's shadow—
And when these black ones huddle together
They are easily clubbed with a stick;
Their bodies then are thrust in the bag.
As the gray crab tugs at the malo's fold;
As he stands mid the heaped-up coral,
While round him wave the pods of rough moss,
Or he rests on the flat coral plate;
As, taken from the bag, he's chewed into bait,
So men spit forth their bitter words.
How many guests at awe, Sir Crab?
Four gods, is the answer returned,
Tortoise, and Turtle, and Kukuau,
And Hinalea, and with them are
Apu-hihi and Hihi-wai, along with
Loli-pua and Loli-koko,
And Loli-ka'e and Lele-a.
Lele-a-makna fathered
The fisherman's god, Kahi-kona.

When he breathed, red as blood poured the rain,
A sign of the power and wrath of the god.
Wonder and awe possess me!

The heavens were turmoiled with rain clouds,
The firmament scaled, earth black as midnight,
At the birth of the princely ones:
The heaven-urging princess was born;
Then came forth a man-child, a prince,
And the blood-red rain poured down.
Then was born Ku-walu and her lord,
Mala-nai, the far-breathing Trade-wind;
And thou, O Pele, then ate of thy land,
Consuming the groves of ohi'a
And Lele-iwi's palms by the sea.
Pana-ewa still was a park;
Ka-u was made a cinder-patch;
By her might Pele threw up a mountain.
Overwhelm your lands, O Pele;
Let your fire-streams flow!
Wonder and awe possess me!

The Mountains
of Erewhon

SAMUEL BUTLER

Samuel Butler (1835-1902) delighted in iconoclasm. In The Way of All
Flesh *he pilloried organized Christianity; in* The Authoress of the
Odyssey *he declared that Homer, who knew so much about weaving, had
to have been a woman; and in his most famous book,* Erewhon—
*"nowhere" spelled backward, almost—he imagined a society taken to ex-
tremes of Social Darwinism.*

*In this passage from that book, he imagines the mountains to be a
place of strange creations.*

I rose with early dawn, and in an hour I was on my way, feeling strange, not
to say weak, from the burden of solitude, but full of hope when I considered
how many dangers I had overcome, and that this day should see me at the
summit of the dividing range.

After a slow but steady climb of between three and four hours, during
which I met with no serious hindrance, I found myself upon a tableland, and

close to a glacier which I recognized as marking the summit of the pass. Above it towered a succession of rugged precipices and snowy mountain sides. The solitude was greater than I could bear; the mountain upon my master's sheep-run was a crowded thoroughfare in comparison with this somber sullen place. The air, moreover, was dark and heavy, which made the loneliness even more oppressive. There was an inky gloom over all that was not covered with snow and ice. Grass there was none.

Each moment I felt increasing upon me that dreadful doubt as to my own identity—as to the continuity of my past and present existence—which is the first sign of that distraction which comes on those who have lost themselves in the bush. I had fought against this feeling hitherto, and had conquered it; but the intense silence and gloom of this rocky wilderness were too much for me, and I felt that my power of collecting myself was beginning to be impaired.

I rested for a little while, and then advanced over very rough ground, until I reached the lower end of the glacier. Then I saw another glacier, descending from the eastern side into a small lake. I passed along the western side of the lake, where the ground was easier, and when I had got about half way I expected that I should see the plains which I had already seen from the opposite mountains; but it was not to be so, for the clouds rolled up to the very summit of the pass, though they did not overlip it on to the side from which I had come. I therefore soon found myself enshrouded by a cold thin vapor, which prevented my seeing more than a very few yards in front of me. Then I came upon a large patch of old snow, in which I could distinctly trace the half-melted tracks of goats—and in one place, as it seemed to me, there had been a dog following them. Had I lighted upon a land of shepherds? The ground, where not covered with snow, was so poor and stony, and there was so little herbage, that I could see no sign of a path or regular sheep-track. But I could not help feeling rather uneasy as I wondered what sort of a reception I might meet with if I were to come suddenly upon inhabitants. I was thinking of this, and proceeding cautiously through the mist, when I began to fancy that I saw some objects darker than the cloud looming in front of me. A few steps brought me nearer, and a shudder of unutterable horror ran through me when I saw a circle of gigantic forms, many times higher than myself, upstanding grim and gray through the veil of cloud before me.

I suppose I must have fainted, for I found myself some time afterwards sitting upon the ground, sick and deadly cold. There were the figures, quite still and silent, seen vaguely through the thick gloom, but in human shape indisputably.

A sudden thought occurred to me, which would have doubtless struck me at once had I not been prepossessed with forebodings at the time that I first saw the figures, and had not the cloud concealed them from me—I mean that they were not living beings, but statues. I determined that I would count fifty slowly, and was sure that the objects were not alive if during that time I could detect no sign of motion.

How thankful was I when I came to the end of my fifty and there had been no movement!

I counted a second time—but again all was still.

I then advanced timidly forward, and in another moment I saw that my surmise was correct. I had come upon a sort of Stonehenge of rude and barbaric figures, seated as Chowbok had sat when I questioned him in the woolshed, and with the same superhumanly malevolent expression upon their faces. They had been all seated, but two had fallen. They were barbarous—neither Egyptian, nor Assyrian, nor Japanese—different from any of these, and yet akin to all. They were six or seven times larger than life, of great antiquity, worn and lichen grown. They were ten in number. There was snow upon their heads and wherever snow could lodge. Each statue had been built of four or five enormous blocks, but how these had been raised and put together is known to those alone who raised them. Each was terrible after a different kind. One was raging furiously, as in pain and great despair; another was lean and cadaverous with famine; another cruel and idiotic, but with the silliest simper that can be conceived—this one had fallen, and looked exquisitely ludicrous in his fall—the mouths of all were more or less open, and as I looked at them from behind, I saw that their heads had been hollowed.

I was sick and shivering with cold. Solitude had unmanned me already, and I was utterly unfit to have come upon such an assembly of fiends in such a dreadful wilderness and without preparation. I would have given everything I had in the world to have been back at my master's station; but that was not to be thought of: my head was failing, and I felt sure that I could never get back alive.

Then came a gust of howling wind, accompanied with a moan from one of the statues above me. I clasped my hands in fear. I felt like a rat caught in a trap, as though I would have turned and bitten at whatever thing was nearest me. The wildness of the wind increased, the moans grew shriller, coming from several statues, and swelling into a chorus. I almost immediately knew what it was, but the sound was so unearthly that this was but little consolation. The inhuman beings into whose hearts the Evil One had put it to conceive these statues, had made their heads into a sort of organ-pipe, so that their mouths should catch the wind and sound with its blowing. It was horrible. However brave a man might be, he could never stand such a concert, from such lips, and in such a place. I heaped every invective upon them that my tongue could utter as I rushed away from them into the mist, and even after I had lost sight of them, and turning my head round could see nothing but the storm-wraiths driving behind me, I heard their ghostly chanting, and felt as though one of them would rush after me and grip me in his hand and throttle me.

Cataclysm

BERTOLT BRECHT

Writing in response to the destruction wrought by World War II, the German playwright BERTOLT BRECHT *(1898–1956) imagines the end of the world not to come with a bang, nor a whimper, but with the birth of a mighty mountain.*

When I saw that the world had passed away
the plants, humans, and other survivors of the surface
    and the floor of the ocean
a mountain grew
bigger than any other mountain
and the highest Himalayas
and it ate up the world as it grew
and wisdom gave it a great hump
    and stupidity a greater one
light made it strong but darkness made it stronger
and so the world transformed itself into a single
    mountain—the greatest it had ever seen

The Hollow-Men and
the Bitter-Rose

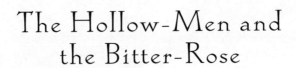

RENÉ DAUMAL

Fascinated by the mysticism of ordinary experience, the French avant-garde poet RENÉ DAUMAL (1908–1944) sought to unite Asian philosophies with European esthetics. His slender collected works show both a devotion to the absurd and a striving for utter self-awareness; had his life not been cut short by illness, he might have been able to complete his unfinished masterwork Mount Analogue *and articulate those concerns more fully, forging a new philosophy in the bargain. His strange "novel of symbolically authentic non-Euclidean adventures in mountain-climbing," as he called it, contains this haunting fable of the mysteries of the world's high places.*

The Hollow-Men live in solid rock and move about in it in the form of mobile caves or recesses. In ice they appear as bubbles in the shape of men. But they never venture out into the air, for the wind would blow them away.

They have houses in the rock whose walls are made of emptiness, and tents in the ice whose fabric is of bubbles. During the day they stay in stone, and at night they wander through the ice and dance during the full moon. But they never see the sun, or else they would burst.

They eat only the void, such as the form of corpses; they get drunk on empty words and all the meaningless expressions we utter.

Some people say they have always existed and will exist forever. Others say they are the dead. And others say that as a sword has its scabbard or a foot its imprint, every living man has in the mountain his Hollow-Man, and in death they are reunited.

In the village of Hundred-Houses there lived the old priest-magician Hunoes and his wife, Hulay-Hulay. They had two sons, two identical twins who could not be told apart, called Mo and Ho. Even their mother got them mixed up. To tell them apart on the day of name-giving, they had put on Mo a necklace bearing a little cross and on Ho a necklace bearing a little ring.

Old Hunoes had one great unconfessed worry. According to custom his elder son should succeed him. But which was his elder son? Did he even have an elder son?

At the age of adolescence Mo and Ho were already accomplished mountaineers. They came to be called the two mountain goats. One day, their father told them, "To whichever one of you brings back to me the Bitter-Rose I shall hand on the great knowledge."

The Bitter-Rose is found only at the summit of the highest peaks. Whoever eats of it finds that whenever he is about to tell a lie, aloud or to himself, his tongue begins to burn. He can still tell falsehoods, but he has been warned. A few people have seen the Bitter-Rose. According to what they say, it looks like a large multicolored lichen or a swarm of butterflies. But no one has ever been able to pick it, for the tiniest tremor of fear anywhere close by alerts it, and it disappears into the rock. Even if one desires it, one is a little afraid of possessing it, and it vanishes.

To describe an impossible action or an absurd undertaking, they say: "It's like looking for night in broad daylight," or "It's like wanting to throw light on the sun in order to see it better," or "It's like trying to catch the Bitter-Rose."

Mo has taken his ropes and pick and hatchet and iron hooks. At sunrise he is already high up on a peak called Cloudy Head. Like a lizard, sometimes like a spider, he inches upward across the high red precipice, between white snow below and the blue-black sky. Little swift-moving clouds envelop him from time to time and then expose him suddenly to the light again.

And now at last, a little distance above him, he sees the Bitter-Rose, shimmering with unearthly tints. He repeats to himself unceasingly the charm that his father has taught him to ward off fear.

He's going to need a screw ring here, with a rope sling, in order to straddle this outcropping of rock like a rearing horse. He strikes with his hammer, and his hand breaks through into a hole. There is a hollow under the stone. Shattering the crust around it, he sees that the hollow is in the form of a man: torso, legs, arms, and little tubes in the shape of fingers spread in terror. He has split the head with the blow of his pick.

An icy wind passes across the stone. Mo has killed a Hollow-Man. He has shuddered, and the Bitter-Rose has retreated into the rock.

Mo climbs back down to the village and tells his father, "I killed a Hollow-Man. But I saw the Bitter-Rose, and tomorrow I shall go to look for it."

Old Hunoes became grave. Far off he saw one misfortune after another coming in procession. He said: "Watch out for the Hollow-Men. They will seek vengeance. They cannot enter our world, but they can come up to the surface of things. Beware of the surface of things."

At dawn the next day Hulay-Hulay gave a great cry, rose up, and ran towards the mountain. At the foot of the red cliff lay Mo's garments, his ropes and hatchet, and his medal with the cross. His body was no longer there.

"Ho," she cried, running back. "They've killed your brother. They've killed my son."

Ho rises up with his teeth clenched and the skin tightening on his scalp. He takes his hatchet and prepares to set out. His father says to him: "First, listen to me. This is what you have to do. The Hollow-Men have taken your brother and changed him into a Hollow-Man. He will try to escape. He will go in search of light to the seracs of the Clear Glacier. Put his medal around your neck as well as your own. Go to him and strike at his head. Enter the form of his body, and Mo will live again among us. Do not fear to kill a dead man."

Ho gazes wide-eyed into the blue ice of the Clear Glacier. Is the light playing tricks on him, are his eyes deceiving him, or is he really seeing what he sees? He watches silvery forms with arms and legs, like greased divers under water. There is his brother, Mo, his hollow shape fleeing from a thousand Hollow-Men in pursuit. But they are afraid of the light. Mo's form seeks the light and rises in a large blue serac, turning around and around as if in search of a door. Despite his bursting heart and the blood clotting in his veins, Ho steps forward. To his blood and to his heart he says, "Do not fear to kill a dead men." Then he strikes the head, shattering the ice. Mo's form becomes motionless; Ho opens the ice of the serac and enters his brother's form like a sword fitted into its sheath, a foot into its imprint. He moves his elbows and works himself into place, then draws his legs back out of the mould of ice. And he hears himself saying words in a language he had never spoken. He feels he is Ho, and that he is Mo at the same time. All Mo's memories have entered his mind—the way up Cloudy Head and where the Bitter-Rose has its habitation.

With the circle and the cross around his neck, he comes to Hulay-Hulay. "Mother, you will have no more trouble telling us apart. Mo and Ho are now in the same body; I am your only son, Moho."

Old Hunoes shed a few tears, and his face showed happiness. But there was still one doubt he wished to dispel. He said to Moho, "You are my only son; Ho and Mo can no longer be distinguished."

Moho told him with conviction, "Now I can reach the Bitter-Rose. Mo knows the way; Ho knows the right gesture. Master of my fears, I shall have the flower of discernment."

He picked the flower, he received the teaching, and old Hunoes was able to leave this world peacefully.

TRANSLATED BY ROGER SHATTUCK

The Ends
of the Earth

⟨ⓑ⟩

ESTONIAN FOLKTALE,

SIR JOHN MANDEVILLE

*What are the mountains at the corners of the earth like? A twentieth-
century ESTONIAN FOLKTALE imagines them to be guarded by Russian soldiers and populated by fearsome creatures.*

The Dog-Snouts live at the edge of the world, where the earth comes to an
end and heaven begins. They must stand guard at the edge of the world, so
that no one may enter into heaven there. . . . The Dog-Snouts at the edge of
the world dwell behind a great mountain. This mountain forms the border
between the land of the Dog-Snouts and that of men. It is necessary that a
company of soldiers, indeed, according to general consensus, a company of
Russian soldiers, stand watch at this mountain, lest the Dog-Snouts come
into this country. . . . Were the Dog-Snouts to succeed in coming over the
mountain, they would tear every man in the world limb from limb. Their
strength is so great that none can resist them.

Although his published work was instantly famous, no one knows who
SIR JOHN MANDEVILLE *was. He is believed to have been born in 1322 and*
to have died fifty years later, and to have spent many years of his life
working in the service of the Great Khan of China. His Travels, *pub-*
lished in 1361, became the first best-selling travel book in history, a fa-
vorite of Columbus, Sir Francis Drake, and other later explorers. Here he
describes, as best he can, the mountainous geography of Paradise.

On the island of Taprobane are great mountains of gold tended by ants, which purify and grade the ore. These ants are easily as big as dogs, and no human dares approach them for fear of being attacked. But the people thereabouts know a trick. When the weather is hot, the ants hide underground for much of the day, and while they are sheltering men ride up on camel-trains and haul away caravans of gold before the ants return to the surface. When the weather is cooler, the men send up mares carrying empty baskets. The ants cannot stand to see anything empty, and so they fill these baskets with gold. The men then release the mares' foals in the fields below the mountains, and they cry for their mothers, who then gallop down to care for them, laden with gold. The ants, you see, tolerate every kind of animal except humans.

Beyond this island none of the lands are inhabited, and they are wildernesses of great mountains and darkness. But beyond these lie Paradise, in which Adam and Eve once lived. East of that place the earth begins. This is not our east, the place of the sunrise, but another place entirely, shaped into mountains and valleys by the great flood that Noah rode out.

Of Paradise I cannot tell you, because I have not been there. I am sorry for that. But I can say what wise men have told me about it. Paradise, I have heard, is the highest land on this earth, so high that it touches the moon, so high that the flood could not reach it. A wall surrounds Paradise, made of materials that are not known to us. The wall stretches from north to south, and there is no way to get over it on account of its being surrounded by another wall of fire, which God erected so that humans could never enter.

In the middle of Paradise lies a spring, and from this spring flow four rivers, which traverse different nations. These rivers rise in Paradise, as I say, but then go underground and resurface. The first is the Ganges, which rises in India below the Himalayas, and runs eastward through India until it enters the great ocean sea. In the Ganges are precious stones and jewels, and the wood we call lignum aloe, and a great quantity of gold in the gravel. The Ganges, also called the Phison, is named for the king Gangaras, who once ruled here. The river is clear in some places, muddy in others, and flows both hot and cold. The second river is the Nile, which rises near Mount Atlas and runs underground all the way to Ethiopia, and thence to Alexandria and the Mediterranean. The third river is the Tigris, which means fast-running, like the tiger, for it is the swiftest river on the earth. This river rises in Armenia under Ararat and runs through Asia until it comes to the Mediterranean. The fourth river is the Euphrates, which means "bearing well," for so many good grains and vegetables grow along its banks. All the other fresh rivers on earth arise too in Paradise, there in the high mountains.

You should know that no one can enter Paradise. No one can travel there by land on account of the ferocious beasts of the wilderness, and because of the mountains and darkness. You cannot go there by water, either, for the rivers flow so strongly that no boat could stand up against the current. Many brave men have tried and failed, dying of exhaustion from rowing or climbing, or made deaf by the roaring of the winds and waters. No one can go there except by God's grace. And so I can tell you nothing more of Paradise.

Selected Bibliography

Aston, W. G. *Nihongi: Chronicles of Japan from the Earliest Times to A.D. 697.* London: Allen & Unwin, 1956.

Auden, W. H., and Louis MacNeice. *Letters from Iceland.* New York: Paragon House, 1990.

Bābur, Zahiruddin Muhammad. *The Baburnama.* Translated by Wheeler M. Thackston. New York: Oxford University Press, 1996.

Bahr, Donald, Juan Smith, William Smith Allison, and Julian Hayden. *The Short, Swift Time of the Gods on Earth: The Hohokam Creation Cycle.* Berkeley: University of California Press, 1994.

Beckwith, Martha. *Hawaiian Mythology.* Honolulu: University of Hawaii Press, 1970.

Benuzzi, Felice. *No Picnic on Mount Kenya.* London: Victor Gollancz, 1952.

Bere, Rennie. *The Way to the Mountains of the Moon.* London: Arthur Barker, 1966.

Berndt, Ronald M., and Catherine H. Berndt. *The Speaking Land: Myth and Story in Aboriginal Australia.* Sydney: Penguin, 1988.

Bleeck, W. H. I., and L. C. Lloyd. *Specimens of Bushmen Folklore.* London: George Allen, 1911.

Bolívar, Simón. *Proclamas y Discursos del Libertador.* Edited by Vicente Lecuna. Caracas: Lit. y Tip. del Comercio, 1939.

Bryce, James. *Transcaucasia and Ararat.* London: John Murray, 1883.

Burnaby, Frederick. *On Horseback Through Asia Minor.* London: John Murray, 1898.

Carmichael, Alexander. *Carmina Gadelica.* Inverness: Gaelic Society of Scotland, 1886.

Chekhov, Anton. *A Journey to Sakhalin.* Translated by Brian Reeve. Cambridge: Ian Faulkner, 1993.

Clark, Ella E. *Indian Legends of the Pacific Northwest.* Berkeley: University of California Press, 1953.

Conway, Martin. *Mountain Memories.* New York: Funk and Wagnalls, 1920.

Curzon, George N. *The Pamirs and the Source of the Oxus.* London: Royal Geographical Society, 1896.

Daumal, René. *Mount Analogue.* Translated by Roger Shattuck. Boston: Shambhala, 1992.

de la Vega, Garcilaso. *Royal Commentaries on the Incas.* Translated by Harold V. Livermore. Austin: University of Texas Press, 1966.

Douglas, William O. *Of Men and Mountains.* New York: Harper, 1950.

Doyle, Arthur Conan. *The Lost World.* London: Macmillan, 1912.

Dundas, Charles. *Kilimanjaro and Its People.* London: Frank Cass, 1968.

Emerson, Nathaniel M. *Pele and Hiiaka: A Myth from Hawaii.* Honolulu: *Honolulu Star-Bulletin,* 1915.

Farquhar, Francis P., and Aristides E. Phoutrides. *Mount Olympus.* San Francisco: Johnck and Seeger, 1929.

Galeano, Eduardo. *Memory of Fire.* Translated by Cedric Belfrage. New York: Pantheon, 1985.

Gaster, M. *Rumanian Bird and Beast Stories.* London: Folk-Lore Society, 1915.

Gilliam, Ann, ed. *Voices for the Earth: A Treasury of the* Sierra Club Bulletin. San Francisco: Sierra Club Books, 1979.

Glacken, Clarence. *Traces on the Rhodian Shore.* Berkeley: University of California Press, 1967.

Gribble, Francis. *The Early Mountaineers*. London: T. Fisher Unwin, 1899.

Hakluyt, Richard. *Voyages and Discoveries*. Harmondsworth, Eng.: Penguin, 1972.

Hatto, A. T. *The Memorial Feast for Kökötöy-Khan*. Oxford: Oxford University Press, 1977.

Hay, John. *Kernels of Energy, Bones of Earth: The Rock in Chinese Art*. New York: China Institute in America, 1985.

Hedin, Sven. *Through Asia*. 2 vols. New York: Harper, 1899.

Herzog, Maurice. *Annapurna*. Translated by Nea Morin and Janet Adam Smith. New York: Dutton, 1952.

Hobbs, Joseph J. *Mount Sinai*. Austin: University of Texas Press, 1995.

Irving, R. L. G., ed. *The Mountain Way*. New York: Dutton, 1938.

James, George W. *The Wonders of the Colorado Desert*. Boston: Little, Brown, 1906.

Jerome, John. *On Mountains*. New York: Harcourt Brace Jovanovich, 1978.

Jochelson, Waldemar. *Peoples of Asiatic Russia*. New York: American Museum of Natural History, 1928.

Julyan, Robert Hixson. *Mountain Names*. Seattle: The Mountaineers, 1984.

Keast, Allen. *Australia and the Pacific Islands*. London: Hamish Hamilton, 1966.

Keay, John. *Where Men and Mountains Meet*. New York: Oxford University Press, 1994.

Kenyatta, Jomo. *Facing Mount Kenya*. London: Secker and Warburg, 1953.

Kerouac, Jack. *Book of Blues*. New York: Penguin Books, 1995.

Kretzenbacher, Leopold. *Kynokephale Dämonen Südosteuropäischer Volksdichtung*. Munich: Rudolf Trofenik, 1968.

Langdon, Merle K. *A Sanctuary of Zeus on Mount Hymettos*. Princeton: American School of Classical Studies at Athens, 1976.

Lange, Harald. *Kilimanjaro: White Roof of the World*. Seattle: The Mountaineers, 1985.

Lattimore, Owen. *High Tartary*. Boston: Little, Brown, 1930.

Lawrence, T. E. *Selected Letters*. New York: Norton, 1989.

Layton, Robert. *Uluru: An Aboriginal History of Ayers Rock*. Canberra: Aboriginal Studies Press, 1989.

Levi, Carlo. *Words Are Stones.* Translated by Angus Davidson. New York: Farrar, Straus and Cudahy, 1958.

MacInnes, Hamish. *Climb to the Lost World.* Harmondsworth, Eng.: Penguin, 1974.

Malcolmson, Scott L. *Empire's Edge: Travels in South-Eastern Europe, Turkey, and Central Asia.* New York: Verso, 1994.

McGuiness, Jamie. *Trekking in the Everest Region.* Hindhead, Eng.: Trailblazer Books, 1994.

McRae, Michael. "Cold Feet over Patagonia." *Outside,* February 1991.

Meade, Charles. *High Mountains.* London: Harvill, 1954.

Miller, Joaquin. *Unwritten History: Life Among the Modocs.* Hartford: American Publishing, 1874.

Mooney, James. *The Ghost Dance Religion and Wounded Knee.* Washington, D.C.: U.S. Government Printing Office, 1896.

Morris, Mary, ed. *Maiden Voyages: The Writings of Women Travelers.* New York: Vintage Books, 1993.

Murray, John A., ed. *Wild Africa.* New York: Oxford University Press, 1993.

Neate, Jill. *High Asia.* Seattle: The Mountaineers, 1989.

Nicholson, Marjorie Hope. *Mountain Gloom and Mountain Glory: The Development of an Aesthetics of the Infinite.* Ithaca: Cornell University Press, 1958.

Norman, Howard, ed. *Northern Tales: Traditional Stories of Eskimo and Indian Peoples.* New York: Pantheon, 1990.

O'Bryan, Aileen. *The Diné: Origin Myths of the Navajo People.* Washington, D.C.: U.S. Government Printing Office, 1956.

Peatfield, A. J. "The Topography of Minoan Peak Sanctuaries." *Annual of the British School at Athens* 78 (1983): 273–79.

Pfeiffer, Ida. *A Lady's Second Journey Round the World.* London: Albert Lane, 1855.

Prejevalsky, Nikolai. *From Kulja, Across the Tian Shan to Lob-Nor.* London: Sampson Low, Marston, Searle & Rivington, 1879.

Price, Larry W. *Mountains and Man.* Berkeley: University of California Press, 1981.

Ramanujan, A. K., ed. *Folktales from India.* New York: Pantheon, 1991.

Read, Kenneth E. *The High Valley.* New York: Scribner's, 1965.

Reader, John. *Kilimanjaro*. London: Elm Tree Books, 1982.

Ruskin, John. *Modern Painters of Truth and Theoretic Faculties*. London: Smith, Elder, 1846–60.

Sakaki, Nanao. *Break the Mirror*. San Francisco: North Point Press, 1987.

Salkeld, Audrey, and José Luis Bermúdez. *On the Edge of Europe: Mountaineering in the Caucasus*. London: Hodder and Stoughton, 1993.

Sarna, Nahum M. *On the Book of Psalms*. New York: Schocken Books, 1993.

Shacochis, Bob. "Bob Versus the Volcano." *Outside*, February 1991.

Shigeru, Kayano. *Our Land Was a Forest*. Translated by Kyoko Selden and Lili Selden. Boulder: Westview Press, 1994.

Simpson, Joe. *This Game of Ghosts*. London: Jonathan Cape, 1993.

———. *Touching the Void*. New York: Harper & Row, 1988.

Spectorsky, A. C., ed. *The Book of the Mountains*. Boston: Appleton Century Crofts, 1955.

Starr, Frederick. *Fujiyama: The Sacred Mountain of Japan*. Chicago: Covici-McGee, 1924.

Synge, Patrick M. *Mountains of the Moon*. London: Lindsay Drummond, 1937.

Tennent, Sir James Emerson. *Ceylon: An Account of the Island*. London: Longman, Green and Roberts, 1860.

Terada, Alice M. *Under the Starfruit Tree: Folktales from Vietnam*. Honolulu: University of Hawaii Press, 1989.

Tobias, Michael Charles, and Harold Drasdo, eds. *The Mountain Spirit*. Woodstock, N.Y.: Overlook Press, 1981.

Tschiffely, A. F. *Southern Cross to Pole Star*. New York: Simon & Schuster, 1933.

Twain, Mark. *Following the Equator: A Journey Around the World*. Hartford: American Publishing, 1897.

Vander, Judith. *Ghost Dance Songs and Religion of a Wind River Shoshone Woman*. Berkeley: University of California Monograph Series in Ethnomusicology, No. 4, 1986.

Wallace, David Rains. *The Dark Range: A Naturalist's Night Notebook*. San Francisco: Yolla Bolly Press–Sierra Club Books, 1978.

Ward, Michael. *The Mountaineer's Companion*. London: Eyre and Spottiswood, 1966.

Whitman, Walt. *Specimen Days*. Boston: David R. Godine, 1971.

Wyckoff, William, and Larry M. Dilsaver, eds. *The Mountainous West: Explorations in Historical Geography*. Lincoln: University of Nebraska Press, 1995.

Young, Geoffrey Winthrop. *The Influence of Mountains upon the Development of Human Intelligence*. Glasgow: Jackson, 1957.

ABOUT THE EDITOR

GREGORY MCNAMEE is the author or volume editor of seventeen books, the most recent of which are *Blue Mountains Far Away*, *The Serpent's Tale*, and *Gila: The Life and Death of an American River*. He is also the author of the texts for two books of photographs, *In the Presence of Wolves* (with Art Wolfe) and *Open Range and Parking Lots* (with Virgil Hancock). McNamee lives in Tucson, Arizona, where he works as a writer, journalist, and editor.